What wrong with our schools?

The ideology impoverishing education in America—and how we can do better for our students

Daniel Buck

First published 2022

by John Catt Educational Ltd
15 Riduna Park, Station Road,
Melton, Woodbridge, IP12 1QT, UK
Tel: +44 (0) 1394 389850

4500 140th Ave North,
Suite 101, Clearwater,
FL 33762-3848, US
Tel: +1 561 448 1987

Email: enquiries@johncatt.com
Website: www.johncatt.com

ISBN: 978 1 915261 53 3

Set and designed by John Catt Educational Limited

Daniel Buck's book opens with a disquieting anecdote. He had read aloud with students from a shared novel, enriched the book with background knowledge, and led a whole-class discussion but Buck's students had never experienced anything like it. That such traditional methods were utterly foreign to his students, whose only experience was in schools informed by romantic and "progressive" theories of education, is the starting point to a book full of observations and reflections that are carefully researched, insightful, and grounded in student welfare. Unbeknownst to his students, Buck's "new" way of teaching drew on traditional concepts of instruction informed by research into cognitive and social science. This is a profoundly thoughtful and important book.

Doug Lemov, author, *Teach Like a Champion*

I have followed Daniel Buck's work for years. He is emerging as an indispensable and engaging voice on education. If he writes with more authority than most, it's because his views were formed not in an ivory tower, but as a classroom teacher who takes seriously his responsibility to other people's children. *What is Wrong With Our Schools?* will bring his insights to the broader audience he richly deserves.

Robert Pondiscio, senior fellow, American Enterprise Institute

There's plenty in this smart, hard-hitting book to make anyone feel pessimistic about the state of American education. But optimism is still in order, because Buck has picked up the mantle of traditionalism for a new generation.

Michael Petrilli, president, Thomas B. Fordham Institute

CONTENTS

To Ethan and Jason, for teaching me how to write.

Part I.
The History and
the Argument

1. A CONFLICT OF VISIONS

OPENING ANECDOTES

I did everything the university told me to. I let students choose their books. I conferenced with them one-on-one. I opted for conversations over consequences. I worked closely with an instructional coach to ensure I implemented a workshop model to fidelity. I let students into my room during lunch to build relationships. I communicated with parents and sought out student interests to guide my instruction. My classes wrote and agreed to their own behavior codes. I provided alternative seating out of my own pocket. Nonetheless, misbehavior abounded and reading growth stagnated.

One thing, however, functioned supremely well: I read out loud for a few minutes every day. When I brought out the book, spun a desk around, sat on top, and cracked a page, I didn't have to remind anyone to quiet down or find a seat. Students sat back and eagerly awaited the next chapter from whatever book we were reading. From these moments came our most robust conversations. Sometimes an impromptu question came to my mind, and at other times a student would raise their hand and begin the discussion.

Over the years, I have slowly renounced the workshop model—an approach to a literature class where students select their own books and design their own writing projects—dedicating less and less of my time and energy to its imposition on my students. It has been nerve-racking to do so. The messaging in support of student-directed learning is strong: if students pick their own books, they'll come to enjoy them, no? Doesn't a teacher-selected text kill the love of reading? Students act out in response to the imposition of rules from outside themselves; allow them to design their own rules and co-create class expectations and they'll start to run it themselves, surely?

However, when I began to dive into the research and to read more traditionalist theories of education, I started to do things differently. I chose the text. I developed clear classroom expectations—obviously variable depending on the activity. I taught grammar. I had students write a five-paragraph essay and gave them a multiple-choice test. I read Shakespeare. I asked students to work silently. I required them to memorize a poem.

Lo and behold, contrary to what the educational mainstream would predict, my students flourished—academically, socially, and emotionally. One young woman came up to me—after we had a long, engaging, at times even tense conversation about what Juliet ought to do after her father threatens to disown her—to tell me that this was the first book that ever really "got" her; it spoke to her life. My students practiced and recited poetry while playing four square together, even welcoming in another student who tended to sit on the social outskirts; they finally had something in common. Another boy, who had been expelled for a semester after he instigated a lunchroom brawl, said, "I know *exactly* how that feels" when we worked through the lines from *Romeo and Juliet* about quenching rage. He connected to the interfamilial conflict and street violence of the play, listened intently as we read and watched it, and in a final lesson admitted that he needed to work on his own anger.

Allow me one last anecdote before I lay out the thesis and intent of this book. At the end of each year, I give students a survey—a chance to provide critical feedback to their teacher. This past year, one student wrote that she enjoyed this "new way of teaching." I spend my classes reading classic books that I choose, discussing and analyzing them together as a class, and concluding units with traditional assessments like exams and essays. My "new way of teaching"—new to me and apparently also to my students—is only a rediscovery of tradition.

SO WHAT IS WRONG WITH OUR SCHOOLS?

When addressing this question, most commentators focus on policy. What role does the federal government play? How ought we to allocate funds? Do schools even have sufficient funds? Are unions too strong or too weak? Daily, I grow more skeptical of the ability of these policies to holistically improve the system. We could change the structure around as much as we want in either direction, but like a car with a new frame and wheels, it will not run if it lacks fuel. What is that essential fuel? The pedagogy and instruction that happen within the classroom.

And that brings me to answer the question that forms the title of this book: *the problem with our schools is fundamentally ideological, not systemic.* Our reforms must focus on pedagogy and instruction, not just policies. Arguments over class size, funding, school choice, unions, teacher certification, and other fads dominate the discourse, but each of these are golden calves. We lay our support and tax dollars at their altar, and they provide little to nothing in return. They provide nothing because our instructional practices, philosophies, and curricula are based upon false first principles. We fill a car with vegetable oil expecting it to run and our schools with faulty theories expecting them to educate. Reflecting on it now, months later, that student's note on my "new way of teaching" saddens me. It implies that her primary years were spent in a model of education that aligns with neither contemporary research nor human nature understood through classical philosophy and a liberal arts tradition.

There is something of a conflict of visions. On one side are the progressives or romantics. This typifies the discourse in our schools of education. It's the ideology endorsed and advanced by unions, universities, and administrations. Don't believe me? Suggest on social media that critical thinking is a silly concept, Shakespeare ought to be read universally, or that expulsions remain a necessary tool and see what happens.

Standing on the other side are those I'll call the neo-traditionalists. They place a primacy on teacher authority, knowledge transmission, and orderly schools. The 20th century educational progressives leveled thoughtful critiques at traditionalist pedagogies—that they paid little attention to student needs and taught rigid information, isolated from real-world applications; the neo-traditionalists took account of these concerns but maintained their commitment to classical first principles.

They also applied social scientific techniques, not just philosophy, to confirm commitments to things like direct instruction. If traditionalism teaches content and progressive education teaches students, then neo-traditionalism teaches content to the student.

This dichotomy is at the root of the changes I made to my teaching. The system around me didn't alter, but my philosophical views and thus instruction did. Like a child's snack, we can change the packaging, include more or less, and give them choice over it, but if the bag has potato chips inside then it will still provide little nutrition. Education happens in the classroom, and so its success or failure hinges upon what happens there.

More specifically, pedagogies based in romantic-era thinking with little to no rigorous evidence for their efficacy dominate our classrooms. Project-based learning, student choice, restorative justice, and the like—practices with at times detrimental results—edge out direct instruction, sequenced curricula, historically significant and challenging books, and other traditionalist approaches—practices with a proven track record. My professors of education began with the assumption that student control of curriculum was beneficial. My professional development didn't even postulate that direct instruction could be beneficial. When our schools run on these assumptions, it does not matter what amount of choice families have or how big classes are.

I'm not the first to hold this conviction. In his ambitious book *Visible Learning* (2008), Professor John Hattie undertook the largest ever synthesis of meta-analyses in education. While we can take his data with some skepticism, after reviewing hundreds of meta-analyses Hattie comes to one conclusion worth reflecting on: "One of the fascinating discoveries throughout my research for this book is discovering that many of the most debated issues are the ones with the least effects."[1] He mentions class size, tracking, retention, school choice, summer schools, and school uniforms. It wasn't that these policies proved positive or negative. Rather, in either direction, their effect was minimal. Instead, the most important changes happen *within* schools, like instructional and behavioral reform.

Before I continue, I have to acknowledge that I do not intend here to catastrophize. On a historical scale, our attempt at universal education is a new undertaking and a profoundly difficult one. For most of human history, society relegated book learning to the aristocracy while the majority of the human race wallowed in poverty and illiteracy. Even as we established systems of education, laws barred individuals from entry based on their race, class, and gender. According to Our World in Data, a project from the University of Oxford, the worldwide literacy rate in 1820 was about 12%; by 2015 that had risen to 86%.[2] This is a vaunting human achievement that we must keep in mind before leveling any critiques.

That being said, our system can do better. It can achieve more than base literacy. To do that, we must unstick a blob, and this blob is an assumed ideology. It finds expression in pithy phrases like "teach the student, not content" and "critical thinking skills." It assumes that the best learning happens through doing, through student choice without adult-imposed standards, and through a renunciation of tests, memorization, or drill. Criticism of this blob brings on accusations of hating children, killing the joy of learning, and old-fashioned schoolmarmery. All the while, the blob slows down everything and everyone. This book intends to identify what exactly this blob is and to isolate its first principles, so as to unstick it and allow more effective ideas, pedagogies, and practices to flourish.

WHAT ISN'T WRONG WITH OUR SCHOOLS

It's beyond the bounds of this book's introductory chapter to cover every suggested policy that *wouldn't* improve our schools, but a few examples—school choice, funding, and class size—may prove illustrative. If pedagogy is more important than policies, it's worth addressing the shortcomings of a few hobbyhorse policy reforms.

Consider class size. One headline from *The Nation* boldly declares "To reduce inequality in our education system, reduce class sizes."[3] On its surface, this proclamation seems plausible. Fewer students might promote easier classroom management and more opportunities for individualized feedback and instruction. It simply isn't that clear, however. I have worked with classes ranging from eight students up to 32. In many ways, the class of eight was harder to manage; the students were friends and a smaller class provided less positive peer pressure. Furthermore, I was a novice teacher when I had my class of 32. My own professional development and adoption of traditionalist educational practices matter far more than the number of students in my room. More learning would happen in a class of 32 students with an experienced teacher than two classes of

16 with inexperienced teachers. Research seems to bear these personal observations out.

Class-size reduction does not happen in a vacuum. We cannot snap our fingers and achieve smaller classes—it requires personnel. Two researchers, Christopher Jepsen and Steve Rivkin, have published papers about class-size reduction policies with teacher experience in mind. When newly created positions brought inexperienced teachers with emergency licenses into the profession, there was "a short term increase in the share of teachers lacking experience and a persistent increase in the share of teachers lacking full certification, both of which were larger in higher poverty, higher minority enrollment schools."[4] When states broadly implement class size reduction policies, new teaching posts in privileged districts draw the best teachers away from schools in poor neighborhoods, thereby creating a disparate impact. Affluent schools improve and poor schools stagnate. The effect of new teachers filling posts "partially or, in some cases, fully offset the benefits of smaller classes, demonstrating the importance of considering all implications of any policy change."[5]

According to another study, "as class size decreases achievement scores increase. However, in elementary schools ... only a slight impact ... was found. No significant relationship was found at middle school grade level." And although the study did find a correlation at high school level, the authors admitted that the "results may be questioned."[6] They concluded: "[This study] reinforces the literature research finding that increases in direct classroom expenditures per student have little impact on student achievement scores."[7]

These conclusions appear over and again across the literature on class size. "We find that there are relatively few high-quality studies, and that these studies show mixed results" reads one report from the Brookings Institution.[8] According to another review, "studies have found mixed effects in California and in other countries, and no effects in Florida and Connecticut."[9] Class-size reduction is efficacious at lower grade levels and on the scale of seven to 10 fewer students per class. But even so, the hiring of new teachers necessitated by class-size reduction policies could actually set learning *back*. And this analysis doesn't even touch on the monumentally expensive undertaking that class-size reduction would prove to be. An increase in class size of one pupil per class would save the

American education system $12 billion in teacher salaries, about equal to the entirety of Title I funding, itself the largest K-12 spending program.[10, 11]

On the opposite side of the partisan aisle is school choice—a policy that I support, although I acknowledge it is no panacea. Even if a system of choice came to run American education, our institutions, teachers, professional development, and curricula would remain. Give a chef only the ingredients for a bacon, lettuce, and tomato sandwich and they might be able to construct something other than a BLT, but it would still taste a whole lot like a BLT. Even with choice, we would function with the same educational ingredients. It may be a more just means of apportioning funds and school attendance, but it alone will not deliver a pedagogical revolution.

And what about funding? Surely our schools lack sufficient resources: stories abound of buildings with crumbling foundations, drafty windows, and classrooms furnished with a teacher's own spending. International comparisons complicate this initial analysis. According to the National Center for Education Statistics, the US spent more than $14,000 per student per year in 2017-18.[12] That's more than just about any other country in the world except for Luxembourg, despite the fact that many countries outperform us on international tests. Put simply, education funding matters *up to a point*. Obviously, schools without a single dollar could do little, but over a certain threshold, adding another dollar to budgets yields a diminishing return. The researchers at Our World in Data conclude that "above a certain national income level, the relationship between PISA scores and education expenditure per pupil becomes virtually inexistent."[13] They point to a compelling graph from the Organisation for Economic Co-operation and Development (OECD) that demonstrates this visually (turn the page to see the graph). Up to about $50,000 per student over the course of their entire education, every additional dollar spent correlates strongly with improved outcomes. Above that, the trend line largely flattens.

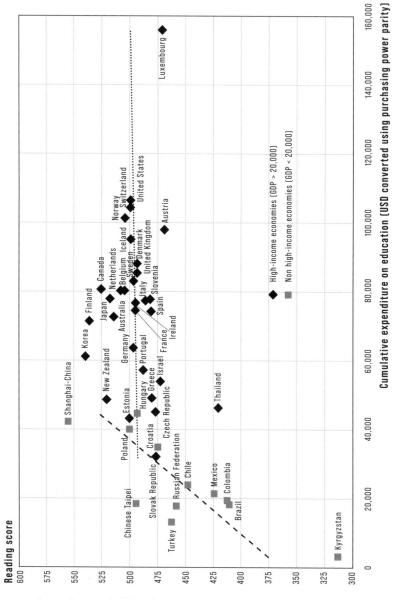

Average reading performance in PISA and average spending per student from the age of 6 to 15.
Source: OECD. (2010) *PISA 2009 Results: what students know and can do – student performance in reading, mathematics and science, volume 1*, p.34

If we zoom in on US policies, the data shows that much of our allocated monies are ineffectively used. Regarding the use of Title I funds, the largest single federal program, authors at the Brookings Institution cogently summarize the problem:

There is little evidence that the overall program is effective or that its funds are used for effective services and activities. Large proportions of school principals report using Title I funds for teacher professional development, which many studies have shown to be ineffective and which teachers do not find valuable. Other services on which principals spent Title I funds include after-school and summer programs, technology purchases, and supplemental services, which also have been shown to be ineffective, and class-size reductions, which are unlikely to be of the size needed to generate effects found in previous research.[14]

In short, *how* money is spent matters far more than *how much* is spent, at least at current levels in the US.

This analysis could continue with ever more policies, each of which may have some value or worth, but they are not panaceas. If implemented to fidelity, their results would be modest, if they achieved much at all. None of these will accomplish much so long as faulty instructional practices persist. American schools need an ideological revolution, not a structural one.

SHADOWBOXING

Judging by the response I see to many books in the same ideological bent as mine, one rebuttal to my thesis worth addressing outright is that progressivist theories of education don't have much of a hold on our system; traditionalism is the predominant philosophy. And I concede: our system is a hodgepodge of both. Even so, progressive ideas in education have an outsized purchase.

As a traditionalist within the system, I see it most simply in the things people say. "Teach the student, not content." "We must foster critical thinking skills." "We should teach students how to think, not what to think." The focus is on academic skills, not content knowledge. This is reflected in the buzzwords that carry positive or negative connotations, like "experiential learning" and "student choice" versus "drill and kill" or "rote memorization." However, passing observations don't amount to much empirically, so let's look at a few concrete examples.

First, the curricula of schools of education across the US demonstrate the commanding position of progressivism within the university. Students encounter Paulo Freire, a radically progressive pedagogue, perhaps more than any other theorist. His book *Pedagogy of the Oppressed* (1968) has sold more than a million copies—an astounding number for a niche book of education. Also topping the list of commonly assigned authors are John Dewey and other educational progressives.[15] David Steiner, the executive director of the Johns Hopkins University Institute for Education Policy, has called teacher training curricula "intellectual barren."[16] If any students of education encounter the ideas of E.D. Hirsch, a profoundly influential traditionalist, it is likely only with derision. In my own course of study, we had one five-week class on the learning sciences—the one class where I and many of my fellow students felt like we were actually learning the craft of teaching—and, ironically, my methods instructor gossiped about that professor. Progressivism is the prevailing philosophy in universities across the country, and this alone could suffice to prove the dominance of progressivist philosophies. If the institutions that train our teachers are progressivist in nature then it's safe to assume that the day-to-day practices of these teachers will reflect that philosophy. But what of K-12 schools?

State- and even federal-level curricula reveal a progressivist understanding of teaching and learning. In my own state of Wisconsin, the curriculum for social studies asks that students learn to *evaluate* primary and secondary sources and *analyze* significant historical events.[17] That gives me as much direction for what to do in my classroom as a city map without street names. In the 67-page document outlining these standards (endless lists of skills), concrete topics to be covered account for a whopping three pages. The focus is entirely on skills, not content.

It's not mere incompetence that leads to such vague phrasing. Rather, when the purpose of learning is the development of academic skills, as the seminal philosopher of education John Dewey would have it, curricula then amount to a list of skills in place of facts, eras, or works of literature worth knowing. Where my state does attempt such clear guidance, it suggests "the modern era" or the "meeting of peoples and cultures."[18] It's the same story with Common Core, a list of skills asking students to analyze, evaluate, and identify in place of clear topics worth learning. Learning is implicitly defined as doing, not knowing. When progressivism undergirds our curricula, it will permeate our classrooms and discussions about teaching and learning.

As one last example, one of the most popular English language arts (ELA) curricula in the US is Lucy Calkins' Units of Study. I used it for a number of years. Students picked their own books and spent most of the class cloistered off; where direct instruction occurred, it came in short spurts and amounted to vague suggestions for habits that students ought to practice, rather than clear, explicit explanations of grammar, structure, rhetoric, or anything of the sort. In reality, Units of Study isn't much of a curriculum at all. Like the aforementioned state standards, it outlines no clear knowledge worthy of instruction. Rather, it is an approach to the literature classroom called the "workshop model" systematized and packaged for sale. The Fountas and Pinnell intervention system follows a similar philosophy of learning to read, and together these are two of the top five most used curricula in the country—that's millions of students and thousands of teachers using a progressivist approach to teaching and learning in the ELA classroom.

Our schools remain a hodgepodge of traditionalism and progressivism. Schools run choice units and still teach George Orwell's *Animal Farm* as a whole-class text. They lecture about science concepts and run class labs. They foster skills and teach explicit content. I make no claim that the progressivist ideology alone runs our schools, but that it is one voice—arguably the loudest—that many people listen to and it is very often wrong. From the university down to the classroom, educational progressivism permeates American education.

THE PURPOSE OF THIS BOOK

One hope for this book is to create a counter-narrative. Much of the dominant progressivist discourse wraps itself in self-righteous language, and so opposition appears in opposition to all good things. What monster would oppose "student-centered learning?" Don't we want to empower students to construct their own knowledge and classroom culture? Take, for example, a union leader who said in 1916, "I believe that every child should be happy in school. So we have tried to substitute recreation for drill."[19] This statement assumes that drill and happiness, rigor and joy, cannot co-exist. A *New York Times* bestselling book on education conceives of traditionalist pedagogy as: "Children read textbooks, memorized their contents, and studied each subject … hunched over a desk."[20] Traditionalism is joyless, leaving no room for self-expression, engagement, or activity—or so runs the argument.

The reality is that these assertions are mere rhetoric. A few counter-examples may help to elucidate my point. Individualized instruction means each student receives appropriate attention in their zone of proximal development, correct? In reality, individualized attention, in a large class, all too often means individualized neglect. When I'm conferring with one student, that means 29 others are left to themselves without teacher direction. Conversely, whole-class instruction means *every* student receives a teacher's expert guidance. Take another example. To place primacy on self-expression in writing over structure and grammar leaves students without the linguistic capacities they need to communicate. Mastery precedes and facilitates self-expression. When an actor memorizes and rehearses their lines, that is not an impediment to self-expression but a means to it.

More examples abound. To renounce adult-enforced rules leaves students vulnerable to the passions, frustrations, and misbehavior of their peers. Without the memorization of basic facts and the automaticity that comes through rote practice, students are unable to achieve the critical and higher-order thinking that we so claim to revere.

Despite their euphonious framing, the progressivist theories of education are not humanistic, not holistic, not empowering. They leave students ill-equipped, lacking knowledge, and without the capacity for critical thought that their advocates claim they engender. In reality, it's the traditionalist approaches to education that achieve these ends. Achieving this reframing requires a few steps.

First, I begin this book with a history of educational thought to identify the philosophical ideas that undercut both traditionalist and progressivist theories of education. Living in our specific time and culture, it's all too easy to accept as fact the contemporary platitudes and understandings about the purpose of education. A survey of educational thought will help to show that the things we accept as so commonsensical as to be unquestioned were—throughout history—questioned, unaccepted, ignored. How philosophers treated ideas throughout history has no bearing on the actual veracity of such ideas, but knowing so accomplishes two goals: it identifies the current assumptions in education, and gives us a sense of humility and a willingness to critique even that which we considered beyond critique.

In part II of the book, I dedicate a chapter each to knowledge, learning, and character, comparing how traditionalist and progressivist theories of education understand each of these broad topics and what they mean for classroom practice. These three chapters are based on a framework set out by John Dewey[21]: any learning encounter involves the content, the context, and the student. The chapter on knowledge asks *what* we ought to teach to students, the chapter on learning asks *how* teachers can best teach so that students learn, and the chapter on character discusses the best systems to put in place *where* students learn.

Part III includes three chapters. First, I discuss how these theories manifest in real-world schools and classrooms. Next, I re-examine and interrogate several contemporary cliches in education, not only to expose their shortcomings but also to demonstrate how a traditionalist approach could make better sense of the ideas behind them. Finally, I lay out a new canon of educational thought. If ideology is at the root of our educational woes, we need to embrace the books and thought that point us in a better direction.

Another way to conceive of the structure of this book is moving from philosophical analysis in part I, to an explication of the social scientific studies and randomized controlled trials in part II, and on to a discussion of these ideas in action in part III. To unstick the "blob," to vivify our education system, requires an identification of these progressivist ideas, a critique of them, and the provision of an alternative. It's no use deconstructing the dominant narratives in a system if no alternative takes their place. The whole purpose of deconstruction is to build back something better.

Perhaps most importantly, I hope this book to be something of an introductory overview. When I graduated and began my teaching career, I had reservations about the progressivist pedagogy into which my university trained me. Shouldn't we be teaching students what's outside of their typical interest? Don't lectures have a place? Can't students be wrong in their own perceptions or preferences? Are there no behavior expectations that are appropriate? Surely a detention or suspension has some place in a school? I had reservations but I knew no alternative. I intend for this book to sketch out such an alternative, from the philosophical first principles through the academic studies and classroom practices. By the nature of one single 200-page text, it cannot possibly cover everything. It will be too short on the philosophy for some, on the research for others, and on the practical recommendations for yet more. However, to make a convincing case, to establish a substantive alternative, requires that I touch on at least all three.

This book is the culmination of my rediscovery of education, from my first faltering attempts at a workshop model to a robust, teacher-centered classroom with a central text and knowledge-rich activities. There are other authors who have better mastered the cognitive science underlying these ideas. Yet more have fancy degrees. Some focus specifically on teacher development, producing "recipe books" on how to craft a rigorous, meaningful, traditionalist classroom. I'm none of these. I'm a visiting fellow at a think tank but I am no super-credentialed scholar.

However, I am a practicing teacher. I've read more books and scholarly articles while writing this one than I did throughout my own master's program. I've observed lots of teachers, taught lots of classes, and seen problems worth solving. I don't just debate these ideas in the abstract; I have also put them into practice in a classroom and seen the results. I've broken up fights, had my class interrupted by a tooth that fell out, and played four square with students. I've cried after a lesson gone awry, pulled myself together, reflected on went wrong, and faced the next class with a smile on my face.

REFERENCES

1. Hattie, J. (2008) *Visible Learning*, Routledge

2. Roser, M. & Ortiz-Ospina, E. (2013) "Literacy," Our World in Data, https://ourworldindata.org/literacy

3. Haimson, L. (2021) "To reduce inequality in our education system, reduce class sizes," *The Nation*, www.thenation.com/article/politics/school-class-size

4. Jepsen, C. & Rivkin, S. (2009) "Class size reduction and student achievement: the potential tradeoff between teacher quality and class size," *The Journal of Human Resources*, 44(1), pp. 223-50

5. Jepsen, C. & Rivkin, S. (2002) "What is the tradeoff between smaller classes and teacher quality?" (working paper), National Bureau of Economic Research, www.nber.org/papers/w9205

6. Nyhan, R.C. & Alkadry, M.G. (1999) "The impact of school resources on student achievement test scores," *Journal of Education Finance*, 25(2), pp. 211-27

7. Ibid.

8. Chingos, M.M. (2011) "Reviewing the evidence on class size," Brookings Institution, www.brookings.edu/opinions/reviewing-the-evidence-on-class-size

9. Chingos, M. & Whitehurst, G. (2011) "Class size: what research says and what it means for state policy," Brookings Institution, www.brookings.edu/research/class-size-what-research-says-and-what-it-means-for-state-policy

10. Ibid.

11. Dynarski, M. & Kainz, K. (2015) "Why federal spending on disadvantaged students (Title I) doesn't work," Brookings Institution, www.brookings.edu/research/why-federal-spending-on-disadvantaged-students-title-i-doesnt-work

12. National Center for Education Statistics. "Fast facts: Expenditures," https://nces.ed.gov/fastfacts/display.asp?id=66. Accessed July 2022

13. Roser, M. & Ortiz-Ospina, E. "Financing education," Our World in Data, https://ourworldindata.org/financing-education. Accessed July 2022

14. Dynarski, M. & Kainz, K. (2015) "Why federal spending on disadvantaged students (Title I) doesn't work," Brookings Institution, www.brookings.edu/research/why-federal-spending-on-disadvantaged-students-title-i-doesnt-work

15. Schalin, J. (2019) "The politicization of university schools of education: the long march through the education schools," The James G. Martin Center for Academic Renewal, p. 53, www.jamesgmartin.center/wp-content/uploads/2019/02/The-Politicization-of-University-Schools-of-Education.pdf

16. Steiner, D. (2005) "Skewed perspective," *Education Next*, 5(1), www.educationnext.org/skewedperspective

17. Wisconsin Department of Public Instruction. (2018) *Wisconsin Standards for Social Studies*, https://dpi.wi.gov/sites/default/files/imce/standards/New%20 pdfs/2018_WI_Social_Studies_Standards.pdf

18. Ibid.

19. Goldstein, D. (2014) *The Teacher Wars: a history of America's most embattled profession*, Doubleday

20. Ibid.

21. Dewey, J. (1963) *Experience and Education*, Macmillan

2. A HISTORY OF EDUCATIONAL THOUGHT

At my old school, few English teachers still taught their ninth-grade class the entirety of a novel. *To Kill a Mockingbird* suffered the chopping block and the movie filled in the details. Students got only a few scenes from *Romeo and Juliet*; a "textversation" adaptation with emojis and textspeak (brb, ttyl, lol) made its rounds. "It just wasn't that important," one teacher told me, as the "skills" students would learn took precedence over actually finishing a book. Where teachers attempted complete works of fiction, this took the form of choice units where students selected their own books to read independently. From my observations, few of them actually read a whole book. They hid their phone between pages, covered it when the teacher happened to look, and resumed the endless scroll when eyes were again cast aside.

Education has descended from the aristocratic ideals of the Greek academe to the scent of marijuana drifting down my halls; from Loyola's first attempts to systematize a classical curriculum to movements to deconstruct them; from Shakespeare and Aristophanes to *Diary of a Wimpy Kid* and *Divergent*; from Plato's celebration of an education that teaches us to love what is beautiful to bell hooks encouraging "teaching to transgress." Forgive my early-onset curmudgeonliness when I say that education ain't what it used to be. There has been a decline and fall that cannot continue.

What has caused this decline? Various individual thinkers and movements have, like guideposts, pointed our teachers and theorists off course, while others have, thankfully, directed them back on. In this chapter, I trace a handful of these intellectual traffic cops through

Western educational thought, from our classical Greek foundations up to our modern critical theorists.

In brief, though, our system has renounced the Greco-Roman and then Christian traditions of education that valued instruction into the good, the true, and the beautiful. This approach needn't be religious. Phrased differently, early pedagogues and teachers valued education as it directed their students to something beyond themselves. They wanted their students to learn the intellectual truths of the world and align their actions to an objective morality, be it religiously imposed or otherwise. Over the course of history, however, the emphasis on objectivism has faded into either an obsessive focus on the self, in the case of progressive education, or an attitude that seeks to destroy and deconstruct, in the case of critical pedagogues.

In tracing these philosophical shifts, I hope to show that many of the assumptions we now consider self-evidently true were not always so, and in many cases run contrary to historical thought. Identification of these differences does not immediately verify or discredit them. However, as examples and non-examples help students to learn new concepts, through a comparison of historical ideas it's easier to identify and isolate beliefs, and hold them at arm's length for critical consideration. We can never quite get an objective look at modern sentiments, but attempting to view our contemporary moment through a historical lens will get us as close as we possibly can.

In other words, I want to look at the history of educational thought in order to critique the present. If we know that the common beliefs of education today are a historical aberration, they will be easier to debunk. It will be easier to compare, contrast, and critique our current assumed incontrovertible truths. Returning to my original metaphor, we can look back at the course we took, think about where we're going, and decide how far we've deviated, where we need to continue, and where we need to turn back.

1. A TOWERING IDEAL: THE TRADITIONALISTS

The Greeks

Arguably the first tract of education philosophy in the West is Plato's *Republic*. Plato believed that education would help to establish a well-ordered society, so, although ostensibly a book about justice, *The Republic* contains much discussion of what the students in his ideal Republic ought to learn.

Perhaps the best inroad to Plato's thought is his "allegory of the cave." In Plato's writing, which takes the form of a Socratic dialogue, the protagonist, Socrates (Plato's teacher), asks his interlocutors to imagine people chained within a cave, with their backs to a fire and their eyes on a wall. He describes people walking by holding statues such that the light of the fire casts shadows of horses, humans, and objects upon the wall. The imprisoned spend their days watching these shadows and, knowing nothing else, they mistake them for reality. The purpose of education in Plato's mind was to unshackle these individuals and introduce them to the world as it really is.

Central to Plato's philosophy is his "theory of forms." In his epistemology, people can hold beliefs and knowledge but the ultimate goal of education is consideration of the forms—idealized versions of all things. Take cats, for example. There may be hundreds of millions of cats in the world of various shapes, sizes, and colors, but there is one perfect idea of a cat. It's why Greek sculptures always represent idealized individuals; art helps us to consider things as they ought to be, not as they necessarily are. Plato's allegory of the cave reflects this idea: we proceed from falsehood (watching the shadows), to knowledge of physical reality (observing the world outside the cave), to grasping truth itself (viewing the sun).

While modern minds rightly reject the esoteric theory of forms, there's still much we can learn from this philosophy if we think of it metaphorically. The role of education and the educator is to introduce students to the truth of the world. Throughout our lives, we adopt and accept beliefs that are verifiably false. Children call things by the wrong name or simply lack knowledge about that which is outside their immediate experiences, like historic events or scientific discoveries. It is the role of the educator to lead students beyond their insular interests and beliefs.

Plato insists that we carefully select the stories to which we expose our students. He knew, like Paul the Apostle, that if we reflect upon that which is corrupted, our lives will follow. Whereas if we spend time considering what is beautiful or lovely, our lives will be likewise. Plato provides the image of sheep grazing. If we surround the sheep with poisonous plants, the animals will quickly sicken and die, but if we provide them with nourishing food, they thrive. So, too, the capacity of our students for deep thought will wither if they are fed immoral or flimsy tales. Take, for instance, Achilles. Though a noble hero, he is rash and violent. Similarly, many individuals in various epics are insubordinate, vain, and proud. If our students lionize characters such as these, they are apt to become rash, violent, insubordinate, vain, and proud.

We needn't accept Plato's authoritarian recommendation of state-sponsored censorship, but the first principle is worth reiterating: the literature to which we introduce our children will shape their views, ethics, and personalities. Some tales are more worthy of instruction than others. Any English teacher will tell you that some books facilitate more robust discussions; other books contain one-dimensional characters, giving rise to only hollow instruction and equally one-dimensional reflection. Taken further, not *all* tales are worthy of instruction. Teachers and adults select those that will encourage children to pursue justice, venerate courage, and so on. Plato tells us that "the object of education is to teach us to love what is beautiful."[1] A student who has left the cave will love and enjoy that which is good, be it a story, song, moral action, or right living.

It's not only the tales that are important, but who selects them. In Plato's allegory, the shackled individuals need a guide to help them out. Effective teachers ought to be experts in their fields of study, introducing children to the poetry of Shakespeare, the sublimity of astronomy, the elegance of mathematics. Students imbibe their teachers' joy and excitement, and so learn to love what is beautiful. They come to appreciate the precision of mathematical arguments, the fresh imagery and striking wordplay of great authors, or the descriptive power of a scientific formula.

After Plato came Aristotle. A student of Plato, Aristotle's vision for education often reflects his teacher's. Where he explicitly discusses education in his book *Politics*, it's mostly a repetition of Plato's ideas. We can gain more insight from his *Nicomachean Ethics*. Along with the Stoic philosopher Marcus Aurelius, Aristotle touches on something that is astoundingly controversial to assert today: that there is a right way to live.

Aristotle and Marcus Aurelius would not impose a daily routine, religion, or anything so prescriptive on their students. Nonetheless, Aristotle argues that it is incumbent upon us as moral beings to apply virtues such as honesty and courage to our lives. How can a father be courageous in his parenting? How can a mother gently correct her child's misbehavior? What does temperance mean for a shopkeeper or banker? Each virtue manifests differently in application to an individual's life, but the undergirding ethic remains. Going further, Aristotle would say that certain actions are right or wrong regardless of circumstances, as they align with or run counter to objective moral law. We humans do not construct our ethics, morals, or knowledge; rather, we consider an objective standard and apply it to our subjective lives.

In his *Meditations*, Marcus Aurelius argues the same: an action is right if it's courageous; a speech is appropriate if it's humble; a day is best spent with proper self-control. Notably, in both authors' works, these virtuous actions are not expected only of heroes and kings; daily habits and small deeds matter just as much to right living. I expose the depth of my nerdiness here when I say that Gandalf, Tolkien's wise wizard, provides a cogent summary:

> *Saruman believes it is only great power that can hold evil in check, but that is not what I have found. I have found it is the small things, everyday deeds of ordinary folk, that keep the darkness at bay; simple acts of kindness and love.*[2]

It's the everyday activities that best determine our virtue and make the greatest impact on this world; we spend the majority of our time in small, daily pursuits, after all. How we make our breakfast, the words we use to greet those around us, the routines we establish in a classroom—these small habits matter. It's essential that we consider how to express objective morality even in our smallest actions.

That fundamental belief in an objective moral law has far-reaching consequences for education that I could not possibly cover in a single book. For the time being, I want to continue engaging with Aristotle and his advocacy for habit as it facilitates the expression of virtue. The modern understanding of habits defines them as that which we do without thinking. They are rigid and unconscious; they lack any defined goal. My students habitually tap their pencils. We ask our children to habitually say please and thank you. The coffee I brew in the morning is a habit; I do not stand before my coffee pot every morning and ponder the ethical implications of drinking a cup.

Aristotle thought habits were far more robust. They can be consciously chosen and formed. They are as much a chosen disposition as a thoughtlessly acquired tic. If the little actions are important for ethical living and we can train ourselves into these actions, it's imperative that we do so. Plato, too, was concerned with self-mastery. He acknowledges that humanity is capable of great good and great evil, writing: "When the better has the worse under control, then a man is said to be master of himself."[3] This mastery takes practice and temperance.

Teachers can help students to develop these habits. Remembering to bring a pencil indicates that they will be conscientious adults who remember small details later in their lives at work. Working silently now encourages focus of thought and respect for others. Of course, as adults, these children can critically consider these habits and change them as they see fit. However, we do them a disservice in the present and the future if we do not help them to develop productive, respectful, and virtuous habits as students.

And so the Greeks leave us with two first principles worth remembering: there is content worth knowing that it is incumbent upon adults to share; and there are right and wrong actions about which we must teach and habituate our students. Teaching our children to be self-controlled and patient is better than encouraging impulsivity and rashness, not just because these qualities will better help them to secure a job in the future, but also because these habits of action are objectively superior.

Modern Traditionalists

Since Plato and Aristotle, countless academics, scholars, and philosophers have advanced, defended, explicated, and clarified these classical foundations. Central to their belief is that some things—like the Grand Canyon or Chinua Achebe's *Things Fall Apart*, for example—are worthy of our admiration. To think otherwise betrays a fault in ourselves, not the object. C.S. Lewis wrote that he did not "enjoy the society of children" but recognized this as a "defect in myself."[4]

I always disliked Joseph Conrad's *Heart of Darkness*, but assumed I had missed something rather than blaming the book. Then I read an edition with explanatory notes that helped me to understand its beauty and significance. I needed a guide to teach me to love it. Similarly, if a class is left disliking Shakespeare, I question the instruction, not the Bard. I've observed too many teachers read *Romeo and Juliet* in a dull monotone, without guiding questions or vivifying discussions. Echoing Plato, the explanatory edition of *Heart of Darkness* revealed the beauty in it—and we are to help our students likewise.

Underscoring the inherent worth of certain knowledge is what Lewis refers to as the Tao, an objective reality built upon "the belief that certain attitudes are really true, and others really false, to the kind of thing the universe is and the kind of things we are."[5] Courage is venerable, lying to be avoided, murder abominable, and justice to be sought. Lewis updates Plato's theory of forms to something our modern pretensions can accept.

Whether or not one believes that this objective reality exists—in the physical world or in the abstractions of morals, ethics, and aesthetic value—fundamentally alters our understanding of the role of education. Rejection of it leaves us with job training, critical sentiments, or arbitrarily justified values as our only conceivable goal. Belief in it points us to something beyond ourselves. Beautiful literature, the triumphs and failures of history, the wonders of the world discovered through science— these things direct us to this objective reality. Man can no more conceive of a new value or virtue than we can change the color spectrum. It is our duty only to discover the Tao.

Literature is full of compelling expressions of this approach to education. We've asked all the questions, G.K. Chesterton quips, and it's about time we start looking for answers.[6] "The disappearance of prejudices simply means that we have lost the answers on which we ordinarily rely without even realizing they were originally answers to questions," writes Hannah Arendt.[7] "Skepticism only has utility when it leads to conviction," argues William F. Buckley.[8] These thinkers express the idea that education is not just about inculcating a capacity for critical consideration, but also about instruction into truth and virtue, as best as we can currently conceive them. We open our minds to close them again around something concrete.

A brief foray into epistemology may further explicate this point. The theory of truth to which most of these thinkers ascribe, whether overtly or not, is correspondence theory, which posits that true statements are those that align with reality. We can have beliefs that do not align with reality, like a child who thinks storks deliver babies. There are also truths that we simply don't know, like a child who has never heard of Napoleon. Finally, there is knowledge: beliefs that align with reality.

A common criticism has it that correspondence theory is inadequate because we as humans are situated within a culture, a context, a period in history that shapes and distorts our beliefs. As such, regardless of the existence of truth or actual reality, we cannot possibly come to know it with any real certainty. The best we can do is to construct biased perceptions of the world. Although this criticism is valid—we are biased by time, place, and culture—it does little to refute the ontological assertion that objective reality exists. Even if our contextualized and historical biases cloud our ability to determine with certainty anything about this world, to give up on the pursuit of truth and knowledge is to erase the purpose of education altogether.

Alongside objective reality—whether it is termed the Tao, knowledge, or true belief—traditionalists also revere the past. The totality of human knowledge comes from those who lived before us; from their scientific discoveries or literary expressions of the human condition. This totality of human knowledge, sifted and winnowed through time, is tradition. History acts as a sort of winnowing fork. Countless individuals, critics, authors, teachers, historians, and so on have deemed writers ranging from Shakespeare to Marx as minds worth reckoning with. Even if we ultimately disagree with or dislike these writers, to ignore the endorsement of millions of minds before us is a rather arrogant proposal.

From the past, we also get worldviews alien to our own. If we value diversity of thought and culture then the past is an ideal place to look. In many ways, I have far more in common with contemporary students of mine from different cultures than any of us do with Aristotle or St. Augustine. Exposure to works from the past places our worldviews under greater pressure than modern contention. Modern minds share many experiences and first principles, even if they seemingly disagree on the surface. In other words, nothing allows us to critically consider the present quite like reading old books. Through them, we encounter ideas, arguments, and lines of thought contrary to what we accept as common sense. When I read Edmund Burke forcefully defend hereditary monarchy in his *Reflections on the Revolutions in France*—not only as the best form of government but as the most ethical and humanitarian— it forces me to question contemporary dogmas. Burke is wrong but his writings can expose shortcomings in our modern assumptions, like our unquestioned allegiance to liberty and democracy as ends in themselves.

A Jewish proverb from the Old Testament tells us that as iron sharpens iron, so one person sharpens another. I would extend that metaphor to the past. When our own ideas and ideologies confront the arguments of history, we sharpen our own intellect like a knife on a whetstone. And if we don't look to the past, we leave ourselves blind to our own dogmatisms. The present creates a stronger bias than any skin color or political affiliation. In reading old books, a torrent of unique ideas spill over on to our contemporary attitudes, knocking down those that are weak and exposing the strength of others.

A passage from Lewis is worth quoting in full. In it, he discusses two textbook writers who he calls Gaius and Titus, and the implications of their disregard for the past.

> *In actual fact Gaius and Titus will be found to hold, with complete uncritical dogmatism, the whole system of values which happened to be in vogue among moderately educated young men of the professional classes during the period between the two wars. Their scepticism about values is on the surface: it is for use on other people's values; about the values current in their own set they are not nearly sceptical enough.*[9]

It is the very reason for this ancestry of educational thought. If we look only to contemporary debates, we'll miss the criticisms and contentions offered by the past. And if education is the training of the mind then our students ought to encounter thinkers who lived far before their time.

2. THE EDIFICE CRUMBLES: EDUCATIONAL PROGRESSIVISM

Jean-Jacques Rousseau (1712-78)

Rousseau was the first to question these paradigms—the value of specific knowledge, the teacher's centrality, human imperfectability, and the like. In his tract *Emile: Or on Education* (1762), he outlines a philosophy that directly opposes the classical beliefs that came before him. The book's central conceit is that Rousseau is writing a letter to a young woman, instructing her in the best methods for raising her son. His book progresses chronologically—from the birth of its central protagonist, Emile, to his eventual marriage. Through it, Rousseau advances a mistaken understanding of human nature, freedom, and the value of book learning, which together established the foundation for contemporary progressivist theories of education.

When it comes to our educational maladies, most if not all roads lead back to Rousseau. He is the progenitor of what E.D. Hirsch has dubbed "educational romanticism."[10] Rousseau injected the ideological framework of the Romantic movement—a reaction to the cold rationalism of the Enlightenment and the urbanization of the Industrial Revolution—into the philosophy of education. Namely, he introduced what has since been dubbed the naturalistic fallacy: that whatever is natural is "good." He contends throughout *Emile* that children ought to follow their own nature and that any impediment to these natural inclinations is immoral. Children naturally play and so their learning must never involve any contrived lesson planning or rote practice.

What comes naturally may be best, or it may not be. Lots of things happen in nature that humanity rightly decries as abhorrent and many of our greatest advances have come by way of unnatural technological achievements. We cannot call that which is natural "good" or "bad" any more than we can technological advancement. All things must be weighed independently in light of the consequences that follow.

Rousseau makes his fundamental mistake in the opening to his work *The Social Contract*. He writes that "man is born free and everywhere he is in chains."[11] This pithy phrase contains a substantive view of human nature and the crux of Rousseau's naturalistic fallacy: that human beings are inherently good but our institutions, society, politics, and interactions corrupt us. Man is not broken; only that which he has created is. As such, the ideal education removes the child from society, from its social norms, from the control and direction of authorities, and allows them to instead follow their own inborn goodness. "The first impulses of nature are always right," Rousseau writes in *Emile*. "There is no original sin in the human heart."[12]

As such, from the beginning, Rousseau emphasizes an ultimate freedom that permits the child to pursue their desired outcomes without reservation. He writes, "The education of the earliest years should be merely negative. It consists, not in teaching virtue or truth, but in preserving the heart from vice and spirit of error."[13] The sole purpose of education until the child reaches the "age of reason" is merely to allow them to play and pursue their own inclinations, free from the corrupting influences of society.

Rousseau goes so far as to deride the constriction of a baby's movement through swaddling. According to him, infants cry from restriction, and when left to move instead they can walk well within the first few months. As they age, Rousseau advances a similar belief about the centrality of freedom, suggesting that "the perpetual restraint imposed upon your scholars stimulates their activity; the more subdued they are in your presence, the more boisterous they are as soon as they are out of your sight."[14] As a baby supposedly cries at the restriction of a swaddle, children develop a spirit of rebellion and misbehavior in response to the constraints placed upon them by a tutor or society. Like forcing down a spring, when the restraint is finally released, the spring bursts out. As such, Rousseau advances a vision of freedom and early education that permits students to do whatever is "in their nature," a phrase he returns to again and again.

While Rousseau's condemnation of swaddling is a bit obsessive, it's a salient example, both literally and metaphorically. In reality, babies calm at the sense of security that a swaddle provides. Swaddling prevents them from harming themselves before they know better than to not scratch their own eyes. In rare cases, we even need something as contrived as a cast, sling, or harness to help a child's bones and joints grow properly. As the restraint of a swaddle protects and calms a child, routines and expectations foster a safe environment and a comfortable sense of normalcy for students. When schools have clearly defined and enforced rules, students can attend without having to worry about a physical confrontation at the doors. They can focus on their math instead of worrying about what harassment awaits them at lunch. They know they will have moments of silence in their day. The question shouldn't be if we have routines and expectations, but rather *what* should be our routines and expectations. No time in school is as hectic as the freewheeling indoor recess.

Ultimately, Rousseau's idealistic view of humanity is suspect. Be it Christian conceptions of original sin, Thomas Hobbes' declaration that the life of man is "solitary, poor, nasty, brutish, and short,"[15] or simple skepticism of the faculties of a mind developed through the mindless process of natural selection, most philosophies agree there is something rotten in the state of man. Even if we could somehow craft a perfect system, middle school boys would still pick fights and conversations would still get catty or outright cruel.

Some misbehavior stems from cultural conflict or unnecessary restraint, surely, but not all does—and that is an essential point. The theologian St. Augustine offers a useful anecdote from his own childhood for this discussion. Augustine and a few friends wandered into a local orchard, stole a number of pears, ate a few, and destroyed the rest. Notably, Augustine comments at the end of this story that they did not commit this minor crime because they were hungry or frustrated, but because they reveled in the joy of doing something wrong.[16]

The simple reality is that humans aren't perfect, and it's both naive and pernicious to leave ourselves and, in particular, our students without healthy restraint. When teachers and educationalists accept Rousseau's vision of freedom—a definition of freedom merely *from* external restraint—some inherently good nature does not then direct the child to all things good. To quote Jonathan Porter, the former deputy head of Michaela Community School in London, "like energy, we cannot remove authority; we can only move it elsewhere."[17]

To remove the constraints that adults, parents, and teachers have knowingly and lovingly placed upon a child leaves the child prey to other, often unknown authorities: the internet, social media, unhealthy passions, the strongest child in the group, arbitrary cultural norms. Dismantle a carefully chosen and constructed system of rules and norms and a more pernicious authority often takes its place. Echoing Plato's call for self-mastery, a removal of norms can leave us enslaved to ourselves, in a sense.

Most people remember *The Strange Case of Dr. Jekyll and Mr. Hyde* for the final plot twist—the protagonist's split personality. However, Robert Louis Stevenson's novella is more than its intriguing plot twist; it is a profound reflection on the duality of human nature and personal freedom, and a compelling example of the implications of ultimate "freedom." The final chapter is a 40-page reflection on human passions and the rotten side that most philosophers agree exists, whatever they may call it. The protagonist, Dr. Jekyll, alludes to his mind now being "enslaved" to his desires. Through his transformation into Mr. Hyde, Jekyll had thrown off the arbitrary constraints of Victorian society only to then be powerless before his vices—drink, anger, sensuality, pride. As the story progresses, Jekyll loses control of Hyde, and his final renunciation of social norms does not end in Rousseauian freedom but a more malign enslavement.

A more robust understanding of freedom embraces not merely *freedom from* but also *freedom to*—the power for people to consciously choose their actions. When I read *Dr. Jekyll and Mr. Hyde* with students, I have to think of examples other than Stevenson's coy allusions to sensuality to keep it child-friendly. We discuss freedom as it relates to health and media addictions. Regarding health, freedom is not eating whatever one wants, but the self-control to choose celery or the donut, a relaxing afternoon or exercise, as best fits the current moment. As the discussion relates to media, my students have few constraints before the first bell rings. Most of them use this time to play video games almost compulsively. They are free from adult constraints for this quarter of an hour, but watching rows of kids stare blankly into screens hardly evokes a sense of freedom.

Part of the *freedom from* advanced by Rousseau comes through a repudiation of habit. Rousseau wants his student to learn none. Rather, he will form Emile's willpower through observation and experience. He gives the example of a teacher lecturing their student over and again about the damages wrought by anger. However, allow the child to see a man fly off the handle, discuss this experience once, and the student will learn a far more lasting lesson. Rousseau believes this learning through experience, free from constraints, will accomplish the *freedom to* that I speak of far better than any contrived habit.

However, mere convincing isn't enough. I know social media is addictive and yet I still spend too much time on it. We've all been convinced time and again that too many baked goods are bad for us and yet our will falters whenever donuts make their way into the staff lounge. We can show students the effects of cigarette smoke on a human lung and yet many will choose to smoke regardless. Paul the Apostle touched on something profound when he wrote, "For I do not do the good I want to do, but the evil I do not want to do."[18] Rather, it is through habit and carefully chosen restraint that we can train our minds and bodies to do what we will. As the Greeks suggest, habits are essential.

Mere *freedom from* is not empowering. Consider freedom as it relates to music. A teacher could have a child sit at their piano and provide no directives or constraints, asking the child to play whatever comes to mind. The student may plunk away at a few notes but little would come of it. Conversely, with a schedule and exercises to practice scales, that student will eventually be able to play whatever their heart desires, be it Chopin's nocturnes, Beethoven's concertos, improvisation over bebop chord changes, or the melodies in their own mind. Rousseau would see the child "free from prejudices and free from habits."[19] In reality, habits and constraints facilitate more robust freedom; a more empowered liberty than that provided by Rousseau.

Rousseau's fault lies not just in his vision of human nature, but also in his views about book learning. He instructs tutors to "give your scholar no verbal lessons; he should be taught by experience alone" and argues that students should "learn nothing from books that they can learn from doing."[20]

Beneath these invocations is a faulty epistemology. Rousseau differentiates between a student grasping images, memorization, and mere sensation and a student making connections, learning, and understanding. To explain his meaning, he gives the example of a student who may have learned countless facts about a city like Paris but is unable to navigate his way around upon arriving there. Mere facts are not understanding, suggests Rousseau. However, flip this example around and its flimsiness becomes apparent. A person may grow up navigating around a city like Paris, but will have a poor understanding of it without factual knowledge of its history, government, or the names of its major locations.

There is some knowledge that we learn through direct experience—language, gross motor movements, and the like. There is a lot of knowledge, and much of it quite valuable, that can only be learned through books. There is plenty that we cannot pick up from experience alone: the influence of the Greeks or Romans upon us, the ways of distant cultures, the functions of our government, advanced mathematics, reading and writing—the list goes on. We cannot acquire the complex knowledge that accompanies the culture in advanced societies solely through play and experience; it requires focus, work, and effort. Understanding something demands factual knowledge of it.

Rousseau does level one thoughtful critique. A disconnected curriculum of facts and ideas is a poor curriculum. An ideal education would layer facts with experience: learning about a city before traveling there; covering a historical time period before attending a relevant museum; practicing grammar constructions before employing them in an essay. Similarly, a thoughtful curriculum will sequence new knowledge such that it can be understood in context—a class may read Frederick Douglass' autobiography while learning about the antebellum South in history, for example. However, to subscribe to Rousseau's belief that a child learns *nothing* from books is both anti-intellectual and undermines any purpose of a system of education beyond mere babysitting.

Rousseau advances an idealized vision of humanity and so an education that provides little in the way of direction or, well, education. If humanity is perfect and so is nature, why impose limits or encourage learning from written sources? He's right to criticize learning that is removed from any experience, but little would come of his ideas but ignorance and vice.

John Dewey (1859-1952)

Rousseau's ideas remained largely the interest of individual tutors until Dewey popularized his progressive theories of education at Teachers College, Columbia University, in New York City. Like a superspreader event, this institution then trained thousands of teachers and bestowed upon them the professional airs that come with an official degree. Accordingly, romanticism came to be perceived as the superior ideology in American education.

To his credit, although an educational progressive, Dewey maintained elements of a classically minded educator. He saw that the purposes of the young do not always match that of the old or society itself. As such, education is something of a formative process whereby society shapes individuals for its norms and systems. While not a direct repudiation of Rousseau's naturalism, Dewey advanced at least a pragmatic endorsement of some anti-naturalism and the need to shape the young. Social norms like handshakes lubricate social interaction, allowing us space to consider more important things, and laws like which side of the street to drive on, however arbitrary, facilitate safety. Dewey knew that society needed a means to induct children into its norms, but this is where any reflection of the classical ended. And even this idea is suspect. Dewey took a pragmatic defense, arguing that we should shape and mold children not because there are certain abstract virtues, but for society and their inclusion in a modern economy.

Dewey introduced two flaws into our thinking: that no content is in itself worth learning; and an "experience"-driven method of teaching and learning. Ironically, many of his ideas continue today as if they are new or noteworthy: project-based learning, inquiry learning, student-directed classrooms, workshop models, going gradeless, and so on. Each one bruits itself as the latest innovation. These trends are not new and notable, but rather the reanimated corpses of old ideas that would be better left to rest.

Dewey's first guidepost to steer us off course was his treatment of traditional content and curricula. In his book *Experience and Education* (1938), he wrote that "there is no subject that is in and of itself ... such that inherent educational value can be attributed to it."[21] His criticism undercut the classical justification for education—that schools had something important to teach. Neither Tolstoy nor Shakespeare, germ theory nor individual rights, are worth teaching in themselves—or so goes the argument. To Dewey, the content itself was irrelevant so long as it maintained student interest and thereby acted as a medium to teach "skills." He popularized the "tools" concept of education wherein we teach students the academic skills that can supposedly be generalized across domains.

This emphasis on general academic skills persists today. My own state's history curriculum asks students to "analyze significant historical periods" and "evaluate a variety of primary and secondary sources."[22] Where it does attempt to outline specific content, the language remains vague, like "meeting of peoples and cultures" and "the modern era."[23] It is irrelevant within Deweyian thinking whether an op-ed, novel, or tweet is used to teach the skill. Teach students to evaluate and analyze and they can use these skills to learn about history on their own later. Content be damned.

There are two critiques to level at Dewey (which I discuss in depth in chapter 3). First, some content simply is worth learning in itself. I read Shakespeare and Frederick Douglass with my classes because these are authors worth knowing. The year of Covid-19 demonstrated that our society would benefit greatly from a general understanding of virology, the mechanisms by which immunizations work, and the difference between viruses and bacteria. Regarding historical content, I would call any education that forgoes instruction about Auschwitz, America's founding, or the Atlantic slave trade to be a poor one.

Second, Dewey's suggestion that we focus on abstract skills, appealing though it may be, fundamentally misunderstands how the mind thinks and learns. Critical thinking is not an abstract skill but a knowledge-dependent process. A constitutional lawyer could critically consider an impeachment process because of their vast knowledge about constitutional processes, former examples of impeachment, various litigations that relate to the controversy, and more, but that same lawyer would be useless when faced with a problem of bridge mechanics. Our intellectual skills are not, in fact, skills at all. Rather, the content of learning only enhances our inborn ability to think. The knowledge that we accrue, not abstract skills, is the tool we need to analyze and evaluate the world. If I want students to analyze and evaluate a contemporary law, they would be better off if I taught them about America's founding documents, similar historical bills, and a basic grasp of political theory than any practice of analytical skills.

This line of argument can continue further, but for this section I'll focus on what has been lost: the pursuit of and instruction into virtue and aesthetic ideals. Dewey trained children into the economy; he thought their ultimate aspiration should be to produce goods and services as workers in America's factories and industries. He chipped away at the foundational idea that education ought to pass along the best of humanity to the next generation, and without that corpus of worthy knowledge for transmission he also conceived of a new means of instruction—his second misdirecting guidepost.

In place of a teacher guiding a class through a predetermined curriculum, Dewey would have the child learn from doing. He uses the example of a scientist throughout his book *Democracy and Education* (1916). A child could learn the content of science, or they could carry out experiments to learn the process of science—again calling to mind the "tools" concept of learning. The school is to mimic real life as much as possible. If a child is to learn about physics, they should design a bridge. If they are to learn about the theater, they should script and perform a play. If they are to learn about chemistry, they should run an experiment. Children learn best through doing the practice itself, suggests Dewey. "An ounce of experience is better than any theory," he writes.[24]

Invoking Rousseau, he encourages schools to facilitate "authentic" experiences. Rousseau acknowledged fundamental differences between children and adults, but thought it unwise to relegate "living" to adulthood. It is unnatural to keep children penned up in schoolhouses; a child is to live their authentic life as much as an adult. To Rousseau, this meant open play and exploration; to Dewey, this meant mirroring professional practice in the classroom.

However, educational progressives misunderstand what cognitive psychologists call primary and secondary learning. Primary learning is those things that the human brain is primed to learn, seemingly without effort: spoken language, object permanence, and the like. Secondary learning is everything else: juggling, reading, scientific concepts—the list is endless. Progressive theorists mistake the two, applying principles of exploration and play to the classroom in the form of project-based or inquiry learning, when secondary learning necessitates explicit instructions and at times rote practice.

Regarding the expert and the novice, Dewey wants students to act, live, and work as if they are in the professional field. Modern conceptions of Dewey's thought manifest in phrases like "I want my student to think like a historian." However, we wouldn't teach a child to play their instrument by pushing them onstage in Carnegie Hall, or to do gymnastics by first performing a back handspring. Rather, there are preliminary skills and bits of knowledge that a novice must learn and that the expert takes for granted. The learning of the novice and the actions of the expert are fundamentally different, and to force the former to act as the latter is to rob the novice of the initial and very necessary instruction into any content or vocation.

Progressive thought also places an emphasis on intrinsic motivation. Give the student an authentic (see: natural) project and their motivation will develop. Give them a contrived (see: unnatural) activity or lecture and they will grow bored. Modern iterations focus less on the nature of the work and more on the topic in question. If the student can relate to the project or if the content is relevant to their immediate experience, they will find the instruction more naturally engaging. However, it is astounding to me that we consider an "authentic" real-life project or issue in a student's neighborhood somehow more intrinsically interesting than nebulas, elves, or medieval knights from a distant land. Such an emphasis on surface-level relatability is facile.

A great teacher can make even the most "boring" content engaging. We need to stop blaming the content. Narrating the importance of rote skills when connected to engaging content can make their practice seem worthwhile. We need to stop pretending that the practice of basic skills upon which more complex competency depends is inauthentic. Exposure to broad ideas far beyond a student's immediate experience may pique their interest in a topic that they didn't even know existed. Motivation is an impossibly complex phenomenon that depends on relatability, a sense of purpose, a sense of competence, values, and more. To suggest that authentic projects or relatable content can solve that Gordian knot alone is simplistic.

3. DISMANTLING THE EDIFICE: CRITICAL PEDAGOGY

While Dewey rejected many of the principles of classical and traditional education, he at least maintained a belief in the system itself. He knew that our system had a role to play in maturing our students and preparing them for society, and at the very least for the economy—a utilitarian belief devoid of soul but a belief nonetheless. However, without a robust commitment to tradition, knowledge, wisdom, beauty, and character, Dewey's hollowed-out vision for education is something of an ideological vacuum. Without objective virtues and truths worth teaching, what is the point?

Any vacuum in nature fills quickly, and in the mid 20th century a far more radical vision for our schools seeped into the void left by Dewey. Critical pedagogues began to fill departments of education, and the most consequential of them was Paulo Freire. Whereas traditional education sought to transmit the best that humanity has to offer, critical pedagogy seeks to transform society itself. Whereas Dewey questioned the educative value of various contents, critical pedagogy questions the very idea of "educated." Freire and the later critical theorists completely reconceived what it means to have and receive an education. He critiqued what he termed the "banking concept" of education, wherein teachers transmit to students the literature, history, science, and arts that they ought to know.

Using weather as a metaphor, traditional theories of education seek to furnish students with the clothing and wherewithal to bear the weather that they will face outside their own walls. When they read Shakespeare and Douglass, their education arms them with the garments—the arguments, sentiments, and ideas—that they need to exist within society and live a fruitful life. Conversely, critical theory hopes to change the weather itself. It turns the school building into a place of social action, not learning—ironically leaving students devoid of the very education they would need for effective social change.

Dewey acknowledged that education could have something of a socially transformative effect as it molded the next generation. He wrote:

> *They endeavor to shape the experiences of the young so that instead of reproducing current habits, better habits shall be formed, and thus the future adult society be an improvement on their own. Men have long had some intimation of the extent to which education may be consciously used to eliminate obvious social evils through starting the young on paths which shall not produce these ills, and some idea of the extent in which education may be made an instrument of realizing the better hopes of men.*[25]

Few, I imagine, would contest this vision for education. We all hope that the next generation will avoid our mistakes. Freire, however, brought the transformative power of education to the present and radicalized it. He no longer recognized the goal of improving society into the future, but saw any teacher's role as working with students to transform society in the present, and in a definitively Marxian fashion. As Hannah Arendt warned us, all totalitarian regimes begin with the education of children.[26]

Paulo Freire (1921-97)

More than a million copies of Freire's book *Pedagogy of the Oppressed* have been sold since its publication in 1968, a rare feat for a niche book on education. According to one review of education schools curricula in the journal *Education Next*, it's one of the most assigned texts within teacher training programs.[27] To say it has reached iconic status is an understatement. Academic journals dedicate entire issues to it, and university libraries host special events for it.[28,29]

Unfortunately, within the pages of this influential work, its author endorses the Maoist Cultural, Russian, and Cuban Revolutions as fine examples of his thought in action. Invoking Marx and Hegel, Freire bases his thought on a dichotomy: oppressor vs. oppressed. However, instead of applying this dichotomy to the self, as Hegel does, or to historical epochs, as Marx does, he brings it to the classroom. Whereas classical philosophers conceived of education as a means to pass along, from adult to child, a *paideia*—the best of humanity—Freire portrays this approach as oppressive. To clarify his thought, he details a number of dichotomies present within such a conception:

- *The teacher teaches and the students are taught.*
- *The teacher knows everything and the students know nothing.*
- *The teacher thinks and the students are thought about.*
- *The teacher talks and the students listen—meekly.*[30]

And so on for a handful more. To Freire, the traditional conception of education, wherein teachers have something worth teaching, is fundamentally oppressive. He writes:

In the banking concept of education, knowledge is a gift bestowed by those who consider themselves knowledgeable upon those whom they consider to know nothing. Projecting an absolute ignorance onto others, a characteristic of the ideology of oppression, negates education and knowledge as processes of inquiry. The teacher presents himself to his students as their necessary opposite; by considering their ignorance absolute, he justifies his own existence.[31]

Freire maps his oppressor-oppressed dichotomy on to the teacher-student relationship. So long as this dynamic exists, in Freire's mind, education cannot occur. He famously caricatures a traditional conception of education—that a teacher is to transmit a corpus of knowledge to a student—as "banking" education. Even if his critique were valid, it only matters if his alternative approach is superior.

Ironically, Freire's magnum opus is almost silent on actual pedagogy and practice. Rather, it is a political tract about how to spur the proletariat in small Brazilian towns into action. His goal is not instruction into history, science, mathematics, and literature as we currently conceive of liberal education, but rather consciousness-raising.

As far as Freire does provide clear directions, he encourages revolutionary leaders to travel from town to town, observe local needs, and ask probing questions to encourage workers into discontent and thereby action. He mentions discussion circles wherein he shows workers pictures to get them to question their subservient status. He cites Che Guevara as an example of a loving teacher and the Maoist Cultural Revolution as his thought when systematized. He's not interested in teaching academic subjects, but political action.

Freire is considered the progenitor of critical pedagogy from which came feminist, postcolonial, critical race, deconstructionist, and Marxist pedagogies. In a sense, he is the Martin Luther to an ever-expanding number of radical pedagogy "denominations." Examining critical race theory (CRT) in particular can further explicate the nature of critical pedagogy in general.

Richard Delgado, an early scholar of CRT, and Jean Stefancic write: "...critical race theory questions the very foundations of the liberal order, including equality theory, legal reasoning, Enlightenment rationalism, and neutral principles of constitutional law."[32] Where its proponents will defend CRT as only teaching accurate racial history or using race as a lens to understand society, the issue is that CRT is not *just* these things. Rather, it is using race and our history as a lens through which to condemn Western values. And each branch of critical pedagogy proceeds accordingly, using race, gender, class, or any other signifier as a means to interrogate and condemn our commitment to classically liberal values.

Now, most bespectacled librarians and smiling kindergarten teachers harbor no revolutionary intentions. They are in the classroom to teach phonics and how to find a book using the Dewey Decimal System. Nonetheless, Freire's ideas have had knock-on effects, particularly in terms of his deconstruction of the teacher-student relationship. When the teacher is no longer considered a conduit to a body of knowledge worth knowing, the nature of curriculum and instruction flips. The student, not the teacher, comes to direct the classroom, with the teacher present merely as a "guide on the side." If the past has no value, if there's no wisdom to be found in tradition, then student interest comes to be the compass upon which a class directs itself.

How this affects classroom structure takes many forms. In the English classroom, with teacher authority and the body of knowledge de-centered, a "workshop model" often comes to the fore. In this model, students select their own books—more often than not young adult fiction novels—and partition themselves off in their own isolated corner. When whole-class novels are used, teachers read them through various "lenses." Authorial intent takes a back seat to what a book read through a Marxist or feminist lens exposes about oppressive structures or prejudicial sentiments. Novels and poems are no longer polemics with meaning in themselves, but cultural artifacts to be used to interrogate systems of oppression. In a classroom of "action civics," students spend their time researching problems in their own community to then plan out policy proposals or even protests for social action.

Other activities take a more radical format: a math curriculum in Seattle that centers concepts like identity, oppression, and liberation, encouraging students to reflect on how they can use their math to advance their activism; or mock communist rallies in fifth grade.[33, 34] The goal of these activities is not the transmission and acquisition of knowledge, but consciousness-raising and political transformation.

It's essential to understand that the goal of critical pedagogy is not to prepare students for careers as activists. That is really just another model of banking education—a teacher instilling the right ideas and sentiments into students; education as training and instruction *for the future*. Rather, the goal is to make students activists in the present. Critical pedagogues want students working to change the world *now*.

Most teachers recoil from Freire's revolutionary pretensions but still credit him for his supposedly salient critique of banking education— that learning should not involve a teacher guiding students through predetermined content. However, if we reject banking education then we risk leaving our students defenseless against the very oppressive forces Freire so decries. He, for some reason, seems to suggest that knowledge is oppressive. Francis Bacon (apocryphally) said that knowledge is power.

Both constructions fail. Knowledge is not oppressive, as Freire contends, but rather liberatory. And it's necessary for more than just power, as Bacon contends. Knowledge is *essential*.

Critical pedagogy is a wholly destructive philosophy. Through reading and the study of history, we learn of genuine, robust alternatives to the present. Allan Bloom wrote that without the study of old books, students "lack what is most necessary, a real basis for discontent with the present and awareness that there are alternatives to it."[35] The great irony of Freire's pedagogy is that when his disciples have razed society to the ground, they will lack a vision for the good life or a just society to build in its stead.

More practically, Freire takes cues from John Dewey but applies a radical bent. Dewey would have his students design and complete projects that resemble real-life work, learning the skills and content as if by osmosis. For Freire, in place of designing miniature bridges or performing plays, his "projects" involve political action.

This activist project approach returns to the categorical mistake between the expert and novice. A physicist cannot solve a complex problem without the basic Newtonian laws they learned in high school; a mathematician cannot attempt advanced calculus until their math facts are essentially automatic. It's hard to imagine Matt Damon's character in *Good Will Hunting* winning any academic awards if he's stuck counting on his fingers. We accept this categorical difference in sports and music. A seminal paper by Paul Kirschner, Jon Sweller and Richard Clark (which I will cover in more detail in chapter 4) finds that this dichotomy extends to academic pursuits as well.[36] In order to achieve mastery, students require explicit teaching wherein an expert explains basic concepts and guides structured practice.

Unfortunately, when people think of "banking education," they think of Ben Stein's economics teacher in *Ferris Bueller's Day Off* rambling disconnected facts in a monotone before asking "Anyone? Anyone?" of a silent room of sleeping high-schoolers. In reality, Stein's portrayal remains satire. Many so-called "no excuses" charter schools rely on knowledge-rich curricula and teacher-centric classrooms to build intellectually engaging and empirically successful systems. Teachers drive instruction that is full of robust discussion, clear examples, compelling anecdotes, partner talks, structured practice, and engagement with meaningful texts.

Societal change is difficult and requires incredible mastery to effect. The knowledge of math and physics needed to build clean energy systems is built over years of strenuous and, at times, boring learning. If teachers adopt Freire's philosophy, they might produce activists, yes, but these activists would lack the knowledge and skills to make a positive change in this world. The greatest social activists throughout history have had a vast bank of intellectual capital. To read Martin Luther King Jr. is to read a bibliography of the great thinkers. Alas, placards are easy.

One media-grabbing example from 2019 exposes the ultimate flaw in Freire's approach. A group of students accosted the US Senator Dianne Feinstein in a hallway, hoping to pressure her into signing a piece of legislation. When the students offered little more than slogans and empty rhetoric, Feinstein rebuffed them and presented the various electoral, political, and monetary complications of which they were unaware.[37] The students' teacher would have better spent her time imparting the basics of science and American political processes, thus empowering her students with the knowledge and skills necessary to make changes when they enter the workforce. These young people expressed zeal but lacked any substantive knowledge with which to furnish that passion—a dangerous combination.

Freire challenges the traditional means and ends of education. Rather than training students to love what is beautiful, he would train them to deconstruct what exists. In place of a teacher guiding students through the best that is thought and said—arming them with the knowledge they need to effect change in this world—he would have students debating whatever social cause is trending on Twitter. I'll choose to give my students Shakespeare and mathematical equations over placards and bullhorns.

REFURBISHING THE EDIFICE

Each new movement, from the classical to the Romantics to the critical theorists, has introduced errors in our thinking about education, directing our system, like a confused traffic cop, down a wrong turn. Fundamentally, we have changed our view on human nature and society, and so how institutions of education ought to relate the two. Traditionalists see an inherently civilizing power within existing institutions, the arts, and sciences. It is right and good that students are molded by them. However,

Rousseau's belief in the inherent goodness of man severed us from our need to connect to the past. If society is corrupting but man's natural inclinations are good, then abstract rationalism in the present suffices—teaching critical skills for the present, not arguments of the past—and any adherence to established norms will only degrade a student. The best we can do is to separate them from society.

The critical theorists took this understanding and made it militant. Not only should we separate the student from society, but we should also allow them to turn around and change society itself. Don't just avoid tradition and existing institutions, but question them and tear them down. We allow our natural perceptions and desires to direct society, not the other way around; we are not to escape the structures of society but to remake them in our own image. If we equate education to a garden, traditionalists would bring students into the backyard to show them the garden and teach them the practices that their family has been using for ages. Progressivists would have students experiment about before bringing them back inside to play around. And critical theorists would have them burn down the house and trench the garden.

That being said, from each movement come critiques that traditionalists would be wise to heed. From progressivism, the criticisms are many. While students needn't have complete control of curriculum or classroom practice, it is right to empower them within the classroom. The occasional book-choice unit is comparatively innocuous and smaller decisions can be devolved, like how they want to read for a day—in small groups, independently, or as a class. While the isolation and practice of basic skills are important, students do need summative projects like essays and scientific labs in order to apply these skills and recall this knowledge holistically. Projects cannot be our only source of motivation or practice, but they are a useful one. Finally, knowledge is ultimately useless if students do not acquire it for themselves and apply it to their own life. After parsing the meaning of a reading, teachers must encourage students to reflect from time to time on what it means to them, or to directly connect a historical event to a similar modern event. What use is knowledge if students never employ it?

Regarding critical theory, our system is rife with injustice. Racial disparities persist in behavior consequences and academics. Although the

West has created some of the greatest works of literature and scientific advancements, it is not alone in these achievements and our curricula should reflect that—not to mention the multicultural nature of America. It is right that we should update our curricula to center all races in the American story. Similarly, some of the greatest works of American literature are written by non-white authors, and perhaps it's time to reconsider their place or lack thereof on American curricula. However, it's important that we maintain a commitment to aesthetic ideals and the teacher's role as expert guide; perhaps we can replace the proverbs of Solomon with the Tao Te Ching and Shakespeare with Chinua Achebe, but we should not allow our students to select young adult fiction over Tolstoy.

Such critiques expose blindspots within traditionalist thinking, but they do not thereby justify a wholesale rejection. Rather, traditionalists ought to accept such criticisms without subsequently renouncing direct instruction, teacher authority, adult-determined curricula, and clear consequences. To their credit, most of the traditionalist thinkers and schools that rely upon the lines of thought that I cover in my final chapter do just that. They teach Jacqueline Woodson and Frederick Douglass alongside Shakespeare and George Orwell—works of literature both contemporary and classic, within the cultural mainstream and outside of it. They provide lunch detentions but also require teachers to hold a restorative conversation after the fact. They are what I call neo-traditionalists.

One more development sets neo-traditionalists apart from their forebears: the now preponderance of evidence, scientific and comparative, in defense of their positions. Throughout the rest of this book, I will seek to defend the traditionalist stance not just from a philosophical but also from an evidence-based grounding—both ends of the barbell, so to speak.

I have here traced out a few of the misdirecting guideposts in the history of education—from the vaunted task of introducing students to knowledge and beauty, to a pedagogy of self-direction and skills practice, to a pedagogy that deconstructs the very idea of something worth knowing. From a theory of education that believed students needed shaping and molding, to one that believed the student was perfect and only required gentle guidance, to one that allows the student to enforce their will upon society itself. From the teacher as the expert, to the teacher as a guide, to the teacher handing their students the levers of power.

To me, many of these latter contentions are obviously incoherent. Surely students need some nudging in the right direction and it's the adult's job to do so. Surely some books are better than others and scarce class time is best spent reading the best books. Surely a student who forgets to wash their hands of Cheeto dust before using a laptop ought to have their control of the classroom, let alone the systems of society, curtailed. We've taken wrong turns in education and sometimes, when you've taken a wrong turn, the quickest way to get to your destination is to do an about-face. Progressive and critical education brought us down the wrong road, and it's time we found our way back to the right one—for the sake of our students.

REFERENCES

1. Plato. (1974) *The Republic* (translated by Desmond Lee), Penguin

2. Jackson, P. (2012) *The Hobbit: An Unexpected Journey* (film), Warner Bros. Pictures

3. Plato. (1974) *The Republic* (translated by Desmond Lee), Penguin

4. Lewis, C.S. (1974) *The Abolition of Man*, HarperCollins

5. Ibid.

6. Chesterton, G.K. (2007) *Orthodoxy*, Barnes & Noble

7. Arendt, H. (1978) *Between Past and Future: eight exercises in political thought*

8. Buckley, W.F. (1951) *God and Man at Yale: the superstitions of academic freedom*

9. Lewis, C.S. (1974) *The Abolition of Man*, HarperCollins

10. Hirsch, E.D. (1996) *The Schools We Need and Why We Don't Have Them*, Doubleday

11. Rousseau, J-J. (2005) *The Social Contract*, Barnes & Noble

12. Rousseau, J-J. (1979) *Emile: Or on Education*, Basic Books

13. Ibid.

14. Ibid.

15. Hobbes, T. (1651) *Leviathan*, part 1, chapter 13

16. Augustine, St. (1963) *Confessions of St. Augustine* (translated by Rex Warner), The New American Library

17. Porter, J. (2020) "Michaela — a school of freedom" in K. Birbalsingh (ed.) *Michaela: The Power of Culture*, John Catt Educational, pp. 39-58

18. Biblica. (2011) *The Bible,* New International Version

19. Rousseau, J-J. (1979) *Emile: Or on Education,* Basic Books

20. Ibid.

21. Dewey, J. (1963) *Experience and Education,* Macmillan

22. Wisconsin Department of Public Instruction. (2018) *Wisconsin Standards for Social Studies,* https://dpi.wi.gov/sites/default/files/imce/standards/New%20pdfs/2018_WI_Social_Studies_Standards.pdf

23. Ibid.

24. Dewey, J. (2015) *Democracy and Education,* The Free Press

25. Ibid.

26. Arendt, H. (1978) *Between Past and Future: eight exercises in political thought*

27. Steiner, D. (2005) "Skewed perspective," *Education Next,* 5(1), www.educationnext.org/skewedperspective

28. *Concept.* (2018) "Special anniversary issue: Pedagogy of the Oppressed," 9(3)

29. UCLA Library. (2018) "Pedagogy of the Oppressed: 50th anniversary in print and UCLA Pedagogy Today," www.library.ucla.edu/events/pedagogy-oppressed

30. Freire, P. (1970) *Pedagogy of the Oppressed*

31. Ibid.

32. Delgado, R. & Stefancic, J. (2012) *Critical Race Theory: an introduction,* New York University Press

33. Buck, D. (2021) "Wokeness comes for math in Seattle," *Chalkboard Review,* https://thechalkboardreview.com/report-wokeness-comes-from-math-in-seattle

34. Rufo, C.F. (2021) "Bad education," *City Journal,* www.city-journal.org/philadelphia-fifth-graders-forced-to-celebrate-black-communism

35. Bloom, Allan. (1988) *The Closing of the American Mind,* Simon and Schuster

36. Kirschner, P.A., Sweller, J., & Clark, R.E. (2006) "Why minimal guidance during instruction does not work: an analysis of the failure of constructivist, discovery, problem-based, experiential, and inquiry-based teaching," *Educational Psychologist,* 41(2), pp. 75-86

37. Guardian News. (2019) "Dianne Feinstein rebuffs young climate activists' call for Green New Deal" (video), YouTube, https://youtu.be/jEPo34LCss8

Part II.
Three Key Ideas

3. KNOWLEDGE: WHAT SHOULD STUDENTS LEARN?

One question above any other has affected my philosophy of teaching: what even is critical thinking? Popular conceptions of critical thinking conceive of it as some abstract capacity that can be taught and trained; a tool that can be applied across contexts and contents. As such, the argument goes that schools should foster critical thinking as their main goal, while facts and knowledge can come as necessary. Just as someone could practice using a screwdriver on any manner of projects, a student could practice their critical thinking skills with a contemporary op-ed, tweet, or Greek text in hand. All that matters is that the content is engaging and provides students with opportunities to practice their skills. Google's existence has only heightened this tendency: why know 1776 or absolute zero when we can just look them up?

I used to be a proponent of such conceptions of critical thinking. Before planning a unit, I would decide on a final summative assessment and spend time brainstorming all the practical skills that a student could learn. If a unit ended with an essay, the students would need to know how to categorize facts and quotes, craft a thesis statement, analyze figurative language, and the like. This list informed my lesson plans, with each skill taking a few days of modeling and practice. I even led colleagues through professional development seminars based upon this type of unit planning. We needed to isolate the skill, identify an activity that would help students to practice it, model it, and set them to work.

My skepticism began over drinks. A family member spoke about how hospitals were starting to focus less on degrees or official training and more on critical thinking skills. Society was changing so fast, the argument ran, that any knowledge or formal skills a school could teach would be outdated by the time a student graduated. Focus on critical thinking instead and a student can learn whatever they need once they are older. A nurse or doctor would better serve a variety of patients if, in place of rigid learning and memorized facts, they had problem-solving skills adaptable to various issues.

I began to ask myself: what actually were these hallowed academic skills? Even so-called reading comprehension skills—asking questions, identifying the main idea, making inferences, and so on—seemed suspect. My attempts to isolate skills for a unit always felt like Tantalus reaching for a fruit that wasn't there. For example, I tried to break paraphrasing down into steps, but no amount of scaffolding or process instruction helped. Struggling students stared blankly at Elizabethan English, while other students comprehended and paraphrased passages with ease. Ever present in my mind was a simple question: how can one actually teach somebody to make an inference?

All the while, many of the criticisms typically leveled at the so-called banking method of education felt just as relevant when aimed at Deweyian skills-centric education. Why would students need to paraphrase later in life? Who cares if they can analyze a metaphor?

I sought out books that tried to discover exactly how we think and, more importantly, how teachers could teach critical thinking skills. After finishing a stack of texts, I had come to a startling conclusion: critical thinking is a nonsense concept. In fact, many of the academic skills touted as important are chimeric. It was the genesis of an investigation that ultimately led me to write this book. I hope to show in this chapter that critical thinking—if we seek to maintain that anachronism—is not an abstract skill that can be learned and applied across contexts, but rather a natural capacity that can only be strengthened through the application of knowledge.

THE PROBLEMS WITH SKILLS

Dewey attempted to explicate the nature of critical thinking in his book *How We Think* (1910). Like my own efforts to identify and sequence specific skills, Dewey tries to isolate the individual components of critical thinking. According to Dewey, critical thinking is the "active, persistent, and careful consideration of any belief or supposed form of knowledge in the light of the grounds that support it and the further conclusions to which it tends."[1] Critical thinking *doubts* any preconceptions, *seeks* out facts and data that do or do not support it, and ultimately comes to a *conclusion* about that which is true. Critical thinking doubts, seeks, and concludes. This is a compelling attempt to break it down into elemental steps; nonetheless, a cursory interrogation of each of these verbs exposes its flaws.

Dewey begins by emphasizing the importance of doubt: "If the suggestion that occurs is at once accepted, we have uncritical thinking."[2] Surely anyone would balk at the recommendation that we accept any idea unquestioningly; such suggestions only appear in the dystopian fiction of George Orwell and Ray Bradbury. Even so, what exactly does thoughtful doubt entail? A reflex to doubt everything risks cynicism. How can we doubt well?

A famous website decries the prevalence of dihydrogen monoxide in our society. To any informed observer, dihydrogen monoxide is simply the chemical name for water, but the website identifies its presence in cancer cells and other toxic materials. Teachers often use this site as an example of why their students ought to remain skeptical of the information they find. Through demonstrations like these or more thoughtful units that require students to research both sides of an issue, we can inculcate within them a tendency to doubt; we can extol the virtues of critical skepticism. However, I'm wary of an overemphasis upon doubt. Genuine doubt takes extensive knowledge. It was only after a life of unceasing thought, discussion, and study that Socrates declared that he knew nothing.[3] Allan Bloom playfully quips that now every high school student makes this same declaration. "How did it become so easy?" Bloom asks.[4]

Doubt without requisite knowledge is cynicism. Consider religious doubt. Any adolescent may question the faith in which their parents raised them, but a thoughtful doubt of religion beyond mere teenage misgivings requires extensive knowledge of a faith's creeds, common justifications like the ontological or teleological arguments for and against the existence of God, the rhetoric around the problem of evil, the history of various religions, theories for the creation of matter, scriptural familiarity, and so on. A predilection for doubt is certainly an important disposition for any critical thinker, but it remains just that: a disposition. Critical doubt is the application of research and knowledge to this disposition.

The next step in Dewey's process of critical thinking is "seeking," wherein he himself affirms the centrality of knowledge. He writes: "Even when a child … has a problem, to urge him to think when he has no prior experiences involving some of the same conditions, is wholly futile."[5] If a student knows nothing of a topic, they cannot think about it. Futility would be asking them to critically consider the implications of Ghana's current president if they don't even know the capital of Ghana. According to Dewey—and here I agree with him—we must seek out and fill our minds with pertinent, relevant information about a topic before we can think well about it. Because I can think critically about the modernist novels that I read in college does not mean that I can think well about astrophysics.

Dewey's final step in the process of critical thinking is coming to a conclusion. He's vague about how we actually do this. Both Dewey and Rousseau make much of thinking beyond mere recall to instead make connections between things. As such, coming to a conclusion would involve connecting the disparate facts and weighing the validity and import of each, but this is another natural process. Even a game relies on some abstract ability to think, doubt, consider, and seek, as well as a broad knowledge of the game's standard strategies, attacks, and defenses. Any master chess player has memorized countless board configurations, famous games, and typical openings and endgame scenarios. Chess is a knowledge-dependent game, as all thought is a knowledge-dependent process. As we learn and take in information, we automatically connect it to what we already know.

The children's book *Fish is Fish*, by Leo Lionni, demonstrates this surprisingly well. It opens with a friendship between a tadpole and a fish. The tadpole grows into a frog, explores the world on land, and comes back to tell the fish about the adventures it has had and the things it has seen. From the frog's descriptions of humans and birds, the fish pictures humanoid fish and birds; fish standing on two legs or flapping wings. The fish connects this new information to what it already knows. Connection is the process by which we learn. Teachers can facilitate this process by introducing new concepts as they relate to former concepts— through analogies, a sequenced curriculum, or the provision of relevant background knowledge. Our brains make connections naturally. More important than training a reflexive habit to make connections is the provision of content knowledge that our students do not already have. We cannot connect what isn't there.

If I were to teach a course on current events and my final goal was for students to critically consider a president's impeachment, no amount of abstract consideration would lead them to a thoughtful analysis of the issue. A well-designed unit would not have them practice asking questions, but would first require them to read the Constitution of the United States and cover scholarly definitions of "high crimes and misdemeanors." The teacher would read a federalist paper or two with students to discover the founder's original intent for impeachment and, obviously, make sure students knew the full details of the impeachable crime in question. Once the teacher had provided that relevant information and theory, then and only then would students be able to *critically* think about impeachment and reach a conclusion. Give them the knowledge and the connections come.

The other definitions of "skills-based" critical thinking often allude to the application and instruction of formal logic. While I'll admit that I'm more sympathetic to this definition of critical thinking, I remain skeptical. An academic biologist could think far more critically about their chosen discipline with or without formal training in logic, while a philosophy major capable of reproducing complex syllogisms could do little. Furthermore, logical syllogisms require that we furnish the propositions with knowledge, facts, theories, anecdotes, statistics, and studies to determine their veracity.

Dewey attempted the most robust explication of critical thinking as a skill that I have encountered. Even so, it fails. He envisions a man walking on a fine day who notices a chill in the air, clouds darkening on the horizon, and concludes that it will likely rain soon. This man *doubted* if the sunny weather would continue, *sought* relevant knowledge in the temperature of the air and status of the clouds, and *concluded* that soon clouds would overcast the sun and rain would begin to fall. If this thought experiment is all that critical thinking is then, well, it's not much. It's a process that we all possess naturally—even animals have this capacity to some extent. My own dog will hear a noise and remain alert for a few minutes on my doorstep to decide if a threat is nearby or if she should return to chasing the ball. She doubts her safety, seeks relevant information, and draws a conclusion.

No, the thing that sets critical thinking apart from mere thinking is the application of knowledge. Critical thinking isn't a skill; rather, it is content-specific knowledge applied to a simple process—the very process that Dewey sets out of doubting, seeking, and concluding.

THE IMPORTANCE OF KNOWLEDGE

The value of knowledge to thinking, learning, and understanding is easy to demonstrate with a short anecdote. I showed a documentary to my students about the Great Depression in the US. I included a reflection question asking which country many Americans moved to during this era and why this might be. I even prompted them to listen about a minute before the documentary made reference to workers fleeing the US in search of work in the Soviet Union. After the documentary finished, I tried to start up a discussion about why Americans would go to the Soviet Union. The class gave me the silent stare that so many teachers dread. No students had any thoughts. I asked myself: had I framed the question poorly? Did I have an adequately accepting classroom culture? Then a student asked a simple question that exposed the real problem: "Is the Soviet Union a country?"

These were freshmen. They had learned a smattering of US and ancient history. A few other teachers likely worked in a few other eras, but our district's curriculum saved extensive instruction about the World Wars and the Cold War to later in high school. How could I possibly expect them to think critically about the Great Depression and the Soviet Union when they knew next to nothing about it? I might as well ask them to water a garden with an empty pail. The tool is useless without substance.

To think well, we must have something to think about. There is the cliche: "I don't want to teach students *what* to think, but *how* to think." In reality, the how *is* the what. The content is the skill. We must first give them the *what*, something to actually think about. Nothing comes from nothing.

The importance of knowledge to academic processes extends far beyond just critical thinking. Perhaps the best example is reading. Although the initial phase of learning to read is in fact a skills-based process (learning letter sounds and the basics of English grammar), knowledge is at the heart of quality reading, which is reading comprehension and analysis. When learning to read, students must first master letter-sound pairs and these are best learned when explicitly taught. It's a process accomplished without much meaning. It's why we can pronounce and read meaningless words such as "sclub" or "shleby."

However, once students learn this process, reading ability relies upon broad content knowledge and vocabulary. The importance of knowledge in reading is easily demonstrated with a review of a few studies, and I'm in debt to E.D. Hirsch's book *Cultural Literacy* for my first introduction to these.

The "baseball study" is a seminal piece of research in cognitive psychology and reading instruction.[6] The study was simple. Researchers gathered groups of children and determined their so-called reading level as well as their knowledge of baseball. They then gave them a paragraph about baseball to read. They found that the students' prior knowledge of the sport determined their comprehension far more than their reading level did. Words and phrases like "double," "change up," "outfield," "third base," "grounder," or "loaded bases" have meanings specific to baseball and a child unfamiliar with the game would struggle to read a paragraph about it.

Similarly, I fancy myself a pretty strong reader, but I brought up a few BBC articles about cricket while researching for this book and found myself at a loss to comprehend them, littered as they were with unfamiliar terms like "wicket" or "run chase." I have no idea of what the cricket field looks like, the rules of the game, the names of teams and the places they represent, or strategies of play. I read the likes of Plato, Rousseau, and Aristotle for this book but a low-Lexile short read on an English sport leaves me dumbfounded.

In another study, the researchers John Bransford and Marcia Johnson devised a clever little activity to demonstrate the importance of knowledge to reading comprehension. They presented the following paragraph to the participants:

The procedure is actually quite simple. First you arrange things into different groups depending on their makeup. Of course, one pile may be sufficient depending on how much there is to do. If you have to go somewhere else due to lack of facilities that is the next step, otherwise you are pretty well set. It is important not to overdo any particular endeavor. That is, it is better to do too few things at once than too many. In the short run this may not seem important, but complications from doing too many can easily arise. A mistake can be expensive as well. The manipulation of the appropriate mechanisms should be self-explanatory, and we need not dwell on it here. At first the whole procedure will seem complicated. Soon, however, it will become just another facet of life. It is difficult to foresee any end to the necessity for this task in the immediate future, but then one never can tell.[7]

Devoid of context, this paragraph is near impossible to comprehend and even harder to retell or sequence. However, if I provide the context and tell you that it's actually a paragraph about folding laundry, the ability to comprehend it immediately improves.

This demonstration has implications for reading. My students can provide plenty of analysis and inferences about celebrity news, a Snapchat trend, or a meme that flies past my understanding because I lack their knowledge of pop culture. In an academic context, many of my ESL (English as a second language) students missed the subtle jibes about various Christian denominations in *To Kill a Mockingbird*, because they grew up in Muslim-dominant countries and didn't know a Baptist from a Jehovah's Witness. No amount of modeling inferences could have developed the analytical skills they would have needed for that insight. Asking students to identify allusions or make inferences without relevant background knowledge is akin to asking them to find a tardigrade in a haystack without even telling them what a tardigrade is.

To continue the example of missed biblical allusions, when I worked at a public school teaching English to Somali refugees, they struggled to identify biblical allusions because they knew little about the Bible. Meanwhile, the students at my Catholic school saw the allusions to scripture like a neon light. However, even these Catholic students missed Harper Lee's Protestant in-fighting because they hadn't yet learned about the Protestant Reformation. They only knew their Catholic theology. Had I focused on teaching inferences to my Somali students like some sort of skill, I would have robbed them of adequate knowledge to understand and interact with the culture and society in which they now lived. That doesn't mean conversion or assimilation—we can understand beliefs to which we don't subscribe. Their comprehension of the text required me to explain the differences between Catholicism and Protestantism, the role of the church in the South, and other such cultural touchpoints. This lecture often took some time, but one student raised his hand and said it was far more interesting and useful than anything they had learned in their history class.

Understood so, progressive education's insistence on skills seems a lot like asking students to guess at an answer that they don't know. To return to the tools metaphor, we can practice using a drill all we want but it's useless until furnished with an actual bit. Instead, we as teachers need to provide the content—the dates, the theories, the themes, the stories, the names, the *stuff* of learning—so that students have something concrete to think about.

If we understand knowledge and academic skills as such, there are implications for the purpose of schooling. We can wax poetic about the purpose of education and its role in society—I wrote a whole damn book about it—but I'd wager most people would consider a school a failure if its students were unable to comprehend a major newspaper. A minimum expectation of our system ought to be that it leaves students capable of understanding the typical article in *The New York Times* or *The Wall Street Journal*. If that is a reasonable practical goal then the tidbits of facts, knowledge, images, impressions—whatever Rousseau wants to call them—are quite important. Dewey contends that "to fill our heads, like a scrapbook, with this and that item as a finished and done-for thing, is not to think."[8] He's right. Memorization, rote learning, and facts are not thinking, but they do provide the content of thinking. Food on a plate is not eating but neither is going through the motions with an empty plate. These traditionalist practices provide the food for thought.

As one last example, the importance of knowledge becomes particularly clear when viewed in its extreme form: expertise. I want to ask the question: why are experts so often wrong?

Our media has an entire branch based on fact-checking. Politicians, professors, reporters, and commentators are so often wrong that there's a whole industry dedicated to correcting them. How is it that they, our societal experts, are so quick to make basic factual errors?

I think about a since-deleted tweet from Nikole Hannah-Jones that identified school choice as originating in the era of Jim Crow racism. Now, regardless of one's opinion of school choice, this contention is patently false. John Stuart Mill and Thomas Paine both proposed systems of voucher funding for schools far before America's segregationist laws. After them, Milton Friedman popularized the idea as a means to *foster* integration without top-down mandates. Finally, many segregationists actually came to oppose school vouchers because of their equalizing effect. How did Hannah-Jones, an acclaimed journalist, make such a simple error?

The answer, as you might have guessed, returns to knowledge. When considering questions of racial oppression in modern society, she has a wealth of knowledge that she brings to bear upon such questions like a sledgehammer against a concrete sidewalk. However, when it comes to the minutiae of libertarian education policies, she misses basic facts that a scholar at the Cato Institute would take as common knowledge.

Critical thinking mastered in one domain—science, history, the arts—does not then transfer across domains. A chemist might make an above-average biologist because there is much crossover in the content and knowledge within each domain. However, mastering philology does not guarantee that a columnist for *The New York Times* will comment authoritatively on the workings of eastern European geopolitics.

WHAT KNOWLEDGE?

At this point, few who are aware of the debate dispute the centrality of knowledge. However, far more teachers simply never learn of its importance. Where Freire is commonplace in schools of education, Hirsch, the professor who really began the knowledge-rich movement and whose thought is the foundation of this book, rarely gets a mention. Rather, a far more difficult and contentious question is: *which knowledge to teach?* Time isn't limitless and so decisions must be made.

Through the Common Core, the US *almost* began a wholesale shift towards a knowledge-centric education. The fine print in the English language arts standards includes the lines:

> *By reading texts in history/social studies, science, and other disciplines, students build a foundation of knowledge in these fields*

that will also give them the background to be better readers in all content areas. Students can only gain this foundation when the curriculum is intentionally and coherently structured to develop rich content knowledge within and across grades.[9]

That's about as concise a summation of knowledge-rich ideas as they come. Unfortunately, the rest of the standards do not follow suit. They are instead a list of "skills" that ask students to make logical inferences or determine what a text says. Common Core expresses the heart of Hirschian ideas but the actual standards avoid them. Why?

The reason is itself a question. Should students learn the capitals of every country? Should they also know mountain ranges and rivers? Should they read Tolstoy or Edgar Allan Poe? Should they learn the parts of a cell and plant structures? We cannot read every book, learn about every scientific concept, and cover every historical epoch. Reading Shakespeare may not leave time for Orwell. The French Revolution may supersede the War of 1812. What to include and what to leave out are necessarily contentious and even political decisions, so it's far easier to list vague skills than to make the hard choices of what to include in the curriculum. As such, in place of swinging for a home run and risking a miss, we bunted the ball and settled for a single. The importance of knowledge is settled. Rather, we must discuss two questions: what do we include in the curriculum and who decides?

The progressivist answer centers on student interest. If the skills are our goal then the actual content is of secondary importance. If music engages them, let students learn their vocabulary through it or design math problems around it. If students like basketball, help them to develop a project to chart and thereby learn the physics of a basketball's parabolic arc through the air. Their interest in the topic develops intrinsic motivation and so they learn naturally. According to Dewey, give students "real situations of experience" and they'll learn.[10] Student interest determines what little knowledge gets emphasis.

There are many flaws with this approach, both philosophical and pragmatic. First, should students not encounter ideas that lie outside their insular interests? Ibram X. Kendi wonders, "What if we measured intelligence by how knowledgeable individuals are about their own environments?"[11] Perhaps we could just leave students to stare into mirrors, then. If the goal is the ability to read and comprehend a newspaper then students must understand things beyond their own environments. In place of staring into mirrors, we ought to invite kids out of the house and into the world, introducing them to that which is outside their own reflexive interest. Besides, in my experience, students almost universally consider their hometowns boring. You know what students don't consider boring? Galaxies, supernovas, deep-sea creatures, predators and prey, medieval knights, fights in Verona's streets, the battles of history, and ancient civilizations.

A second question: how much intrinsic motivation can a cursory interest actually foster? And how far does that go? I enjoy woodworking, but there's a half-finished project in my garage at the moment because my flippant enjoyment of the hobby sometimes isn't enough to motivate me through the tedium of drilling in 60 screws. Perhaps a student enjoys swimming, but will content related to their sport motivate them enough to finish the difficult tasks of learning? To think that a student's obsession with basketball will thereby encourage them to complete grammar activities related to it or even read a book about it seems idealistic.

I wonder whether personal interest is the only avenue to the enjoyment of content. I ask my students about their favorite book they have read all year. The majority identify a book that I chose, not one from a book circle unit or one they read at home. Some name a book from a choice unit, but usually it's exposure to a new genre, class discussions, and, yes, inspiration from a teacher that really sparks their interest.

There are yet more practical difficulties around letting student choice control and dictate curriculum. I haven't read the entire corpus of human output. If students pick whatever book they want, most will necessarily pick something that I haven't read and so my ability to push their thinking will be functionally zero. One-to-one conferencing will accomplish little when I haven't read the books that my students are trying to parse. Students have asked me clarifying questions about books they have chosen, but I'm left with little to offer them.

So, regarding our question about "who" ought to determine the knowledge, student interest perhaps could determine content for a few units, but it is an inadequate foundation upon which to construct the entirety of our schooling system. Schools, local governments, teachers, and administrations—in other words, adults—ought to make the final decisions.

The next question is: what knowledge, content, facts, history, science, and books ought to be on that curricula? There are a number of answers to that question and I'll cover a few here. But, in short, the functional utility of knowledge, the beauty of certain literature, tradition, aesthetic ideals – all these are better foundations for curricular construction than whatever happens to catch a student's attention that day.

Despite many practitioners' tendency to shun the word, tradition remains a vital determinant of school curricula. G.K. Chesterton famously wrote:

> Tradition means giving votes to the most obscure of all classes, our ancestors. It is the democracy of the dead. Tradition refuses to submit to the small and arrogant oligarchy of those who merely happen to be walking about.[12]

In Chesterton's mind, history is something of a long-term art critic. In the US alone, upwards of a million books are published each year and there are as many new historical events as there are individual lives. Inevitably, some of those books will be better than others and some of those events will be of more consequence to a greater number of people. Tradition consists of those books, events, and bits of knowledge that people throughout history have deemed important. Those books that have left the most number of people saying, "Oh, that was just exquisite."

Edmund Burke called tradition an inheritance: the great and beautiful literature that most eloquently distills the human experiences and expresses the ideas worth knowing, the heroes and villains of histories worth emulating and fearing, the events that shaped our society, and the body of science that has allowed us to advance as far as we have. Our institutions and traditions and customs amount to a stack of accumulated wisdom that we ought to hand on to the next generation. Just as we all read Dr. Seuss as children and remember him fondly amid other miscellaneous children's books that we have forgotten, certain traditions and customs make it through time for a simple reason—they are better and we want to share them with our children. Burke also referred to tradition as an intellectual capital that we hand along to future generations.

Both Burke and Chesterton respected tradition because they saw the fallibility of the thought of the present. With our flawed visions and biased perspectives, we in the present are apt to make mistakes. While we needn't take it as capital-T truth, tradition can provide a pertinent corrective, opening our eyes to the shortcomings of present thought. As we value the advice of our elders, so should we value the wisdom of our ancestors. To think only of the present is a short-sighted and arrogant thing.

Dewey—and Rousseau—balked at teaching tradition qua tradition, suggesting that content only has value as it relates to the present. In a sense, this is correct. Education is valueless if students do not incorporate that which they learn into their own minds and characters. However, the works of Beethoven, Shakespeare, and Miguel de Cervantes have value in themselves regardless of their relation to the present. The events of World War II and the Enlightenment influence the modern-day regardless of our cognizance of them. Food provides a useful analogy. A carrot only has value in so far as we eat, digest, and process it, yes. However, it has value to our bodies because of the nutrients and calories in the carrot itself. So it is with classic works of literature and art. They have value to the present because they express something beautiful and true. They only have value as we read, listen, and incorporate them into our lives, yes, but they are worth incorporating into our lives because of the value they carry in themselves.

The reality is that, as an animal may not understand its reliance upon the oxygen all around, we exist within a tradition. We cannot escape it; we can only choose to become conscious of it. To ignore our traditions is not to open our minds to what's before us, but to blind ourselves to what came before. In a joint op-ed for *The Washington Post*, Cornel West and Jeremy Tate write, "Even the choice of no tradition leaves people ignorantly beholden within a language they didn't create and frameworks they don't understand."[13]

Tradition provides the language and arguments we need to understand the present. *Macbeth* helps me to understand power-hungry politicians. The arguments between Booker T. Washington and W.E.B. Du Bois, Martin Luther King Jr. and Malcolm X help us to understand current debates over racial justice. These works provide the very language that we use in our current debates. We cannot emancipate ourselves from tradition any more than an animal can emancipate itself from air. Even extremists who would tear down civilization owe an intellectual debt to the thought and models of revolutionaries before.

Another way to determine what we ought to teach relies on a less controversial and loaded term: historically significant texts. Trace an ancestry of thought starting with any contemporary thinker—who inspired who—and similar names will appear again and again: Du Bois, Socrates, Shakespeare, Tolstoy, and so on. To read Plato is not just to hear the words of Socrates, but also to understand the philosophical groundings of the American Constitution, the philosophers who came after him, the foundation of our education system, and the like. The reality is that certain texts and historical events carried larger effects and influences than others, even if they aren't inherently better or more important in the sense of some abstract, platonic ideal.

Hirsch wrote much about what he called cultural literacy—that literacy and communication within a culture that require familiarity with certain texts, regardless of their value in themselves. He strikes a middle ground between the traditionalist and progressivist approaches. He wouldn't say that Beethoven is necessarily superior to modern pop music, rather that the composer's influence is greater and familiarity with his music will better help us to appreciate other genres and hear references to him. We shouldn't read Shakespeare because he's great necessarily, rather because doing so is better for our literacy. The US Declaration of Independence may not be the greatest piece of political theory ever written, but any American needs to know its basic proclamations and ideals to comprehend most debates over current events. If mathematics is sequential—one must learn addition before multiplication—reading and critical thinking are cumulative. The more one knows, the more one can understand.

Professional writers assume a certain level of background knowledge. Otherwise, newspapers would have sentences constructed out of endless appositive phrases and clarifications. Even something as simple as "start the water for coffee" assumes that I put it in a pot on the stove and begin to boil it for a caffeinated drink popular in America. These assumptions get ever more complex as we speak about more complex topics. A writer in *The New York Times* will assume that we know certain foundational texts, major figures from history, general country locations, and much more that they will not clarify. It would take too much time and too many words to do so. As such, it is imperative that we provide students with access to the most common and useful knowledge in any society.

This contention approaches the debate on breadth versus depth of knowledge. A common argument for project-based styles of learning is that they allow students to acquire far more depth of knowledge on any given topic—a defense of project-based learning that is itself questionable. Students may not learn a complete survey of American history, but that is only meaninglessly scratching the surface anyways; it's better that students fully understand just a few eras—or so the argument runs.

However, literacy requires a broad knowledge of these passing familiarities, and it's incumbent upon educators to identify and instruct them. Knowing every political move from Henry III in England probably wouldn't serve much purpose, but the theory of evolution and linear algebra together influence almost every department in a university.

There's also something of a nationalist means to determine a knowledge-rich school curriculum. I return again to Chesterton for an astute summary of the point. He writes about Pimlico, an area of central London that is rather posh these days but was a slum in Chesterton's time, an area that he calls rather a "desperate thing."

> *It is not enough for a man to disapprove of Pimlico: in that case, he will merely cut his throat or move to Chelsea. Nor, certainly, is it enough for a man to approve of Pimlico: for then it will remain Pimlico, which would be awful. The only way out of it seems to be for somebody to love Pimlico ... If men loved Pimlico as mothers love children, arbitrarily, because it is theirs, Pimlico in a year or two might be fairer than Florence.*[14]

Any nation has certain national texts. A British citizen knows their Charles Dickens and Jane Austen. A US citizen reads Frederick Douglass, Mark Twain, Ralph Waldo Emerson, Langston Hughes, and Emily Dickinson because they are part of their national canon. A US citizen will learn of the Civil War over 16th century Egyptian monarchs because it's their history. What Chesterton gets at is that we love and learn these texts because they are ours and help to develop a positive patriotism. If we love our country, we will seek to reform it for the better.

The word "patriotism" will set off a few reflexive alarm bells and so allow me to clarify. In using the word "patriotism," I do not mean an uncritical, positives-only view of a country. To love my home of America is not to ignore its endless list of historical sins. Rather, I can appreciate the geography that I learned about in school and experience on road trips, the unique cultural creation that is jazz music, and the anti-classicist literary tradition that began with Twain using a rough vernacular and extended beyond Hughes' attempts to capture the language of Beale Street.

A critical love of country, according to Chesterton, inspires us to improve our country like a critical love of our children inspires us to help them improve upon their imperfections. The love that Douglass, Abraham Lincoln, and Susan B. Anthony had for the US inspired them to push for abolition and universal suffrage. Through their writings and speeches, they allude to the ideals within the Constitution and Declaration. In a letter to Henry Pierce, Abraham Lincoln points out that pro-slavery politicians considered the principles set out in our founding documents "glittering generalities" and "self-evident lies." It was in a renunciation of our founding ideals that slave owners and racist politicians justified their positions.[15]

It's honestly a rather Deweyian justification. Public schools are central institutions. They are the place where families with differing worldviews come together under a common purpose. Their football games and musicals are unifying events in many localities. Perhaps more than any other institution, they shape our national character. The texts we read and the history we cover in schools will determine that national character, and it would be wise to select those that espouse the values we hope to engender in the next generation.

The final means of approving what exactly belongs on curricula is far more democratic in nature. The Aspen Institute initiated a project that asked the internet: what should every American know?[16] I think few would take issue with the top 10 responses:

1. Slavery.
2. September 11th.
3. Voting.
4. Human rights.
5. The civil rights movement.
6. The Declaration of Independence.
7. Law.
8. White privilege.

9. US Civil War.

10. Democracy.

The project website also lists the responses of famous thinkers, including jazz, the Stonewall Riots, Douglass' Fourth of July speech, Lincoln's second inaugural address, and the 19th amendment.

This simple site demonstrates a profound means of determining school curricula: leave it to small-d democratic ideals. Be it local teachers, representative samples of individuals from a community, or elected local officials, let communities determine their curriculum for themselves. The important point is that whatever makes it onto a curriculum should not be broad or abstract goals like critical thinking, but concrete, specific bits of information and ideas that our students ought to know.

Although my own political inclinations bristle at federal interventions into local education, Common Core already provides a unique opportunity for such a curriculum. As I mentioned, it is currently a list of those abstract and admittedly rather directionless goals. However, it offers a chance for the US at least to begin this conversation. Alongside the list of skills could be included a compendium of things from which a school can craft its curriculum; a buffet of knowledge from which they can select. Thus, students must not only be able to analyze an argument, but to do so in King Jr.'s "Letter from Birmingham Jail." They must not only identify the main idea, but also know about natural rights theory.

Discussions over which knowledge to include will be rancorous, political, and heated. Keeping the decision-making local could reduce the tension of curriculum-making. One community may value Malcolm X and another Thomas Jefferson. Let each prioritize different things according to their own values and preferences.

It's commonplace to criticize the prioritization of white men and their literary works above equally as consequential and accomplished men and women of color. Considering the multi-ethnic populace of America, in particular, it seems altogether reasonable that we should expand the canon. However, as the philosopher John Searle notes in his essay "The storm over the university," much criticism of the canon is aimed not at its actual content—that we have historically prioritized Shakespeare over Phillis Wheatley—but rather bemoans its very existence.[17] The act of assigning levels of quality to literary work, imposing a rank order from without, is described as "hegemonic," an inherently oppressive act. As such, the argument goes, we should eschew any teacher-imposed curricula and cast off any implication that some books are better than others, instead allowing student interest alone to drive curricular determinations.

The rejoinders are three. First, some books simply are better than others. Surely the novels of Ernest J. Gaines are superior to my first scribbles in crayon, and the improvisation of John Coltrane better than the mindless pencil-tapping of my students. It's a contention that few meaningfully dispute. They may question Shakespeare or other authors traditionally identified as superior, only to recommend something else that they deem, well, better: "Don't read this specific list of books; read this one." Unfortunately, time is in scarce supply in schools. Teachers must make decisions and elisions, and we ought to choose the books with the greatest character complexity, thematic depth, and historical significance to read with our students.

The second response is more pragmatic. The idea that students choose their own books is all well and good until we examine the consequences of workshop or choice-driven units. I'll address this approach to instruction more fully in the following chapter, but to summarize: about reading workshops, Professor Timothy Shanahan said, "I can't find a single study that supports its use."[18] Rather, schools that rely on teacher-directed classrooms and linguistically complex, historically significant texts achieve far greater gains in literacy for all the reasons I've already mentioned: the broad knowledge that students learn from them; the teacher's familiarity with the text and so their ability to meaningfully direct learning and questions; and students' ability to engage with peers and teachers collectively, instead of being isolated in their own little reading corner.

Finally, we can adopt aspects of the critique of traditional curricula within a knowledge-rich approach. Perhaps it's time we let go of our unquestioned allegiance to Shakespeare's excellence but at least replace him with something of equal quality. Similarly, we should disavow vague goals like "using race to interrogate society"—which suffers the same flaws as "critical thinking"—and instead center robust elements of America's history of race relations. If we want to improve our schools' discussions of race and racism in the US then we should define specific things worth knowing, like the Tulsa race massacre, the life of Malcolm X, or Du Bois' *The Souls of Black Folk*.

I wonder what positive effect this wouldn't have on race relations in America. If students read the searing works of every culture alongside each other—Edgar Allan Poe and Emily Dickinson alongside James Baldwin, Langston Hughes, Gabriel García Márquez, and Shūsaku Endō—this would push against our inborn ethnocentric tendencies without the need for crass consciousness-raising activities as suggested by Freire.

And so we're left with four justifications for the knowledge we choose: tradition, cultural literacy, nationalism, and democracy. Which one most influences each reader will differ, but what they share in common is this: it is incumbent upon adults to sequence and plan a curriculum that covers specific facts, eras, and texts. Some knowledge is too important to students' critical thinking and ability to function in society to leave what we teach up to chance or student fancy.

As Hirsch details meticulously in his book *The Schools We Need and Why We Don't Have Them*, the countries with the most successful education systems all have a core knowledge curriculum. Adults have outlined what students ought to know, and these ideas direct what happens in the classroom. This not only boosts literacy but also allows for smarter planning within schools. Administrations can ensure that students only tackle Stephen Crane's *The Red Badge of Courage* after they have learned about the American Civil War. As such, students can better understand the novel and gain yet more new knowledge.

Teaching at a school where I instruct three grades successively—sixth, seventh, and eighth—has shown me just how powerful a sequenced curriculum is. We refer back to a character or concept from a year or two before and everyone in the classroom understands it. This collective base of referenceable knowledge adds a depth to the conversation that would not exist otherwise. One student references how a character is narcissistic, alluding to a reading from sixth grade. We begin to reference characters as archetypes—he's a Scrooge or an Uncle Andrew. Students compare Dr. Jekyll's struggle with self-control to Mercutio's impetuosity.

Our American pretensions spurn prescriptions and lists as stifling. However, my students have been much more engaged, producing far more thoughtful responses, since my school adopted knowledge-rich theories of education. Taking a sequenced approach—not leaving literary decisions up to the whims of teachers or students—ensures everyone benefits from this cumulative effect. Every student reads this or that book and learns this or that fact; the common complaint of "Well, you should have learned this in elementary school" ceases.

IMPLICATIONS FOR THE CLASSROOM

The implications of centering knowledge over skills in the classroom are manifold. Perhaps the greatest implication is curricular, and I've addressed it in this chapter, but the importance of the knowledge-skills debate touches almost every aspect of education. I'll address a few more here.

Notes on Reading

While many might consider literary theory an academic trifle, an esoteric triviality, how we analyze books in the language arts classroom is no such thing. It is here that students engage with conflicting ideas and shape their worldviews. And not just what books we read but also how we read them play an essential role in the construction of ideas and worldviews. There are three broad theories of reading that I'll address: reader response, critical theories, and traditionalist theories.

The critical theories find their source in the works of Jacques Derrida and other postmodern thinkers. While traditionalist approaches to literary theory—movements like formalism or new criticism—place primacy on the meaning within the text and authorial intent, these postmodern thinkers pushed a radical subjectivity. They posited that texts carry no inherent meaning because language and even individual words are contextually and culturally dependent. All that matters is how a text works on us.

From these critical ideas, in their more innocuous forms, we get reader-response theory. In short, any attempt to determine an authoritative reading of a text is futile. Our only experience of a story is subjective; a book left alone on a shelf is meaningless. As such, our own experience of a story takes primacy. How do we relate to it? How does it move us? What unique perspective do we, the reader, bring to the story? This is not a rigorous textual analysis but neither is it particularly nefarious.

Critical theories of textual analysis move beyond individual experience to the imposition of meaning on the text. As I mentioned in the previous chapter on the history of educational thought, this theory of reading tracks onto the ever-changing end goal of education: from discovering truths of the world to a Rousseauian personal reflection and ultimately the imposition of our personal will and political views onto the world; from education as discovery to education as social change. Michel Foucault's work is an example of critical analysis at the elite level. He considers his work akin to archeology. The texts he analyzed were important not necessarily in the meaning they bore within themselves, but as a means to understand and interrogate society. What does the author's word choice or portrayal of a female character reveal about that era's systems of oppression, hegemony, and power differentials? Who has the power in this text and how is it used oppressively?

In grad school, I remember one activity in particular where we analyzed the same short poem through various lenses—critical race, feminist, postcolonial, deconstructivist, and so on—under the umbrella term of critical theory. In doing so, we questioned society's and our own views about race, gender roles, differing cultures, and power dynamics. What the work had to say itself was ancillary compared with what it revealed about power structures in society.

Unfortunately, we reached the same conclusions with every and any book in hand. Like staring at an elephant from varying angles, you might get a different look at racism or sexism as you walk around it but it's always that same elephant—the same conclusions. This builds confirmation bias into our reading, leading to the same thematic takeaway every time. We learn over and again that oppression and power exist, but never can the books breathe new life, meaning, or means to manage these societal shortcomings.

Our job as teachers of literature is to show students what the great works have to say and offer in themselves; ideas with which our students may contend, wrestle, and either accept or reject. Critical theory turns literature into something of an echo chamber, repeating the same theme with each book. A better approach to discussing a topic like race would be to provide students, again, with books that have something to say about the topic. Place Du Bois and Washington in their hands, parse out what these two great authors have to say, and allow students to draw their own conclusions.

Race, class, gender, cultural power, and other such issues are worthy of discussion and instruction, surely, but we should do so with a book in hand that has something definitive to say about it. We can read Harper Lee's *To Kill a Mockingbird* or Alice Walker's *The Color Purple*. However, it is a mistreatment of literature and an ineffectual classroom exercise to mine such themes out of a book that is indifferent to them. When students' minds are furnished and filled with examples of great thought on these topics, then they will be able to think critically about them.

All this brings me to the traditionalist theories, which seek to understand the ideas within books themselves. "A text's meaning is what it is and not a hundred other things," Hirsch wrote in one of his early books on this topic.[19] Joseph Conrad's *Heart of Darkness* is a harsh criticism of colonial practices, and the works of Dostoevsky are a skeptical albeit pious defense of Christianity; to argue otherwise about them is simply to misunderstand these novels.

T.S. Eliot was a modern defender of traditional approaches to reading, forming a school called "new criticism." In Eliot's mind, the poet or author introduced the reader to ideas themselves. They gathered images, stories, and arguments to form and arrange into aesthetic end products. Almost like a non-fiction speech, books have distinct messages and impressions to leave upon the reader. We'd consider it rather silly if someone attended a lecture on cell phone usage among teenagers and walked away talking about the speaker's opinions on frog mating. So, too, we should focus on what the book itself is trying to teach us, instead of looking only for ourselves or our preferred critical analysis.

An amusing example of these theories in action comes by way of Robert Frost's poem *The Road Not Taken*. Upon our first reading, many students take from it that it's a poem in praise of nonconformity. "Be yourself," read many of the responses that they turn in upon our first review. A "reader response" theorist accepts this interpretation and students are then to apply that to their lives.

However, Frost had a very different intent; the poem resists this reading. In the poem, the two roads are actually quite similar: "And both that morning equally lay / In leaves no step had trodden black," writes Frost. Both roads had been worn down "really about the same." At the poem's conclusion, the narrator looks ahead and imagines he may one day lament having never explored the alternative path. The poem is not about always choosing the road less traveled; rather, it is an almost existentialist meditation upon the necessity of choosing and how many choices necessarily close off others. In fact, Frost wrote this poem as a light mockery of an indecisive acquaintance who struggled to make even minor decisions. In a misreading worthy of a Greek tragedy, Frost's friend misread this poem to mean that he ought to live a nonconformist life; he joined the army and subsequently died in battle.

While our students' misreadings may not have such dramatic consequences, parsing out a correct interpretation leads to more profound insight. "Be yourself" or "take the road less traveled" is really a rather mundane message, and Frost's poem would be something of a failure if it ended there. Instead, upon further review, my students find the alternative and true meaning to be far more interesting and provocative. We then discuss how we can possibly go about making big decisions— what college, what job, what spouse—knowing that one selection almost always closes off other options and that the future consequences of our decisions are unpredictable, just as a road curves out of sight. Students learn more and draw more interesting conclusions because we apply a traditionalist, formalist lens to the poem over a reader-response one.

Ultimately, our children need to read books within a traditionalist framework for their own intellectual and emotional development. The developmental psychologist James Marcia outlined every child's need to both wrestle with and ultimately decide on their beliefs and life choices.[20] To wrestle but never decide leaves a child in a state of *identity diffusion*— think the college dropout who cannot decide a trajectory for their life. On the opposite end is to never wrestle but decide anyways. This is *identity foreclosure*—the child from a strictly religious household for whom the parents made decisions. However, when students have a chance to explore and decide their beliefs and life trajectories, they reach identity achievement and a healthier sense of self.

Young children explore their world first through play. As we age, this identity formation becomes an intellectual affair. When read in a traditionalist frame, books present students with ideas and ideologies for them to grasp, test, flex, consider, and ultimately decide upon. If I put before them the works of C.S. Lewis and excerpts from Rousseau, they can wrestle with forceful arguments for and against the existence of God to find their own personal conviction.

In short, in a knowledge-rich curriculum, we cannot treat books merely as a personal hobby, or cultural artifacts, or a medium through which we can practice other skills. Instead, it is imperative that the teacher focuses on teaching the book itself. For example, in reading "Letter from Birmingham Jail," I want my students not only to have a visceral response but also to understand King Jr.'s arguments about the nature of extremists and how we ought to be extremists for love. I want them to grasp his criticism of the white church, the harsh impacts of segregation on his children's psyches, and his famous quotes: "Injustice anywhere is a threat to justice everywhere." That and nothing else, especially in later grades, is the literature teacher's imperative—to pass along the arguments, images, and language worth remembering and knowing in the stories, poems, and novels themselves.

Standardized Tests

There are implications for standardized tests as well. Too often we ask what *skills* a test ought to measure and forgo asking what content ought to be on the test, but it matters if the passage a student faces comes from Twitter, an opinion column, a textbook, or classic literature. Sit a kid down and give them a passage about errant knights and their success on such a test will have little to do with their actual reading skills, depending more on whether they happen to have read a few books about medieval weaponry or attended a museum from which they learned relevant vocabulary. Even some of my English learners would struggle with something that we consider as innocuous as a passage about breakfast—toast, bacon, platters of pancakes—because these are American cultural mainstays with which students from other countries might be unfamiliar. Hirsch has gone so far as to proclaim that there's no such thing as a reading test. In reality, these are too often arbitrary tests of background knowledge. Whatever the topic of the passage, students will score well or poorly based on little more than a stroke of luck.

Ibram X. Kendi and critical theorists understand this arbitrariness. It's at the heart of many critiques of standardized tests: that they are culturally biased towards upper-middle-class white culture. Accordingly, the ACT and SAT have been neutralized as much as possible. A cursory glance at the practice questions reveals passages from contemporary literature, op-eds, and abstracts to science manuals. In an attempt to remain neutral, unfortunately, the reading passages are then disconnected from student learning and lacking in any substantive value, like kickball bases without a field to play in.

In response, we shouldn't abolish any and all standardized tests—they more than anything else have drawn our attention to the inequalities in the system, putting numbers to the injustices. Rather, we should reform them. One state points to a new way forward. Louisiana has devised a way to balance a knowledge-dependent understanding of reading with the utility of standardized tests, beta-testing an exam that aligns with the curricula taught in schools.[21] As students progress, the reading passages that appear on their test reflect the time periods and genres they have learned about in school in the years prior. As such, the selection of passages is no longer arbitrary; the reading passages feature content that we could reasonably expect a child to have learned. This approach creates a virtuous cycle wherein test writers and curriculum designers work together. "Teaching to the test" no longer resembles bland multiple-choice drills, but is embedded in the very content of the class—teaching the curriculum with effective instruction is synonymous with teaching to the test. The test and instruction speak back and forth in a two-way dialogue.

Literature Instruction

Text selection is the most pertinent issue that arises in a literature classroom when we center knowledge over skills. Through historically significant, complex texts, students will best develop the broad knowledge and exposure to linguistic complexity that they need to develop their capacity for reading. However, it's not just what we read as the central text, but also what we read around it.

One of the most significant alterations I made to my language instruction after reading Hirsch was the introduction of supplementary texts to any unit. If we select historically significant texts, we get something of a free-throw opportunity in our classroom. We sink the first shot in the text selection and then get a second opportunity at a shot if we also teach students about the context and history of a book. If we only teach the book without supplementary readings, it's akin to deliberately not taking that second shot.

Supplementary texts can help students to connect a book to the real world. *The Atlantic* ran a long piece recently about the surveillance state in China and its increasing control over the Uighur population.[22] While Lois Lowry's *The Giver* elicits many interesting conversations about the role of memories, books, and freedom of will in society, it all remains abstract to students. When we read about China's AI-powered City Brain software that tracks people's movements and even assigns them a color based upon their criminal track record, students see that these concepts have application in the real world. Add in the Declaration of Independence and students can start to see the real-world benefits and risks that come with liberty. These ideas are no longer abstractions but hard and fast realities.

Supplementary texts also introduce students to concepts they will encounter again and again throughout literature. In *The Magician's Nephew* by C.S. Lewis, there are several narcissistic characters. The protagonist's Uncle Andrew is a hack who stumbles his way upon some magic and thenceforth casts himself as an overwise magician. Later in the novel, the characters encounter a genuinely powerful witch who has destroyed an entire civilization, but in her haughtiness can only make allies through fear and coercion. To help us understand these characters, we read a short retelling of the tale of Narcissus and a medical description of narcissistic personality disorder; later on, we read excerpts from the Bible that Lewis deliberately alludes to. Students' understanding of the novel is furnished with language and concepts they can use to analyze other literature. Sure enough, as the year progresses, my students refer to dystopian aspects of American society, call other characters narcissistic, and catch references to the Creation story in our poetry unit. These bits of knowledge, not abstract skills, become the tools they can apply later on to new learning. Asking them to "find the main idea" is a vain enterprise; introducing them to the Creation story gives them a piece of knowledge with which to understand future readings.

Students often need to understand the history of a book to fully grapple with its meaning. George Orwell's *Animal Farm* is an inexplicably violent fairytale if students don't know about the Russian Revolution. Students might miss Mr. Hyde's true crimes if they are unfamiliar with Victorian prudishness and Robert Louis Stevenson's coy allusions to the reality of what Hyde is doing. In *To Kill a Mockingbird*, I have to cover the history of racial violence during the Jim Crow era for my students to fully understand the mob that attacks Tom Robinson's jail cell at night. When we supply students with this supplementary information, they can better grasp the novel or poem in hand.

This same need for knowledge applies to writing as well. We understand this intuitively and apply the concepts with research papers. With any research topic, we ask students to spend class periods and homework time reading articles, encyclopedia entries, and scholarly essays on a topic so they have enough facts, data, theories, and anecdotes to fill a substantive research paper. So it is with literary analysis. While there's a time and a place to ask students to pull out and analyze a theme from a class novel, it can be difficult to do so because students lack the necessary comparative knowledge. It's easy for me to grasp many of the arguments about theism in Dostoevsky's *The Brothers Karamazov*, not because I'm some grand abstract thinker, but because I can compare his theism to non-fiction works I've read by Lewis and the atheistic novels of Albert Camus. Like painting, it's easier to notice the fine differences in colors when we have a whole palette to choose from. Our students have only read so many books and engaged with themes so many times. They need other colors to compare.

We can introduce them to supplementary materials that engage with the same theme. With *Romeo and Juliet*, my final essay for students tasks them with answering the simple question: is this a love story? Before asking them to do that, however, we read various passages and theories of love, so they needn't rely on whatever philosophy of love they happen to have picked up from popular media. I read with them the famous wedding passage from 1 Corinthians 13 ("Love is patient, love is kind..."); excerpts from Lewis describing how love cannot simply be an emotion but requires action; a scientific explanation of the chemicals that pass through our brain as we fall in love; and a short reading about the different words the ancient Greeks used for love. *Philia* is brotherly love, *eros* is passionate romantic love, *storge* is family love, and so on. Only after having read these pieces do I feel comfortable asking my students to answer even that most basic of questions in long-form.

In the end, they wind up producing some unique and insightful writing on the play. When they have the language of eros versus agape to describe love, Romeo's suggestive jokes connect to philosophic ideas. Lewis' differentiation between falling in love and a mature love that is far more than a feeling gives them another context in which to discuss Romeo and Juliet's love. At least one student every year takes the reading on the Greek words for love and analyzes various relationships from the play, exploring the love of friendship, family, romance, and more. In place of drab, uninspired essays, students produce unique insights that no amount of practicing the identification of main ideas or connection-making would have allowed.

Field Trips

Unfortunately, with our misunderstanding of reading as a skill, field trips have fallen into disrepute. When a standardized test score determines the quality assigned to a teacher or school, and we assume that only book practice of skills improves reading abilities, field trips become something of an unnecessary frill—an indulgence. Surprisingly, the academic benefits of field trips have been little studied.

However, one such study is revealing.[23] The researchers posed questions that checked for factual knowledge and analytical ability to 10,000 students who had and had not attended a field trip to a local art museum. Even weeks after the trip, students remembered factual elements they had gleaned from paintings and the tour with up to 80% accuracy. They remembered explicit bits of knowledge, like what the Harlem Renaissance was, the significance of Rosie the Riveter, or that one painting showed a farmer destroying his crop to control prices during the Great Depression. These students are thus primed to understand and analyze future class activities and assessments that relate to the Harlem Renaissance, World War II, and the Great Depression. Field trips are an effective means to obtain and maintain the broad knowledge requisite for a robust literacy.

Regarding analytical skills, the researchers asked the control group and museum group to analyze a painting that neither had seen before.

The analyses were then sent to experts at the museum to rank according to their depth and complexity. Having watched their tour guide model analyses of paintings throughout the day, students were later more inclined to think critically about the example painting before them. In particular, students who attended the field trip were likely to identify more details—more in both number and specificity.

Surely this historical empathy of sorts is useful when comprehending and analyzing any historical text or work of fiction. Tactile exposure to images and history facilitates this thinking, not mere practice. And this extends beyond field trips. Sometimes the best literacy instruction happens in math, science, history, art, and gym classes. If we coop students up for hours a day in "literacy blocks," they spend time practicing needless comprehension skills when what they really need is exposure to knowledge from the real world.

REFERENCES

1. Dewey, J. (2019) *How We Think*, Anodos Books

2. Ibid.

3. Plato. (1992) "Apology," *The Trial and Death of Socrates*, Dover Publications

4. Bloom, A. (1988) *The Closing of the American Mind*, Simon & Schuster

5. Dewey, J. (2019) *How We Think*, Anodos Books

6. Recht, D.R. & Leslie, L. (1988) "Effect of prior knowledge on good and poor readers' memory of text," *Journal of Educational Psychology*, 80(1), pp. 16-20

7. Bransford, J.D. & Johnson, M.K. (1972) "Contextual prerequisites for understanding: some investigations of comprehension and recall," *Journal of Verbal Learning and Verbal Behavior*, 11(6), pp. 717-726

8. Dewey, J. (2015) *Democracy and Education*, The Free Press

9. National Governors Association Center for Best Practices & Council of Chief State School Officers. (2010) *Common Core State Standards for English Language Arts & Literacy in History/Social Studies, Science, and Technical Subjects*, p. 10, www.corestandards.org/wp-content/uploads/ELA_Standards1.pdf

10. Dewey, J. (2015) *Democracy and Education*, The Free Press

11. Kendi, I.X. (2019) *How to Be an Antiracist*, One World

12. Chesterton, G.K. (2007) *Orthodoxy*, Barnes & Noble

13. West, C. & Tate, J. (2021) "Howard University's removal of classics is a spiritual catastrophe," *The Washington Post*, www.washingtonpost.com/opinions/2021/04/19/cornel-west-howard-classics

14. Chesterton, G.K. (2007) *Orthodoxy*, Barnes & Noble

15. Lincoln, A. (1859) "Letter to Henry L. Pierce and others"

16. Aspen Institute. "What every American should know," www.whateveryamericanshouldknow.org

17. Searle, J.R. (1990) "The storm over the university," *The New York Review of Books*, www.nybooks.com/articles/1990/12/06/the-storm-over-the-university

18. Shanahan, T. (2019) "What do you think of the reading workshop? Or how not to teach reading comprehension," *Shanahan on Literacy* (blog), www.shanahanonliteracy.com/blog/what-do-you-think-of-the-reading-workshop-or-how-not-to-teach-reading-comprehension#sthash.QEUwalPm.dpbs

19. Hirsch, E.D. (1967) *Validity in Interpretation*, Yale University Press

20. Marcia, J.E. (1980) "Identity in adolescence" in J. Adelson (ed.) *Handbook of Adolescent Psychology*, Wiley, p. 159

21. Pondiscio, R. (2018) "Louisiana's remarkable reading test," Fordham Institute, https://fordhaminstitute.org/national/commentary/louisianas-remarkable-reading-test

22. Andersen, R. (2020) "The panopticon is already here," *The Atlantic*, www.theatlantic.com/magazine/archive/2020/09/china-ai-surveillance/614197

23. Greene, J.P., Kisida, B., & Bowen, D.H. (2014) "The educational value of field trips: taking students to an art museum improves critical thinking skills, and more," *Education Next*, 14(1), pp. 78-86

4. LEARNING: HOW SHOULD STUDENTS LEARN?

We've all done it. We learned that a good teacher designs lessons such that their students discover new theories, facts, and analyses on their own. We set them to work. We probe their understanding. Nonetheless, when the final discussion comes around, their literary analysis is lacking or their grasp of the scientific concept, while ingenious, is wrong. And so what do we do? We close the door and explain it.

I still feel guilty about this at times. Just this year, I planned a discussion of Robert Frost's beautiful poem *Stopping by Woods on a Snowy Evening*. The poem is both a rumination on man's relationship to nature and an allegory of our journey through life—full of beauty, sadness, toil, and ultimately rest. Previously, these circle discussions had lasted entire class periods, with students putting forth compelling analyses of the literary works in question. This time, the discussion was stilted, awkward, and teacher-driven. Finally, after a painful 10 minutes of forced conversation, I cut in and just explained the darn poem.

It felt like a failure. The animated atmosphere that we teachers so crave was absent that day; it stayed at home in bed. And still, when the end of the unit came, many students marked this poem as their favorite and mimicked many of its qualities in their own poetry. A few chose to memorize it. Perhaps there's something to be said for just giving students the answer from time to time, instead of leaving them guessing and grasping for the whole class period.

If the last two chapters were something of a philosophical overview of different approaches to learning, this chapter will hone in on the research, studies, and scholarship of education. There are tendencies to both over-philosophize and over-scientize education. The former gets lost in abstractions without an emphasis on what works. The latter often fails to convince, leaving people's first principles unchallenged. I hope to do both. I've laid out many of the philosophical justifications for progressivist theories of education, and as much as sometimes I want Rousseau or Dewey to be correct, a preponderance of scholarship suggests otherwise. But first, it's important to hone in on what exactly progressivist theories of instruction look like.

LEARNING BY DOING?

As with every educational misconception, all roads seemingly lead back to Rousseau. From his glorification of childhood, he draws false conclusions about how children learn. As he watches and observes the fictional Emile, Rousseau concludes that children learn through play and that "they only learn what is of use."[1] A similar sentiment is expressed in a quote attributed to Pablo Picasso: "Every child is an artist. The problem is how to remain an artist once he grows up."[2] If we allow children to explore the world around them, they will discover knowledge and skills naturally—or so runs the argument. They are filled with creativity and curiosity, and our institutions can only deprive their childhoods of freedom; any imposition of adult expectations will mess up this natural process. If the child is to learn about worms, they should go play with worms. If they're curious about water, an adult can help to design little experiments for them to learn about water.

In one of his famous TED talks, the late educationalist Ken Robinson gives the example of Gillian Lynne, a renowned dancer and choreographer, who was something of a problem child until a doctor recommended that her mother enroll this squirmy little girl in dance classes.[3] Only then did she discover her passion. Rousseau would cheer: her inner perfection persisted despite the school's best attempts to squash it.

A few concerning conclusions follow from this perception of childhood and the teacher's role in it. First, I'm hesitant to draw too many conclusions from Robinson's sole anecdote. I'm glad this woman discovered her passion and graced our lives with the choreography for *The Phantom of the Opera*. Nonetheless, when Robinson then alludes to people who have to "move to think" or draws conclusions about what this one story means for our education system as a whole, I'm skeptical. To me, this is the story of a girl who needed a little more exercise and a hobby, not a story to condemn the work of thousands of teachers and administrators within a system that has been built over hundreds of years.

Second, if we accept this belief, what is the point of education? Classes are reduced to mere babysitting. The teacher exists as something of an archeologist, digging out and dusting off every child's natural inclination. It's funny, though, how many speakers who denigrate traditionalist approaches to education make use of formal English. It's grand that one child became a famous dancer, but we also need engineers and doctors trained in the hard sciences. Even something as abstractly creative as art, without a grounding in classics and formal styles, is reduced to mere colors and shapes.

Finally, it's hard to know how to systematize such ideas. There are countless stories like that of Gillian Lynne; Robinson himself provides many throughout his TED talks. We must consider what these ideas actually amount to when put into practice before we deem them as wisdom. One system that seems to ground itself in these Rousseauian first principles would be the "workshop model" in English language arts. It is how I learned to teach at university and is the approach used within Lucy Calkins' Units of Study, which I referenced in chapter 1. Within this reading curriculum, students choose their own books and learn "strategies" for reading, like spotting differences or asking questions. The child's natural interest and personal will come to direct the curriculum, and we as teachers are there only to react.

Unfortunately, there's little research to suggest that such an approach works well for most students, not to mention that it's a rather isolated affair. In place of whole-group readings and discussions, students partition themselves off into various corners of the room to read their own books independently. I compare that with a lesson every year where I read Tom Robinson's guilty conviction in *To Kill a Mockingbird* out loud, so students can experience the build-up and disappointment together. Every year, someone lets a "No!" slip out; when the bell rings, my students walk out of the classroom talking about just how affecting that scene is. There's a communitarian aspect that is lost in an English language arts classroom when it transitions to Rousseau-influenced workshop models. The individual child's interest is so centralized as to atomize the class; we no longer commune around books.

Dewey modifies this approach and would have the classroom represent real-world "authentic experiences" in place of contrived activities and rote learning. Teachers are not to be a sage on a stage, nor an expert depositing information into the minds of students, but rather curators of activities and experiments that allow students to discover and learn information on their own. Knowledge is only of use when we incorporate it into our own minds—what good is a fact that isn't remembered?—and so it's best that students learn from experience, or so the argument goes.

The most common application of these Romantic ideas is project-based learning (PBL). In a skills-centric approach, students are to design projects that resemble the work of real-world professionals. By doing the work of scientists or historians, the theory runs, they will best learn science and history. Content takes second place to the skills of a historian or scientist that students can apply across topics. When put into practice well, this approach looks like High Tech High, wherein students develop simple machines to represent historical epochs, or practice and perform a play. The situations must resemble real life. As a student experiments by building a bridge or rewriting the Constitution, they learn all the physics or political theory that another child would get through lectures or a textbook. In this case, however, because the students have learned it for themselves, they supposedly retain it better. And as they have autonomy over their learning, motivation supposedly remains high. Students learn in community and through play, and so any mechanistic "drill and kill," contrived lesson plan, or worksheet runs counter to our natural inclinations for learning.

One humorous example from social media outlines the flaw at the root of the project method. A Twitter user now widely known as Bean Dad[4] one day tweeted a long thread about how he continued with a jigsaw puzzle while his hungry nine-year-old daughter tried to open a can of beans. She didn't know how a can opener worked and her father wanted her to study the individual parts and figure it out for herself. He let her struggle for six hours before she finally had it worked out. The collective Twitter response could be boiled down to "Just explain the damn thing already!" What purports to be discovery and experimentation too often amounts to frustration and confusion, and perhaps it's best that the teacher just systematically explains and models the concept.

COMPARATIVE STUDIES

We can bicker all we want in the abstract about the comparative value of teacher-directed versus student-directed classrooms, explicit teaching versus exploratory learning, or whatever other dichotomies you want to employ to differentiate between progressivist and traditionalist styles of instruction. However, since the abstractions of Rousseau and Dewey, researchers have conducted countless comparative studies of the two in countless different contexts in countless different domains, and found explicit, teacher-led instruction superior countless different times. I'll review some of the research here.

In one study, researchers split students struggling in math into two separate groups. Teachers either administered explicit teaching of the math concepts or ran students through inquiry-type activities so they could develop a supposedly deeper understanding of the concepts in question.[5] In the inquiry group, the teacher presented a problem and relied on group discussion to develop solutions—what techniques would the students use? As the students responded, the teacher explicitly identified the strategy in discussion and based instruction upon student responses. When students made errors (suggesting that 15 could be reached by the process 5 + 5 – 5) the teacher relied on student input for correction. Students then spent time practicing problems together, teaching each other in discussion.

In the explicit instruction group, the teacher presented a problem and demonstrated the strategy they would use to solve it. For example, with a basic mathematics problem representing how many wheels two cars have, in place of letting students suggest 4 + 4 or 2 x 2 x 2, the teacher suggested that 2 x 4 was the best representation. Students then practiced numerous problems of a similar type. There was little space for student input, with the teacher always directing them to apply the appropriate strategy to the problem.

Afterward, the students who learned the concepts from a supposedly mechanistic lecture with examples demonstrated better proficiency. The researchers posited that one explanation for the superior achievement was that in constructivist-type classrooms that value student input, students encounter correct and incorrect solutions and processes; this can confuse their own problem-solving. Conversely, in teacher-directed classrooms, teachers can more clearly organize instruction, only presenting correct solutions. If they provide common mistakes or non-examples, these are presented as such and used only as a means to emphasize the correct solutions.

Interestingly, this study also attempted to review how each intervention method affected student motivation. This observation is important because many student-directed theories of instruction rely on their supposed efficacy in stirring intrinsic motivation. Contrary to progressivist predictions, the researchers posited in the introduction that "explicit instruction can increase the motivation of low achievers in addition to facilitating their performance because such instruction enables them to handle difficult tasks and thereby motivates them, in many cases, to attempt new tasks."[6] They used a questionnaire at the beginning and end of the intervention to gauge student interest, self-conceptions, and beliefs regarding math. In this particular study, there was no notable difference in effect between the constructivist and explicit approaches. However, a non-result is telling regardless. When the running assumption in education circles is that lectures and structured classrooms stifle the joy of learning, it's revealing that, at the very worst, there's no difference between student-directed and teacher-directed classrooms.

In a larger trial from the UK-based Education Endowment Foundation, teachers, teaching assistants, and senior colleagues worked together to implement PBL units to fidelity.[7] In their summary of the study, the researchers note: "The existing international evidence on the effectiveness of PBL is relatively weak." For an approach to learning that is so universally praised, it should raise a few eyebrows that little rigorous research has actually explored its efficacy. In the end, the researchers came to a few conclusions, two of which are worth noting:

1. *Adopting PBL had no clear impact on either literacy (as measured by the Progress in English assessment) or student engagement with school and learning.*

2. *The impact evaluation indicated that PBL may have had a negative impact on the literacy attainment of pupils entitled to free school meals. However, as no negative impact was found for low-attaining pupils, considerable caution should be applied to this finding.*

Also worth noting is the researchers' admission that one trial with their sample size and various uncontrollable variables like student attrition should leave any reader hesitant to draw broad conclusions about PBL.

Project Follow Through (PFT), launched in 1968, was the single largest and most expensive education study ever funded by the US government, involving 178 communities, 200,000 students, and 22 different learning models for comparison. Communities selected a learning program, then received funding and support for effective implementation. After nine years, once the dust had settled and the numbers were crunched, direct instruction (DI) emerged as the clear winner, outperforming every other model in literacy, mathematical problem-solving, and even affective measures like student self-esteem. Many of the progressivist models designed to explicitly foster higher-order thinking and self-esteem actually had negative results—a powerful reminder that an educational model's self-proclaimed goals do not guarantee such an outcome. Long-term follow-ups found that students in the DI programs were more likely to graduate, apply for college, and subsequently attend college; these students also had higher-level reading and math scores come the ninth grade.[8] DI achieved not only short-term but also long-term educational attainment. This is significant because a common criticism of teacher-centric models is that they foster steep forgetting curves, wherein students master a concept until the test and then quickly forget what they have learned. These results suggest the opposite.

Also significant is that PFT seems to demonstrate that it *is* the method and philosophy, not just the teacher. It's not that certain personality types or strengths are drawn to a specific model; rather, these teachers had a model foisted upon them and so the models had some causative effect. One analysis of PFT, by Carl Bereiter and Midian Kurland, argues that it is in fact "a battle of the philosophies, with the child-centered philosophy coming out the loser on measured achievement, as it has in a number of other experiments."[9] Returning to the thesis of this book, it *is* a question of ideology and not individual competence or policy framework. It is the "more direct methods [of instruction], involving clear specification of objectives, clear explanations, clear corrections of wrong responses, and a great deal of 'time on task'" that outperform student-directed, progressivist approaches.[10] Bereiter and Kurland further note that "the effects tend to be strongest with disadvantaged children." In other words, DI works for all students and particularly well for kids who are already struggling for one reason or another.

If reframing the narrative—showing that traditionalist instructional practices are more holistic and humanistic—is one goal of this book, then Bereiter and Kurland do a wonderful job of it and write a passage that is worth quoting at length:

> *The behavior that meets the eye [in a student-directed classroom] is instantly appealing—children quietly absorbed in planning, studying, experimenting, making things … But look at the learning activities themselves and one sees a hodge-podge of the promising and the pointless, of the excessively repetitive and the excessively varied, of tasks that require more thinking than the children are capable of and tasks that have been cleverly designed to require no mental effort at all.*

Two common objections arise when PFT comes up. First, though important because of its sheer size, PFT was a messy study—many variables went uncontrolled and unaccounted for. Second, DI was put forth as a basic skills method of instruction. I'll begin with the second objection.

DI as it appears in PFT was a very specific method of teaching. Nowadays, "direct instruction" is thrown around in reference to any teacher-driven, highly structured learning environment, but in PFT the term referred to a specific program, established as a basic skills program by its creator, Siegfried Engelmann. Even though PFT found it also benefits high-order thinking skills, many still wonder if DI and explicit teaching are better for only basic knowledge and skills, or can also foster more holistic learning.

Jean Piaget put forth perhaps the most cogent one-line summary of this counterargument: "That which we allow him to discover by himself will remain with him visibly … for the rest of his life."[11] Although not written in reference to PFT, Piaget's comment underlies a common criticism of explicit instruction in all its forms: the knowledge that students learn, discover, and construct on their own will be of a more holistic, lasting, and transferable nature. Rousseau differentiated between memorization and comparison; Dewey between the learning of images like a scrapbook and holistic understanding. Is there anything to this depth of understanding that comes through discovery learning compared with the supposed mere memorization of direct instruction? Hardly.

One study attempted to answer this question.[12] The researchers sought to teach students about the need to control a single variable in scientific studies. To do so, they used contraptions that rolled a ball down a short slope. Students could modify the height of the slope, its angle, and the ball used; they were either given time to experiment with this contraption or led through explanations of various studies. Afterward, researchers measured their ability to craft single-variable experiments relating to a variable previously discussed and one that wasn't (what effect would a different runway surface have?). Unsurprisingly, students who received explicit instruction far outperformed those who received discovery-based instruction.

However, the researchers included a second step in this study. Once they determined which students had "mastered" the concept of single-variable control, they asked them to apply this skill in a discussion of science fair posters. If the progressivist idea holds true—that explicit instruction only fosters a surface-level understanding—students would show little ability to critically consider the posters. However, students who showed mastery on the test performed as well as the other group in identifying flaws in the experiments of the science fair posters.

In other words, mastery is mastery. Understanding is understanding. Once the students grasped the educational objective—changing one variable in an experiment to determine causation—they could apply it across contexts. There was no magical extra "understanding" power that came when students discovered it on their own. As such, that 77% of explicitly instructed students achieved mastery compared with only 23% of the discovery intervention students is the telling statistic. There is no qualitative difference between these "masteries" and the only important number is the quantitative superiority of explicit instruction.

It's important to note that, overall, students who spent time discovering this concept did gain greater understanding. Students taught in a progressivist classroom will learn. The essential question is whether they will learn better or worse compared with other methods of instruction.

Regarding the first common objection to PFT—that its methods and conclusions are suspect—I say that it's just one more example in a preponderance of evidence against progressivist approaches to classroom instruction. Even here, I only cover a handful of studies as a survey of the shortcomings of discovery learning and project-based learning. However, Paul Kirschner, John Sweller and Richard Clark wrote a seminal paper on the topic that amounts to an exhaustive list of such studies. By the end, they go beyond suggesting that PBL is ineffective to instead warn that there is even "evidence that it may have negative results when students acquire misconceptions or incomplete or disorganized knowledge."[13] There are a handful of studies that suggest PBL can work; I'll address those at the end of this chapter. For now, I'll allow Kirschner, Sweller and Clark to summarize the consensus of research into PBL: "After a half-century of advocacy associated with instruction using minimal guidance, it appears that there is no body of research supporting the technique."[14]

Being an English teacher by trade, I find the workshop model worthy of special consideration amid broader progressivist theories of instruction. Literacy is arguably the primary goal in education—it's the faculty through which most other learning happens. If the workshop model fails, it's a serious weakness in our education system. While the workshop model has a few different iterations, generally the approach has a number of consistent features: students choose their books and writing projects, explicit instruction is kept to a minimum, and time spent in silent reading or writing dominates class time. A typical workshop class might begin with a short read-aloud before the teacher spends about 10 minutes modeling a skill like asking questions or using descriptive words. Then students have a chunk of time (30-60 minutes) to read and write independently, practicing the skill they have learned.

In theory, the model works through a preponderance of practice. If students select their books and topics of writing, the theory runs, then they will have an intrinsic motivation to complete work. As a result, they spend more time reading and writing, practicing both, and so improve in their skills. Although the workshop model does leave space for direct instruction, the time allotted is usually short—no more than 10 minutes.

The justifications for the workshop model are eminently Rousseauian: he suggested that children will only learn what is of immediate use to them, be it the worms in the ground at one moment or medieval knights in another. He speaks of the child's "individual" or "natural bent" and says the teacher is to observe and fit their instruction to it.[15] Thus, workshop models surround students with extensive libraries and allow them to follow their own bents, to learn and discover independently.

Before we even get to the studies that attempt to measure the effectiveness of workshop models, a number of retorts come to mind to undercut the workshop model. First, I don't see how a choice-based literature classroom necessarily guarantees a love of reading. Personally, I was always a reader but teacher selection played a large role in that. For example, in high school, a teacher's lecture on *Moby-Dick* demonstrated to me how literature has so much more to offer beyond mere entertainment. Similarly, many of my own students remark that they enjoyed a book I selected for the class that normally they would not have read. In many cases, these students went on to read more books of a similar genre on their own time. Conversely, it seems that those students who already enjoy reading would thrive in a workshop model, but its ability to foster a new love of reading is minimal.

And this doesn't even touch on the countless other factors that relate to a student's perception of reading—cultural messaging, peer pressure (positive or negative), parental models, previous experiences with books, cultural values, and so on. Daniel Willingham confirms that "reading attitudes are mostly emotional" and difficult to influence.[16] Perhaps choice can foster this love of reading, and many seem to assume that it does so. Intuitively, I don't see it and there's a paucity of research to support this contention.

The assertion that the workshop model boosts motivation is equally suspect. Competence is central to motivation. This connection is a phenomenon so well studied and confirmed as to be almost a simple fact. It makes intuitive sense: we enjoy doing things that we're good at. If we're to struggle, it must be a productive struggle; anything too difficult quickly leads to disengagement. When it comes to reading, students who are better readers tend to enjoy reading more. A superficial interest in the topic of a book will only last so long if a student feels like they're dragging an elephant through wet cement while reading it. As such, the approach to the language classroom that best achieves high levels of literacy seems the best way to establish high levels of engagement and motivation.

Progressivists have it backward: they think that motivation facilitates competency. In reality, competency comes first and motivation follows. If explicit instruction is better at teaching reading and math then it's likely better at instilling motivation in the long run, even if it's superficially boring in the moment. If students have a low sense of self-competency, they won't do it, so if motivation is our goal then whatever best develops literacy must be our means.

While most workshop models do allow for some amount of teacher-led instruction, I question if it's enough. Practice matters but only accurate practice is effective. As Barak Rosenshine notes in his "principles of instruction," if teachers give short shrift to their examples and models, students may either practice incorrectly, thereby establishing bad habits, or may struggle so much through problems that they overload their working memory and so remember little. Rosenshine suggests that the best teacher spends half of class time or more in "lecture, demonstration, questioning, and working examples."[17] If students are struggling through work time then the teacher should pause and retry the next day. Bad practice is not only inefficient but can also work against learning. Only a sufficient amount of direct instruction can ensure effective practice.

A team of professors and literacy experts, including Professor Timothy Shanahan, ran a comprehensive review of Calkins' Units of Study, one of the most popular workshop models in the US. It's worth spending some time reviewing their reflections, which expose the weaknesses of this progressivist approach to literacy instruction and suggest a superior alternative. Their bird's-eye-view conclusion in the executive summary reads thus:

> One of the consistent findings of the expert reviewers, however, is that following the course of Units of Study would be unlikely to lead to literacy success for all of America's public schoolchildren, given the research … The "make your own adventure" design left reviewers skeptical that crucial aspects of reading acquisition would get the time and attention required to enable all students to become secure in their reading ability.[18]

The reasons provided for this inadequacy are legion. The critiques align with an understanding of how the brain learns to read, known as the "simple view of reading." This explanation of literacy breaks the process of learning down into two parts: first, students learn their phonics, then they rely upon a large network of knowledge in order to comprehend and analyze a text. Units of Study is light on both knowledge and phonics.

Regarding phonics, Units of Study does make space for phonics instruction but the time is limited, the instructional plan is scattershot, and the primacy of phonemic awareness is undersold. The curricular materials suggest that "Every minute you spend teaching phonics (or preparing phonics materials to use in your lessons) is less time spent teaching other things."[19] This reflects the progressivism of Dewey, who criticized phonemic awareness thus: "If they originally learned the sensory-motor technique of reading—the ability to identify forms and to reproduce the sounds they stand for—by methods which did not call for attention to meaning, a mechanical habit was established which makes it difficult to read subsequently with intelligence."[20] In other words, Dewey says and the Units of Study suggest that reading is not simply sounding out words. And yet, in the beginning it is, and until that ability to sound out words is automatized, students will struggle to comprehend. It might be easy to walk and chew gum at the same time, but students cannot sound out words and deeply analyze simultaneously.

The second shortcoming relates to knowledge and vocabulary acquisition. As I demonstrated in the previous chapter, knowledge is essential to reading comprehension. Shanahan, in particular, worries that the workshop model will not guarantee the development of an adequate knowledge base over time. With the "make your own adventure" approach, two different students will have markedly different experiences in the same class.[21] One student may while away their hours reading science fiction of low text complexity that does little to challenge them or improve their literacy. Another may select from a variety of genres and text complexities, thereby increasing their literacy and knowledge base.

Furthermore, teachers aid in the development of this knowledge. In the workshop model, write the team that reviewed Units of Study, "students are often left without the teacher supports and scaffolding that are often required to help them build their knowledge of unfamiliar words and knowledge."[22] Without teachers providing necessary background knowledge and explicit instruction of new words, students will be slower to develop the wealth of background knowledge that any fluent reader has.

I'm not a complete enemy of all progressivist approaches to instruction. In fact, if anyone looks into high-performing schools that rely on PBL methods, it's hard to argue with their results. I don't want to claim here that PBL has no validity. Surely an expert teacher of PBL methods will outperform an inexperienced teacher who wants to adopt traditionalist pedagogies. Rather, it's a question of bell curves. In the profession, there will naturally be a distribution of teacher quality, ranging from true duds to Hollywood-worthy successes. When put into place, traditionalist methods seem like they will achieve better results, curtail losses, and find a higher median than their PBL counterparts. I don't want to see a complete lack of PBL in our system; I merely want to question the almost "gold standard" status that it has, and to suggest that it should be an addition to instruction rather than the structure and guiding force of a classroom.

I've watched experienced teachers struggle to keep students on track during literature choice units, with many of their students leaving the class having read no books. In contrast, even mediocre teachers that I've observed have fumbled through central class texts. If we compared expert with expert, I'd put my money on the star teacher running a class collectively through a classic work of literature over a star teacher running a workshop or PBL classroom.

PRINCIPLES OF COGNITIVE SCIENCE

Despite PBL's theoretical appeal—at times I really do wish it worked—the studies find a near consensus on its inferiority. One question remains: why? If PBL makes sense in the abstract then why does it falter when it's put into practice?

At the turn of the century, when Dewey and his compatriots at Teachers College advanced their progressive education, many of the arguments for and against remained philosophical. What was the purpose of education? What might best lead to student learning? How ought we to treat students and content? However, in contemporary times, advances in modern cognitive science provide insight into why the project method fails to measure up. I'll outline a few of the principles of cognitive science that teachers ought to know, explain how they relate to and cause the shortcomings, and sketch out an alternative approach to classroom instruction.

Primary Versus Secondary Learning

Watching my daughter develop in her early months has been a true delight. I spend hours lying next to her on the floor as she reaches about on her play mat. It is fascinating to watch her learn what many of us consider second nature: reaching and grabbing the toys dangling above her head; turning her wrist and curling her fingers as needed; bubbling out her first syllables. Her movements, at first jerky and wild, now have a semblance of coordination to them. She can sweep her hand and curl her fingers with intention. Within another year, her meaningless babble will develop into controlled consonants and vowels to make "mama," "dada," and every parent's favorite word, "no."

These developments are what cognitive scientists and child psychologists call primary learnings. They are the skills and aptitudes that we as humans are primed to learn almost without effort. They include spoken language, motor control, basic psychology, and basic physics (what goes up must come down). However, certain things will never come naturally to her. She cannot learn addition and subtraction without guidance. Learning to read will require concerted effort. No amount of play will ever teach her that Napoleon was banished to a lonely island in disgrace. She may learn motor skills without any aid from me, but she'll need me to teach her all the juggling tricks that I know. These more advanced skills and bits of knowledge are called secondary learnings. They are the things that require effort on the part of the learner and input from some outside source—be it a teacher, a video, or a written text.

To explain why this dichotomy exists—that we learn some things with ease and others through focused effort—cognitive scientists look to evolution. Before society and robust cultures came about, humans only needed verbal language, motor skills, and basic knowledge of the world to function. Evolution brought us to a point and pre-programmed us to learn the things that are necessary for survival. However, as society advanced and developed written language, history, and science, our original faculties no longer sufficed, nor were properly attuned to developing this secondary learning. Interestingly, many of our secondary learnings co-opt certain evolutionary processes to function. For example, the human capacity to identify shapes and patterns allows our brains to decode words on a page. Similarly, when we think of certain written words, like "kick" or "pick," the areas of our brain that control our legs and fingers, respectively, light up.

Dewey approaches this realization. He acknowledges that the more complex a society, the greater the gap between the "civilized" and "uncivilized."[23] His language here is antiquated but I think we can understand his meaning. We can even just think about a child who would be left to their own devices in nature and one who would be expected to function in a modern city or town; the amount of science, history, social norms, math, literacy, rules, laws, and the like—even advanced farming and industrial techniques—that a child left alone could never grasp.

The progressivist error is to mistake the two. Children's early learning comes through play and exploration, and so progressivists suggest that we must maintain that throughout their schooling. Children learn almost through osmosis, so to lecture, assign readings, or provide tests is unnatural. This is a return of the naturalistic fallacy. Progressivists suggest that however children first learn naturally is the way we ought to learn in later grades, too; that whatever the child is naturally inclined to do is right and good. Well, my daughter currently likes to put everything in her mouth, but that doesn't seem like a sound pedagogical approach.

Quite the contrary: secondary learning takes effort. Students must study, memorize, and practice. When push comes to shove, teachers must give clear explanations of the concepts they expect their students to know. I think many of us intuitively understand the difference. It's why, ironically, so many professional development sessions about project-based learning and intrinsic motivation find expression in a lecture format.

Direct instruction can take many forms and I don't think it must take the joy or creativity out of teaching either. In my own class, I rely on readings from various sources as stand-ins for lectures to supplement our class novels. Even when I do lecture, it is designed to keep my students engaged. One student even remarked that they liked my class because I never lecture. I informed them that I do, in fact, lecture almost every single day, they just don't realize it, because the so-called lectures are full of stories to clarify points, analogies for an explanation, diagrams on the board, goofy examples, moments for student reflection, pauses for paired discussion, and whole-group conversations. Engaging explicit instruction requires teachers to find compelling examples and analogies to explain complex processes. It requires that we demonstrate various concepts graphically. It means we must help our students to connect new knowledge to their old knowledge and to the world as it exists today. That, to me, is an intellectually engaging task.

This distinction also underscores the centrality of literacy. I've encountered many teachers, scholars, and advocates who contend that literacy is the single most important aspect of education. I'm hesitant to say it's the most important, but it certainly is of primary importance. By that I mean it's the one capacity by which all other learning comes. We first learn to read, developing phonological awareness and the basic elements of English grammar. From there, we read to learn. We use this initial capacity to read textbooks, primary sources, novels, magazines, newspapers, and on and on and on. If most learning is indeed secondary then literacy is the most important means through which a student accrues additional knowledge. Once a student achieves basic literacy, it's as if a dam breaks and another source of information flows into their life. Reading then has a cumulative effect: as they learn more, they build an ever-expanding schema of background knowledge with which to comprehend more; this, in turn, allows them to comprehend more and the cycle continues. Those who develop literacy early accelerate sooner and so pull ever farther ahead. Without the ability to acquire new knowledge independently through texts, students necessarily must rely on another person. They only have spoken language as a medium of communication and so can only draw information from lectures or videos.

Schema Theory

There's a goofy scene in C.S. Lewis' *The Magician's Nephew* where the new land of Narnia has come into existence and all the freshly created animals are beginning to explore. The main characters are humans and have also just appeared on the scene. Upon seeing a horde of elephants, beavers, tigers, and other critters, one character, Uncle Andrew, faints. The animals are unsure about this unmoving creature. Standing around his unconscious body, they try to determine what animal he is by matching his characteristics to theirs. He has a big nose, so maybe he's a dog, but he also has large front teeth, so maybe he's a beaver. Ultimately, they decide that his limbs look like roots and branches, and so plant him like a tree up to his waist in the ground; the elephant waters him for good measure. This comic relief in the middle of a children's book is a good example of schema theory. Unsure of this new phenomenon, a human, the animals compare his characteristics to what they already know.

Although it's a bit of a simplification to describe it so, we can think of a schema as a network of all the information we already know and how it's connected. We use these schemas to acquire new knowledge, learn new concepts, and make sense of the world. The animals compared Andrew's nose, teeth, hair, and limbs to the schemas they had already constructed in their minds.

It's fascinating to watch young children develop their schemas and to witness the misunderstandings that arise. A child may see a cat and from their parents learn that we call this "furry, four-legged" animal a kitty. Well, "kitty" then means "furry and four-legged," so dogs, cats, squirrels, and chipmunks for a time are also described as kitties. Over time, children develop fine-tuned schemas that help them to categorize different tails, sizes, habitats, facial features, and other defining characteristics as belonging to various furry, four-legged animals.

Schema theory has far-reaching implications for the classroom. E.D. Hirsch popularized the concepts in his seminal work *Cultural Literacy* and often uses the image of Velcro to explain its significance.[24] Knowledge is sticky, he contends; when we know a lot, it's easier to learn more. I recently read a book of 20th century history and followed the author's account of the Russian Revolution relatively easily, because I already had a basic grasp of the timeline, the major players, and how it related to events elsewhere in the world. When the author jumped over to India, I learned and now remember little because I had minimal background knowledge before starting the chapter. When we have a pre-existing schema for what we're trying to learn, it allows us to grasp more of the new knowledge.

When we bring these schemas to bear on problems and concepts, they allow us to critically consider them in a new way; the nodes in the schema become the "tools" for learning. If my students know about the story of Narcissus, they can identify narcissistic personality traits in characters. If they have schemas for utopia and dystopia, they can describe modern laws and societies as utopian or dystopian. Conversely, if students struggle to understand a concept or reading, we often jump to conclude that they lack a certain skill or reading level when they simply might lack sufficient background knowledge. Factual knowledge is something of a boogeyman in education when, in reality, it's a vast schema of knowledge that actually allows our students to think and understand.

Working Memory, Chunking, and Cognitive Load

I think back to my wedding day. I can remember the food that I ate and our first dance, but I can't remember the distant relations that my wife introduced me to, nor the drive to the church. I can remember what I ate on that day, but not last Tuesday's dinner. Why? The answer is surprisingly simple: I spent time and energy selecting the song for our first dance and taste-testing our meals, but considered the name of my third-cousin in-law for just long enough to make it through the conversation. I probably reheated leftovers last Tuesday before focusing on an episode of my current show, conversation with my wife, or a crossword puzzle. In the case of what I remember, these things spent time in my working memory, while in the other cases my attention was focused elsewhere.

Our memory has two broad spheres of activity: working and long term. Our working memory is our conscious brain, our space of active thought—what we're thinking about at the moment. Long-term memory is where we store information. Everything that makes its way into long-term memory passes through working memory. Long-term memory is functionally limitless—even if we can't easily recall everything there—but working memory is limited.

The classic examples used to explain these concepts are numbers and letters. The first thing to know about working and long-term memory is that mental connections and time are imperative. The longer you consider a new concept or the more things it relates to, the more likely you are to remember it. If I gave you a set of random numbers, like *813456*, you would likely be able to memorize it but you would only retain that information for a few minutes afterward. Conversely, many people can recall the first six digits of pi or their first phone number throughout their life. The random set of numbers means nothing, has no connections to other concepts, and you might spend only a few minutes considering it. However, the phone number and pi have connections to other concepts and I, personally, spent lots of time thinking about them. As a result, it's unlikely that I'll ever forget either.

The other thing to know is the capacity of working memory. If I give you a list of letters— *jilnljsodiehwo*—it would take considerable time and effort to memorize them. Cognitive scientists disagree on the exact number but generally assume we have between four and seven "slots" of working memory; we can actively think about and remember four to seven things at a time. It's why that list of letters is difficult to memorize: it exceeds the capacity of our working memory. Thankfully, however, we can "chunk" things together and so allow more slots. A list of letters is difficult to memorize, but you could recall far more if I ask you to remember the letters *ChicagoNewYorkLosAngelesMiami*. In this case, each city name becomes a unit in our working memory and we can chunk the letters together into words. This process of chunking continues to expand and incorporate more information into it. I could also give you four famous quotes to remember and thereby allow you to memorize up to a hundred letters, but in this case they would be chunked in your working memory within the sentences.

This almost-cheat for storing information in our working memory extends beyond simple memorization and into the realm of academics and thinking. Despite my enjoyment of chess, I'm a rather novice player. When my turn comes, I try to think through every possibility; I move from piece to piece and consider every potential outcome, but quickly get lost in what could happen just a few moves out, then forget the moves and possibilities that I'd considered earlier. I struggle because my working memory can only process a few pieces or moves at a time. My friend with whom I play, however, thinks in terms of sections of the board and general flows of play. He chunks various areas, attack, and defense together and balances these out with individual pieces, working within these larger chunks like letters within a word. Finally, compare that with chess masters, who think in terms of entire game possibilities, pre-existing strategies, and theoretical approaches to the game. Their working memories chunk vast stores of information together, while I'm busy thinking about just the pawn, queen, and king that I have left on the board.

Much of the seminal research into working and long-term memory comes by way of chess. In one such study, researchers presented novice and master chess players with real game boards—from both in-process games and ones with pieces randomly placed—and asked them to memorize the positions of the pieces.[25] For the boards of in-process games, the master chess players performed far better. Interestingly, however, for the boards with pieces randomly assigned, the ability of the master chess players was drastically impaired. The researchers used memory and chunking to explain this phenomenon. They posited that the master chess players had memorized tens of thousands of typical boards, strategies, and gameplay positions. As a result, they could easily chunk the board into memorizable bits. However, when presented with randomly placed pieces, they had to work piece by piece, just like novices.

As it relates to academics specifically, we must be wary of cognitive overload—when students receive more input, instruction, and demands than they can functionally process. It's easy for teachers—as cognitive experts who have chunked much of the information and many of the processes in our specific content areas—to provide too much for our students to process all at the same time. I often think about when I ran a homework help class for English language learners. Looking through their math textbooks, a chapter would explain a new concept and then, in the practice questions, students would have to apply this concept in various contexts, within word problems, or with positive and negative numbers. It's demanding enough for them to think through the simple problem—the numbers on the page and the process itself take up working memory—let alone try to juggle that with various curveballs.

In my own language arts classroom, if I'm asking students to attend to a new aspect of essay-writing, we first practice with simple content. They might structure a paragraph about their opinions on school uniforms or practice proper quote-formatting in isolation. To instruct students in new writing skills while demanding that they do so with heady themes and character motives in mind will allow them to think well about neither the writing nor the content; it's too much for anyone's working memory. Similarly, I may provide them with one element of a paragraph, like a topic sentence or the details, and ask them only to provide the missing elements.

Cognitive overload isn't merely a source of frustration but actively inhibits learning. If a teacher presents a student with too much information at once or asks them to perform too complex a task, their working memory will flit between topics or focus on the wrong things. As such, little will make its way to long-term memory, or what they learn will be quite different from the stated learning objective—they may not remember the importance of Claude McKay's poetry but they'll remember how to animate a picture on Google Slides.

Thankfully, as students master certain skills and acquire more knowledge, just as chess players chunk strategies and sections of the board, they can chunk knowledge and automate processes such that the demands placed on their working memories are lessened.

Automaticity

I've observed many high school students still sounding out words that their classmates find elementary or completing basic math equations on their fingers. This places a severe demand on the working memory. When a student is thinking through the sound that a letter makes, a teacher could hardly expect them to deeply analyze a story's meaning let alone comprehend it. When a student is using their working memory for phonics, they cannot attend to these deeper questions.

Math is a useful example of automaticity. With some effort, the average person could likely solve the problem 56 x 73 in their head. There's a number of moving parts to manage in long multiplication—the initial multiplication in the first steps and the addition after—but it's an achievable process. It's particularly helpful when someone has basic math facts memorized (3 x 6, for example) and has practiced multiplication to the point where the steps are second nature. Conversely, a student who has memorized their basic multiplication tables and is still a bit shaky on the steps of long multiplication will find this problem near impossible to do in their head. The basic problem 3 x 6 can take up most of their working memory.

Interventions, especially as they pertain to reading, focus on various strategies for students to employ when the lack of automaticity holds them back. If, instead, the intensive intervention focused on the humdrum but essential development of phonics and mathematical recall, students would automate these processes, thereby speeding up their work and opening up working memory for the mastery of more complex problem engagement. If they are stuck thinking about phonics or basic multiplication, however, they won't have the working memory to also consider the mathematical principles or reading comprehension and analysis.

In other words, we denigrate supposedly basic thinking skills like memorization for their low-cognitive demand. In reality, students require absolute mastery of basic processes before they can tackle more complex problems and cognitively demanding tasks. A saxophonist would do well to master their scales before trying improvisation over John Coltrane's *Giant Steps* and a student needs to memorize their multiplication tables before they attempt advanced algebra.

Leveled Texts

Much of the workshop model relies on matching students with a text of appropriate difficulty. Prepackaged programs like Fountas & Pinnell rely upon letter-graded difficulties, with A being the easiest and Z+ representing adult-level books. Similarly, Units of Study aims for students to read books with a 95% success rate, almost going so far as to discourage students from selecting books that are too difficult. In both cases, motivation remains key. If students read books that are appropriately leveled, they will practice successfully and so improve. In many ways, these arguments mirror cognitive-science-type arguments. Accurate practice leads to improvement and success leads to motivation.

However, there's one little problem: there's little to no research to back up the idea of clearly leveled texts. Intuitively, the idea of matching textual difficulty to a student's competency makes sense; teaching Dr. Seuss over and again to high-schoolers would benefit no one, and neither would a first grader's independent engagement with Chaucer's *Canterbury Tales* in the original Middle English. In broad strokes, the idea of matching textual difficulty to student competency has veracity. Nonetheless, any attempt to pin it down beyond that is suspect.

Put simply, the idea of strictly leveled texts is not backed by research. In one blog post, Shanahan concluded that "we have put way too much confidence in an unproven theory."[26] Similarly, the education professor Juliet Halladay called the 95% cut-off rate for appropriately leveled texts "somewhat arbitrary."[27] These levels are particularly questionable when considered in light of how much of our comprehension depends on background knowledge. A child with a robust knowledge of baseball could likely read far beyond their predetermined level and outdo me, their teacher—a baseball illiterate.

Conversely, the use of difficult, complex instructional texts has a firm footing in research. In one study, researchers implemented 45-minute blocks of explicit science instruction that made use of non-fiction science texts to enhance reading scores and science content knowledge.[28] They based their program on the idea that students require exposure to complex texts and the development of a broad base of core concept knowledge to improve literacy. The teachers explicitly taught science concepts, read science materials with students, and did concept-mapping. The intervention improved scientific aptitude as well as reading comprehension.

In another study, researchers sought to determine the efficacy of "dyad reading," where teachers pair struggling readers with confident readers who then read texts out loud together.[29] The idea is that fluency— the automatic phonemic reading of words—improves literacy as it helps students to string together the words and focus on the meaning of a text. However, the researchers stumbled upon an interesting result: students benefited most from more difficult texts. They write:

> Results indicate that weaker readers, using texts at two, three, and four grade levels above their instructional levels with the assistance of lead readers [more confident third graders], outscored both proficient and less proficient students in the control group across multiple measures of reading achievement.[30]

While discussing an earlier study, they continue this same thought, writing about students using complex texts:

> Delayed readers, who were reading at one or two years below grade level at the beginning of the study, achieved increases in reading level sufficient to bring them to or above grade-level benchmarks after the intervention, helping to close the achievement gap for those readers.[31]

Challenging books will not teach themselves, nor automatically raise scores, but they certainly provide a better opportunity. The research supports the use of difficult texts with support as a more effective path to literacy achievement than arbitrarily pairing a text to a teacher's conception of a student's ability.

In a 2014 paper, Shanahan sought to identify the source of this misconception.[32] He found two studies that seemed to link text levels to achievement, but only in early grades and the results were not repeated. Conversely, he identified 23 studies that support the use of complex challenging texts. In an article for ASCD, Shanahan, Nancy Frey and Douglas Fisher cogently summarize the need for complex texts: "Just as it's impossible to build muscle without weight or resistance, it's impossible to build robust reading skills without reading challenging text."[33]

Perhaps a better question to ask regarding text selection for classrooms is not if a text is appropriately leveled for a student, but rather if a text is worth reading. Are the characters fit for psychological analysis or one-dimensional? Is the language beautiful and original or a piecing together of cliches? Does the story make intelligent commentary or are the themes reducible to simple phrases like "friendship is good?"

There are several ways to answer whether or not something is worth reading. Classical educators would ask the questions above, looking to tradition to parse the great works of literature. Proponents of knowledge-rich education would consider which texts have the most common and useful knowledge buried within—*Moby-Dick* might be painfully boring but the idea of the "white whale" is baked into culture whether we like it or not. Critical pedagogues would consider the power differentials that get an author a place in the canon or not, and perhaps seek out a demographically representative curriculum. Whatever the answer and method of selection, considering a book's worth will lead to a far more rich and interesting curriculum of books than mere text-leveling.

PUTTING IT ALL TOGETHER

Explaining Failure

The common dichotomy presented between teacher-led and student-directed classrooms is that of the "guide on the side" or the "sage on the stage." Is the teacher supposed to be an expert in front of the room explicating complex concepts, or are they merely there to construct and facilitate learning experiences? Comparative studies and research into cognitive science seem to present the sage on the stage as the more effective approach. When presented with unstructured learning environments wherein they design their own learning, students too often encounter misconceptions, find their working memory overloaded with all the moving parts of projects, and lack the repeated practice necessary for automaticity to develop. A master craftsman might work as a less loaded analogy to explain the shortcomings.

In the later Middle Ages, a young adult would spend years learning a trade from a professional craftsman before joining a guild and opening up their own shop. To master any such skill requires direct instruction of some kind. An apprentice could stare at a pile of wood and clobber their way to some semblance of a finished project. In the modern era, a kid might be able to tinker their way into fixing a broken car, especially if they have access to the internet. Even so, in both cases, the process would be incredibly inefficient, riddled with misconceptions and jerry-rigged solutions, and would likely lead to demotivation. These young people would be far better off if a professional explicitly modeled procedures, explaining the names of concepts, correcting misconceptions or errors, and assigning tasks from simple to complex. Even factual knowledge plays a part here. Someone could presumably fix a car without knowing the name of a single part, but the process would be far easier with an expert guide identifying various parts along the way.

I myself stumbled my way into exquisitely amateur woodworking one summer. I picked up the hobby through project-based, discovery learning, and my experience exposes many of the flaws in this approach. I spent countless hours ambling through store aisles trying to figure out the difference between polyurethane and oil finishes, pine and cedar boards, and countless screw types. I got halfway through sections of the project only to realize that I'd made a major error early on. In the end, I finished a bookshelf—and many other projects since then—but it was an endlessly frustrating, inefficient, and often joyless task. Did I learn how to woodwork? Sort of. Would the process have been more efficient and would I have learned better with someone explaining it all to me? Certainly.

In a sense, I did have some direct instruction. Although I didn't have a master carpenter in the garage with me, I found a few YouTube accounts that modeled various skills and explained the differences between various products. A few even recommended drilling basic skills like making a box or creating specific wood joints. These videos and explanations gave me a sense of competence and thereby the motivation that I wouldn't have had otherwise.

The same principles apply to the classroom. Leaving our students to struggle through independent work or discover their way into answers all too often means that they fail discreetly, struggle unnecessarily, and lose motivation. Learning is not doing, necessarily, and neither is doing learning.

The concepts of cognitive science also help to explain this failure, and at the crux of it is working memory, where all our thinking and learning happens. When students are working on a project, their working memory is beyond overloaded. In my struggles through woodworking, my novice brain could barely process what my hands were doing, let alone conceive of the end goal, the steps along the way, or the names of various tools and parts. I spent hours working but I learned and recall almost nothing. There was no space in my mind to deeply consider those aspects of woodworking that I would have done well to ponder and so learn.

The same applies to academic tasks. I asked my students last year to select a writer from the Harlem Renaissance, research their life, select two poems, and craft a presentation to show their classmates. They spent so much time thinking about the colors used in their presentation and various slide transitions that their analyses of the poems were lackluster. That was an exceptionally cognitively demanding task and they spent what little space they had in their working memories thinking about the visual aspects of the presentation, not its content. The same applies to essays. When I ask students to master the structure of argumentative writing and the content in one go, their novice minds can be quickly overloaded. They don't have a schema node that includes all the elements of an argumentative essay, as an expert writer might, and so they struggle to format the words, while complex analysis takes a back seat.

Too often, simplifying tasks is denigrated as, well, making the content too simple. In reality, by reducing the cognitive demands we place on students, we can allow them to focus the entirety of their working memory accordingly. Algebraic problems are already demanding enough; introducing students to a single concept through worked examples ensures they achieve mastery before working in and demonstrating yet more variations. If I ask my students to complete an essay on day one, the task may appear demanding but, in reality, a systemic approach—which takes a semester to focus on each element of writing bit by bit, before turning students loose on a complete paper—would achieve far more learning and allow them to consider the content in a more cognitively rigorous manner. When they learn about theses and then topic sentences and then introducing evidence and so on, there will be fewer false starts, misconceptions, cognitive overload, and learning of inessential side concepts.

If we focus in through sequenced lessons and worked examples, it's like isolating a muscle group. There's a time to put it all together when the game comes around, but strength training requires isolation. Similarly, complex tasks require a mastery of countless skills and factoids that are best passed along through expert instruction. Understood so, the role of the teacher is not to structure activities wherein students incidentally learn the desired content; Socratic-type questioning may have a place but it too often amounts to "guess what's in my brain." Rather, the teacher's job is to construct the clearest explanations, conceive of the most useful analogies, craft interesting examples and visualizations, and sequence knowledge and skills into learnable increments for students.

There are a number of great explanations for what "explicit" looks like in science, history, and math. I'm no expert on instruction in these domains, so I'll instead include books on these topics in chapter 8, which presents a canon of traditionalist education. For this chapter, I want to outline the alternative to the leveled-text, workshop approaches to a literature classroom: the central class text.

I love the central class text, as do my students and their literacy scores. When they engage with complex texts and succeed, it builds in them the sense of self-efficacy that they need for motivation. When they discuss a text together, it builds a community of literacy that further encourages and motivates them. When a teacher selects what books to read, it ensures that students experience a wide range of genres and knowledge domains that they might not have ever known they would enjoy.

In place of the hyper-individualized nature of the workshop model, teachers ought to present students with challenging, historically significant, beautiful works of literature and raise their students to the academic level necessary to master them. Rather than dumb the content down, we must build the student up and provide the supports that they need to access challenging literature. The teacher's role then, as I've said over and again, is not to facilitate a reading room. Rather, teachers must pre-teach the vocabulary that a student might need to read Edgar Allan

Poe; provide the background knowledge necessary to grasp the historical significance of *Animal Farm*; read difficult passages out loud to model fluency and explicitly explain the beauty within; set comprehension questions not as a "gotcha" activity, but to isolate and draw attention to the important aspects of a chapter; and provide any other scaffolds that students need in order to access the text.

When Project-Based Learning Works

As a final caveat to this chapter, I want to emphasize that PBL is not entirely bunk; some schools do implement it successfully. There is, however, as one paper puts it, a "paucity" of research in defense of PBL's efficacy.[34] Accordingly, an earnest attempt among many educational researchers is to perform the first study or trial that secures convincing evidence of its efficacy; who can find the first picture of Sasquatch?

A paucity is not a complete lack. A review of one study that purports to identify PBL's potential can perhaps lead this discussion to a conclusion that is more insightful than just "explicit teaching good, project-based learning bad." This study compared the results of an intensive implementation of a PBL program with the results of standard classroom procedures. The schools in the study structured their AP US government and AP environmental science classrooms around projects, allowing student interest and research to guide the way instead of the teacher's routine approach. According to the study, example projects for the government course included "student debates over historical and contemporary constitutional issues, mock presidential elections, and, for the culminating project, creating a political action plan intended to move an agenda item (e.g., immigration policy) through the political system."[35] At the conclusion of the year, students in the PBL classrooms scored on average 8 percentage points higher than the control group on the AP exam, and 10 percentage higher after a second year's implementation.[36] Convincing, no? Alas, the study is riddled with imperfections; the picture is fuzzy.

To begin—and perhaps this is a commentary on education research writ large—the essential question is how the experimental group did *compared with what*. In this case, the PBL program incorporated "curriculum, instructional materials, and robust professional development supports for teachers."[37] Conversely, the researchers referred to their control group throughout the study as "business-as-usual." In other words, they compared a program with countless factors and influences to a classroom with none of that. In that case, we shouldn't be surprised if any intervention showed success. When teachers receive intensive training and continual support from professors of education, should we be surprised that test scores improve? It would be impossible to discern what was actually the causal factor in these cases—the PBL structure, the program materials, the professional development, the support from researchers, the mere fact that these teachers spent extra time reflecting on their practices, the Hawthorne effect, or something else. A key point in Kirschner, Sweller and Clark's seminal article is that any time researchers compared inquiry-based methods with explicit instruction, not a control group, explicit instruction came out as superior.

We must also look at the group of students in question. These were not middle-schoolers or the average high-schooler. These were AP students. The consensus that comes from cognitive science is not that progressivist approaches to the classroom never work, rather that they are less likely to work for novices. Upperclassmen in an advanced placement course may not yet be experts in their field but they are certainly closer than the run-of-the-mill seventh grader. They have stores of background knowledge and familiarity with many of the academic tasks—essay-writing, presentations, comparative analysis—such that the cognitive load placed on them is far smaller. As a result, they could learn through projects, whereas a younger student in a regular history classroom would be overwhelmed with the factual data, basic skills, and planning and unable to actually retain much information. It's why Greg Ashman has called PBL "a pedagogy of privilege."[38] It works in cases where students already have much academic support and background knowledge.

Better than a simple comparison of efficacy would be asking why, how, and when PBL works. It is when students have already shown mastery of the content and skills in question. Be it from age, prior instruction, or parental support, when students have a firm grasp of the content in hand and the skills necessary to perform the task, they may succeed in PBL. In my classroom, only after I have provided my students with a semester's worth of information, practice with basic topics, and structured essay-writing would I trust that they have the mastery to learn through an academically rigorous essay.

If we want students to create some action plan on a trending social issue, it would require that a teacher first provide substantial amounts of background information and practice with models of the final project on easier topics. It would be hard for them to research immigration if they don't first know what visas are or about various immigration trends throughout US history. One teacher asked me about having students form book groups, read a work of historical fiction, then design a business that could succeed in that era. A better approach might feature a class text of historical fiction accompanied by an abundance of readings, images, and other background knowledge about the historical era, before asking students to complete such a task. Even then, I wonder if they would have the knowledge of business plans and basic economics to devise such a scheme with any meaningful thought.

And even with these projects, it's likely that these students would cement their learning in long-term memory through reviewing the skills and content, but would be unlikely to learn through the process. The project works as a final capstone, not the modus operandi. And that is really as far as the research can bring us. Studies do find that project-based and inquiry learning *can* work, but in isolated contexts and usually not as well as more structured approaches. I don't believe we should *never* implement aspects of PBL in the classroom; however, I would like to see it relegated to a garnish in place of the main course.

REFERENCES

1. Rousseau, J.-J. (1979) *Emile: Or on Education*, Basic Books

2. The Picasso quote originated from this article in *Time* magazine but no source is given. It could be apocryphal but the sentiment is common regardless: *Time*. (1976) "Modern living: Ozmosis in Central Park," https://content.time.com/time/subscriber/article/0,33009,918412,00.html

3. Robinson, K. (2006) "Do schools kill creativity?" (video), TED, www.ted.com/talks/sir_ken_robinson_do_schools_kill_creativity

4. The original tweet thread was deleted so I'll include this amusing analysis from Robert Pondiscio as a source: Pondiscio, R. (2021) "Explicit teaching vs. constructivism: the misadventures of Bean Dad," Fordham Institute, https://fordhaminstitute.org/national/commentary/explicit-teaching-vs-constructivism-misadventures-bean-dad

5. Kroesbergen, E.H., Van Luit, J.E.H., & Mass, C.J.M. (2004) "Effectiveness of explicit and constructivist mathematics instruction for low-achieving students in the Netherlands," *The Elementary School Journal*, 104(3), pp. 233-251

6. Ibid.

7. Education Endowment Foundation. (2016) "Testing the impact of project-based learning in secondary schools," https://educationendowmentfoundation.org. uk/projects-and-evaluation/projects/project-based-learning

8. Meyer, L.A. (1984) "Long-term academic effects of the direct instruction Project Follow Through," *The Elementary School Journal*, 84(4), pp. 380-94

9. Bereiter, C. & Kurland, M. (1981) "A constructive look at Follow Through results," *Interchange on Educational Policy*, 12(1), pp. 1-22

10. Ibid.

11. Piaget, J. (1972) "Some aspects of operations" in M.W. Piers (ed.) *Play and Development*, W.W. Norton & Company

12. Klahr, D. & Nigam, M. (2004) "The equivalence of learning paths in early science instruction: effects of direct instruction and discovery learning," *Psychological Science*, 15(10), pp. 661-7

13. Kirschner, P.A., Sweller, J., & Clark, R.E. (2006) "Why minimal guidance during instruction does not work: an analysis of the failure of constructivist, discovery, problem-based, experiential, and inquiry-based teaching," *Educational Psychologist*, 41(2), pp. 75-86

14. Ibid.

15. Rousseau, J-J. (1979) *Emile: Or on Education*, Basic Books

16. Willingham, D.T. (2017) *The Reading Mind: a cognitive approach to understanding how the mind reads*, Jossey-Bass

17. Rosenshine, B. (2012) "Principles of instruction: research-based strategies that all teachers should know," *American Educator*, 36(1), pp. 12-39

18. Adams, M.J., Wong Fillmore, L., Goldenberg, C., Oakhill, J., Paige, D.D., Rasinski, T., & Shanahan, T. (2020) *Comparing Reading Research to Program Design: an examination of Teachers College Units of Study*, Student Achievement Partners, https://achievethecore.org/page/3240/comparing-reading-research-to-program-design-an-examination-of-teachers-college-units-of-study

19. Ibid.

20. Dewey, J. (2015) *Democracy and Education*, The Free Press

21. Adams, M.J., Wong Fillmore, L., Goldenberg, C., Oakhill, J., Paige, D.D., Rasinski, T., & Shanahan, T. (2020) *Comparing Reading Research to Program Design: an examination of Teachers College Units of Study*, Student Achievement Partners, https://achievethecore.org/page/3240/comparing-reading-research-to-program-design-an-examination-of-teachers-college-units-of-study

22. Ibid.

23. Dewey, J. (2015) *Democracy and Education*, The Free Press

24. Hirsch, E.D. (1988) *Cultural Literacy: what every American needs to know*, Vintage Books

25. Gobet, F. & Simon, H.A. (1996) "Recall of random and distorted chess positions: implications for the theory of expertise," *Memory & Cognition*, 24(4), pp. 493-503

26. Shanahan, T. (2011) "Rejecting instructional level theory," *Shanahan On Literacy* (blog), www.shanahanonliteracy.com/blog/rejecting-instructional-level-theory

27. Halladay, J.L. (2012) "Revisiting key assumptions of the reading level framework," *The Reading Teacher*, 66(1), pp. 53-62

28. Vitale, M.R. & Romance, N. (2011) "Adaptation of a knowledge-based instructional intervention to accelerate student learning in science and early literacy in grades 1 and 2," *Journal of Curriculum and Instruction*, 5(2), pp. 79-93

29. Trottier Brown, L., Mohr, K.A.J., Wilcox, B.R., & Barrett, T.S. (2018) "The effects of dyad reading and text difficulty on third-graders' reading achievement," *The Journal of Educational Research*, 111(5), pp. 541-553

30. Ibid.

31. Ibid.

32. Shanahan, T. (2014) "Should we teach students at their reading levels? Consider the research when personalizing your lessons," *Reading Today*, www.shanahanonliteracy.com/upload/publications/98/pdf/Shanahan---Should-we-teach-at-reading-level.pdf

33. Fisher, D., Frey, N., & Shanahan, T. (2012) "The challenge of challenging text," ASCD, www.ascd.org/el/articles/the-challenge-of-challenging-text

34. Miller, E.C. & Krajcik, J.S. (2019) "Promoting deep learning through project-based learning: a design problem," *Disciplinary and Interdisciplinary Science Education Research*, 1(7)

35. Rosefsky Saavedra, A., Liu, Y., Korn Haderlein, S., Rapaport, A., Garland, M., Hoepfner, D., Lock Morgan, K., & Hu, A. (2021) "Knowledge in action efficacy study over two years," USC Dornsife Center for Economic and Social Research, https://files.eric.ed.gov/fulltext/ED616435.pdf

36. Ibid.

37. Ibid.

38. Ashman, G. (2016) "A pedagogy of privilege," *Filling the Pail* (blog), https://gregashman.wordpress.com/2016/10/10/a-pedagogy-of-privilege

5. CHARACTER: IN WHAT KIND OF ENVIRONMENT SHOULD STUDENTS LEARN?

No one ever really talks about how many fights some teachers have broken up. One memory in particular stands out to me. I walked out of my room on an errand to the office and found a student holding another in a vice-grip headlock. The sound of a kid gagging as another crushes their trachea isn't one you quickly forget. Another sound that has stuck with me is that of a face being punched. No student should have to call security while the teacher holds back another from a physical altercation. Students used to walk into my room weekly watching the latest lunchroom brawl on their phones. After one such event, a student complained, "Why does our school have so many fights? It's embarrassing." And the abuse doesn't remain physical. A colleague checked herself into a psychiatric hospital over the verbal harassment she suffered. In the most egregious case I know of, one young woman had to spend two semesters in class with her sexual abuser after his temporary expulsion ended.

These anecdotes aren't outliers. Horror stories abound of students sexually abusing teachers,[1] students sharing classrooms with their rapists,[2] teachers getting beaten bloody,[3] and general chaos plaguing schools.[4] Many students encounter enough violence in their lives already and it's an injustice that they must face even more when they walk through school doors.

And yet, there's a growing movement to abolish the use of suspensions and expulsions in schools. Districts in California, New York, and Philadelphia have banned suspensions for minor offenses. Across the pond, British MPs like John McDonnell have endorsed this idea as well. This movement deconstructs traditional responses to misbehavior and leaves schools without essential tools to address the violence recounted above. No one wants to exclude a child from their civic right to education via expulsion, but neither should any child have their right to education stripped from them by in-school chaos. Fellow disruptive students are one of the biggest detriments to student learning, after all.[5]

Alongside this absolutist stance, many successful charter schools are ridding themselves of the very thing that allows their success: high behavioral expectations. Uncommon Schools has relaxed its uniform policies and revoked the use of its controversial acronym SLANT (Sit up, Listen, Ask questions, Nod, Track the Speaker). In a similar move, KIPP schools have retired their revered slogan "Work hard, be nice."

Across the US, suspension rates have dropped by as much as half in cities like New York.[6] Progressivist critiques of traditional behavioral systems undergird this change. They do expose genuine flaws; an overreliance on suspensions benefits no one. Nonetheless, punitive discipline, routines and order, and clearly stated behavioral expectations remain necessary measures in any school system.

COMPETING JUSTICES

In his essay "The humanitarian theory of punishment," C.S. Lewis provides a useful dichotomy between two broad theories of justice: retributive and humanitarian.[7] The former seeks to dole out punishment in accordance with the crime and the latter to reform the criminal. A third theory, restorative justice, has risen in popularity and goes further, seeking not only to restore the perpetrator to a healthy relationship with the system and their peers, but also to improve the system within which the offense occurred.

Perhaps the most famous contemporary book to address this topic is Michel Foucault's *Discipline and Punish*,[8] a harrowing journey through the history of punishment in Western society. He traces the development of our penal system from that of public torture to one of mass internment and surveillance. To Foucault, every system of justice yet conceived reduces to power and control. Public executions put the power of the sovereign over its constituents on display to maintain control. Nowadays, schedules, rules, and incarceration accomplish the same ends by different means.

Interestingly, he connects this same imposition of routine, schedules, and rules in prisons to other industries—a factory schedule over its workers, strict routine in the military, and, most notably to this discussion, a school over its pupils. Our systems of behavior and discipline are not about learning, according to Foucault, but mere power and control.

In a sense, Foucault and Lewis agree. Foucault acknowledges that many of our so-called humanitarian systems of punishment are just as retributive as the old, if less barbaric. Our systems of surveillance, prison, and psychological reformation are in fact a means of control and compulsion. We no longer sentence offenders to the stocks for public torture, but to prison, service, or a set of therapeutic sessions in which behaviors are to be modified. Regarding the modern humanitarian approach, Lewis' thought mirrors Foucault's:

> They are not punishing, not inflicting, only healing. But do not let us be deceived by a name. To be taken without consent from my home and friends; to lose my liberty; to undergo all those assaults on my personality which modern psychotherapy knows how to deliver; to be re-made after some pattern of "normality" hatched in a Viennese laboratory to which I never professed allegiance; to know that this process will never end until either my captors have succeeded or I grown wise enough to cheat them with apparent success—who cares whether this is called Punishment or not?[9]

In other words, our new, humanitarian system of dealing with crime is still a punishment. To be given new goals, purposes, and self-conception through counseling may feel just as consequential as a stint in jail overnight, a few days in the stocks, or a week of lunch detentions. In my experience, students perceive a restorative justice circle as a punishment even if adults don't perceive it as such. It is to be "cured" against one's will—a rather disconcerting turn of phrase by Lewis.

Lewis is wary of this almost medicinal language when applied to behavior. He imagines a court judge declaring, "Here are the statistics proving that this treatment deters. Here are the statistics proving that this other treatment cures."[10] In such a system, our individual opinions no longer matter when faced with statistics that prove the success or failure of this or that response. Scientizing punishment removes from it the sense of humanistic justice or rightness. It becomes a matter of predetermined efficacy before which our own moral inclinations must bow. Even during the most atrocious of public executions in former eras, the public could call for mercy. Now our hearts have no say.

Hannah Arendt warned that education all too often functions as a means to compel behavior without force.[11] We inculcate a certain worldview and values, hoping our children will act upon this system of beliefs as they age. And this inculcation of a worldview needn't be some religion or political indoctrination. Even classically liberal principles, like respect for a diversity of views and a belief in the rights of individuals, are in a sense a worldview that we ought to instill in our children.

We must be wary, then, of behavior modification as a goal. In retributive theories, expectations and consequences are or at least *ought* to be clear. A student still has the liberty to cross boundaries with full knowledge of the potential consequences. In humanitarian systems of justice, the desire for control is hidden from view under the guise of reformation. In reality, participation in a restorative justice circle is just as compulsory as detention.

While Lewis' insights are profound, they are not necessarily damning. He only asks us to acknowledge that traditional consequences and humanitarian efforts at reformation have much in common: compulsion, punishment, and control. However, he prefers retributive justice because in his mind it is honest about its expression of power and control, and has a far more clear limiting principle. A detention is done when it's done. Who's to say what reformation entails and when it has been achieved?

And all this equivocates away from the simplest rejoinder to Foucault: discipline and punishment are not simply matters of power and control. Order and authority are not dirty words. They encourage flourishing and creativity. They establish a well-functioning system wherein students can expect safety. They facilitate education, allowing pupils to focus without distraction when necessary, discuss without a cacophony of voices, and play without a descent into chaos. They inculcate virtuous habits. They are a means by which we secure the right of our students to access an education. These concepts are in no way oppressive to a student's flourishing, necessarily, and I have had many students thank me over the years for creating a silent workspace amid a chaotic school day. Clearly defined and enforced behavior policies have twin goals: they protect students from emotional and physical harm, and they secure for students the environment that is most conducive to their learning.

I've taught in poor and affluent schools. I'll tell you what set apart the affluent schools: silence. It wasn't silent all the time; it wasn't even quiet most of the time. Classes got quite raucous. Even so, when the time came for tests, independent reading, or work, students fell silent and allowed each other to focus. Teachers enforced it and parents would get involved if kids never had access to it. Conversely, the unprivileged schools featured near-daily fights, excessive bullying, chaotic classrooms, and an administration that was too weak to do anything about it. It's hard to pull a class back on track after another student screams, "HEY, FUCK YOU!" down the hallway.

Perhaps strict enforcement of behavior policy sounds domineering. Learning is noisy! Kids can teach each other and need cooperative groups for learning! Let them play and enjoy their classroom! However, silence is at times necessary for learning. As discussed in the previous chapter, what we learn must first pass through our working memory. If my students are focused on the fight that happened at lunch, their peer whispering behind them in class, or (as happened in a fellow teacher's lesson) the kid crawling around on the floor passing audible gas, they cannot focus on their work. It would take Herculean focus for even an adult to learn in these circumstances. Some activities require noise; others require silence.

Perhaps even more importantly, well-defined behavior policies protect students from each other. A few years ago, when my district was taking in lots of refugees, we had a meeting with parents and teachers to try to determine how we could best serve this community. One parent asked how their child was supposed to focus during school when they knew they would suffer abuse on their walk home. How could anyone in my friend's class in that same school expect their kid to focus when another child was farting under a desk with impunity?

Behavioral expectations and consequences extend beyond a gratification of desires for control and power. They are the healthy imposition of adult authority. They create safe and productive learning environments for our children.

Our American pretentions tend to spurn authority. We're a democratic country that holds dearly to our democratic values. With every breath, we exhale rhetoric of equality. Unfortunately, that preference for individual liberty and equality seeps into our classrooms, where it doesn't always belong. Civil equality is a societal virtue; equality between adults and children less so. Put simply, there are significant differences between adults and children, and the imposition of a healthy teacher authority is a loving act that children need for healthy development. Arendt wrote, "It is obvious that such an equalization can actually be accomplished only at the cost of the teacher's authority."[12] In other words, many want to remove the natural hierarchy that exists between students and teachers, children and adults. But this leveling out will not result in utopia. Arendt further explicates the real results:

> For the authority of a group, even a child group, is always considerably stronger and more tyrannical than the severest authority of an individual person can ever be. If one looks at it from the standpoint of the individual child, his chances to rebel or to do anything on his own hook are practically nil; he no longer finds himself in a very unequal contest with a person who has, to be sure, absolute superiority over him but in contest with whom he can nevertheless count on the solidarity of other children, that is, of his own kind; rather he is in the position, hopeless by definition, of a minority of one confronted by the absolute majority of all the others. There are very few grown people who can endure such a situation, even when it is not supported by external means of compulsion; children are simply and utterly incapable of it.

> Therefore by being emancipated from the authority of adults the child has not been freed but has been subjected to a much more terrifying and truly tyrannical authority, the tyranny of the majority.[13]

In other words, when we remove adult authority as expressed through consequences, we leave a vacuum behind. Nature hates a vacuum. A utopian sharing of power wherein students and teachers co-learn together does not result. Rather, the strongest students fill the vacuum. This is the result: chaos, anarchy, the strong overpowering the weak. A student of mine that I was mentoring picked a fight after going a long time without an office referral. When I asked him why, he told me he was sick of being bullied and knew our school would do nothing about it. The alternative to consequences is not peace, but students taking authority and defense into their own hands.

Whereas Rousseau believed in some Edenic childhood, reality is quite different. Children are capable of mean, cruel, even wicked acts, especially as they are learning about the effects of their own actions in the world. This returns to an Augustinian view of human nature: are we born perfect and corrupted by imperfect systems, or is there a flaw at the root of human nature? A cursory glance at human behavior seems to suggest the latter. Lewis wrote in his autobiography that the isolation and bullying he experienced in school were worse than his time in the trenches.[14] We should be wary of any behavior policy that risks exposing children to an increase in such abuse.

There is a third approach to justice beyond the retributive and humanitarian. Restorative justice finds expression in Rousseau's saying, addressed in chapter 2, that "man is born free and everywhere he is in chains."[15] Fix the institutions and systems and man will be perfected. Restorative justice attributes misbehavior not to adolescent immaturity or simple human imperfection, but to flawed systems, rules, and instruction. It's summed up in the question one teacher-trainer asked me: "What is your building doing that asks students to change instead of the building?" In other words, our children are without fault; only our building is to blame and misdeeds merely draw attention to it. Misbehavior is merely a communication of any cultural conflict or oppressive system.

Despite its many flaws, let me first address the usefulness of restorative justice. It does have some explanatory power and insightful critiques of an unquestioned use of punitive discipline. Eric Jensen's book *Teaching With Poverty in Mind* details how poverty and trauma can modify brain structures and engender maladaptive behaviors.[16] If a child learns early on that any cry for help is met with abuse, they will toughen up and that reflexive combativeness can last into adulthood. In other words, context, systems, history, and society do bear some blame. Proponents of restorative justice also draw attention to disparities in typical punitive consequences that we cannot ignore. For any number of reasons—historic injustice, current cultural conflict, prevailing racist beliefs—students of color are excluded up to three times as often as their white peers.[17] These are concerning statistics. Meanwhile, students with learning disabilities or who have suffered trauma may act out at higher levels through no fault of their own. However, this is not to denounce detentions, suspensions, and expulsions. To see these shortcomings of punitive discipline and to then suggest a complete abolition of exclusions is akin to removing a tourniquet because it's causing bruising. It may be a necessary stopgap.

In other words, the explanatory power of restorative justice and reservations over punitive discipline do not then justify a wholesale reconsideration of how we respond to misbehavior. Even in a perfect system, kids would still act out. Humanity is not perfect: we are prone to selfishness, anger, ambition, dissension, factionalism, and the like. As we have a political system that enshrines an individual's right not to suffer violence and abuse from fellow citizens, so too our schools need systems in place to protect children from the imperfect natures of their fellows.

When put into practice, restorative justice asks teachers to design behavior standards alongside students and, if a student breaches these collectively agreed standards, a conversation follows. In such a restorative conversation, the perpetrator expresses their justification, the victims voice their grievance, and everyone reconsiders the faults in the behavioral structures. Taking cues from Rousseau, proponents of restorative justice place the blame on the system alone, not the individual.

Dewey's three elements of a learning encounter—the student, the content, and the environment—provide a useful categorization to understand the need for retributive justice. If misbehavior in the environment distracts the student, it keeps them from accessing the content. Thus, to account for inevitable misbehavior that stems from imperfect human nature, punitive discipline is necessary, however unseemly it may be. Retributive discipline like detentions, suspensions, and expulsions exists for the victims as well as the perpetrators. It safeguards the learning of those students who remain in the building and acts as a disincentive to anyone else who may choose to act out. Students who are well behaved are too often afterthoughts in these discussions. The concerns above necessitate a continual reflection on policy and wise application of consequences, but not a complete overhaul of our approach to behavior.

A teacher's authority maintained through behavioral expectations and sanctions arbitrates between competing student interests, protecting individual rights to learn. An abdication of authority leaves the weakest children without an advocate, beholden to the whims of the strongest children and group pressure. The strongest pupils fill the vacuum and a far less benevolent authority, that of the majority, wins out.

A RESTORATIVE CRITIQUE AND FAILURE

Arendt's and Lewis' observations and predictions were just that: observations and predictions. With the advancement of social science and countless case studies of schools implementing discipline reform, we now have concrete evidence that bears out their predictions.

In much literature on this subject, there is a grand mix-up of causation and correlation between suspensions and academic achievement. Students who get suspended tend to fall behind their peers in math, reading, and other academic disciplines. No one disputes this. However, this factual reality cannot prove that suspensions *cause* low achievement; they are merely correlated. Arne Duncan, the former secretary of education in the US, drew attention to the fact that "suspended students are less likely to graduate on time and more likely to be suspended again, repeat a grade, drop out of school, and become involved in the juvenile justice system."[18] It's not clear, though, if these poorer outcomes come from the suspension itself or the fact that the behaviors that lead to suspensions also tend to lessen a student's ability to learn.

One working paper from the University of Arkansas clearly lays out the issue with this line of thinking: "It is unclear whether disciplinary issues precede and 'cause' poor student achievement, or the declining achievement of a struggling student and the associated disengagement from school leads to disciplinary problems."[19] Simply, it's hard to practice problems and listen to the teacher while also shooting spitballs. Perhaps the behavior at issue causes the poor academic performance, not the suspension.

The same researchers attempted to parse out the causation and correlation. In this case, they came to the conclusion that "OSS days have a slight positive impact on the following year's test scores in math … and in ELA."[20] I'll repeat: when other variables are accounted for, they found a *positive* causation between out-of-school suspensions and student achievement the following year. The authors of the paper rightly make no sweeping conclusions, yet their research subverts the assumed causative link between suspensions and poor academic performance. There may be reasons to curtail the use of suspensions but portraying them as a detriment to achievement is a poor justification. The researchers themselves recommend that there are valid reasons to phase out suspensions in schools; however, teachers, policymakers, and parents "should not expect academic gains to follow."[21]

Another study in Philadelphia with a similar intent—to determine the causation or correlation between suspensions and academic achievement—found trends in the opposite direction. Suspensions caused declines in reading and math scores in the realm of .04 to .05 standard deviations, a small but not necessarily inconsequential result.[22] In sum, one paper found a small positive and another found a slight negative effect, so these two studies paired ultimately lead to no conclusion. They do, however, fail to substantiate, at minimum, the worry that suspensions *cause* a dramatic drop in academic achievement.

As with all things, the question should not be if one solution necessarily works but rather if an alternative works better. Somewhere in the distance, the voice of the renowned economist Thomas Sowell echoes: there are no solutions, only trade-offs. In the face of this question, the analysis grows far more interesting and concrete. Does the replacement of a retributive system with something more humanitarian or restorative improve outcomes? We must look at districts that have reduced reliance on suspensions and replaced them with various restorative procedures for this analysis–and the initial prognoses are dim.

In the academic year 2012-13, the School District of Philadelphia implemented a ban on the use of suspensions for "conduct" behavior such as profanity use or a refusal to follow basic school rules. A 2018 review of the results is almost disturbing.[23] Truancy increased from 25% to 50%, math and ELA scores declined, and "serious incidents" of student misconduct increased. In the end, suspensions for minor offenses declined but overall time spent in suspensions actually increased owing to an uptick in other misconduct. Students received fewer suspensions but for longer terms. Los Angeles pursued a similar path to Philadelphia and two academic reviews sought to discern the effects. Max Eden of the Manhattan Institute summarizes the conclusions:

> One [study] controlled for student characteristics and found no effect on reading but a huge harm to math achievement: students at the 50th percentile before a ban would be at the 32nd percentile three years later. Another examined school-level growth in other California districts and found substantial negative effects for academic growth in Oakland, San Francisco, and Los Angeles.[24]

As yet another example, during his time as mayor of New York City, Michael Bloomberg banned suspensions for first-time low-level offenses; his successor, Bill de Blasio, required principals to get written permission from the district's discipline office before a suspension and invested $1.2 million in restorative justice training in schools.[25] Suspensions halved but, in that time, students reported feeling markedly less safe, teachers said their schools failed to maintain order, and violent incidents increased.[26] Students also reported increased drug use and gang activity.[27]

As one final data point, John Hattie suggests in his book *Visible Learning* that the "most powerful effects of the school relate to features within schools such as the climate of the classroom, peer influences, and *the lack of disruptive students* [emphasis mine]."[28] When researchers gave students in a California district quarterly tests and compared them to the suspensions in classrooms, they found a positive correlation between suspensions and math achievement. Their findings "imply that suspensions, when used appropriately, can improve the academic achievement of non-suspended students, particularly for students from vulnerable populations."[29] These policies helped to facilitate calmer, more orderly, more productive classrooms. We can talk all we want about funding and choice, but getting behavior and routines right will afford us the most bang for our buck.

In response to New York's changing behavioral policies, the United Federation of Teachers president Michael Mulgrew rightly acknowledged that we should not measure success by suspension rates, but rather "by the number of schools with an improved climate."[30] This assertion is backed up by the case of my own former school, which employed restorative practices. Fewer students received suspensions but behavior worsened. The administration celebrated the numbers while staff and students suffered.

That we over-suspend students of color is certainly a problem. But in seeking a remedy, we must not accept any proposed solution. Ridding our schools of punitive discipline to solve disparities in suspensions offers a trade-off that we cannot accept. Overcorrections or misapplied remedies can either exacerbate the problem or cause ancillary issues that outweigh the costs of the original problem. In this case, completely ridding a school of suspensions for the good of a handful of students could not only greatly tarnish the environment for hundreds or thousands of other students, but also create an atmosphere that is in fact even worse for those few students we're hoping to help. They may not get a suspension but now, attending a school devoid of adult authority, they are deprived of an education.

If academic mediocrity in classrooms and chaotic schools cause a "school-to-prison" pipeline then suspension bans seem likely to only worsen that problem. In fact, in New York, the schools that saw the greatest increase in misbehavior served predominantly minority students.[31] The move away from suspensions often finds its justification in the disparate impacts they have on poor and minority students. When the data is parsed out, the conclusion should run in precisely the opposite direction. Policies that loosen behavioral norms and remove punitive discipline disproportionately harm the learning of poor and minority students.

As I've noted again and again in this book, the question is always: compared to what? It's not just a matter of whether suspension bans send schools into chaos, but whether alternative systems are better. Alas, these same failures play out not only when districts curtail suspensions, but also when they make intentional efforts to replace punitive discipline with restorative justice. When put into practice, restorative justice loosens the constraints on adolescent impetuosity. Unsurprisingly, the few studies that have looked into the results of restorative justice are concerning. Media outlets celebrated a comprehensive review from the RAND Corporation because the implementation of restorative justice shrunk disparities in suspensions and expulsions.[32,33] Alongside the shrinking disparities came an uptick in bullying, classroom disruption, and misbehavior.

These discussions about the use of consequences in society don't limit themselves to K-12 buildings either. The "Abolish the Police" movement that has gained popularity in recent years is a comparable example in the broader political sphere. Because of disparities in police brutality, advocates recommend the adoption of restorative practices in place of typical community policing—just as they do in schools.[34] When communities adopt these policies, the results mirror what happens in schools. The Harvard economist Roland G. Fryer found that when municipalities decrease their levels of policing, crimes and homicides increase.[35] Policing *saves* lives. Similarly, when police abandoned the area around Seattle's Capitol Hill and protestors set up a police-free commune, crime rates skyrocketed.[36] While we shouldn't take a settlement made by a few sophomoric protestors too seriously, it's telling that its results map onto what we would expect; unless society reaches utopia, it needs protective measures. Police, courts, suspensions, and exclusions all act as necessary limits on humanity's worst tendencies.

As I addressed earlier, restorative justice isn't entirely bankrupt. Many successful schools that rely on suspensions and detentions require that their teachers also partake in a restorative conference with their students after doling out a punishment. They adopt certain practices of restorative justice while maintaining a rigid behavioral frame. Perhaps we overuse punitive discipline in schools—we don't need a return to corporal punishment—but we should not overcorrect and completely rid our schools of consequences.

Finally, and perhaps most importantly, it's imperative that we establish proactive routines and policies that prevent misbehavior. In a compelling article for *Education Next*, the researchED founder Tom Bennett compares this positive prevention to fires.[37] We shouldn't only have systems in place to tackle fires when they arise, but ought to design buildings to prevent them in the first place. If our policies are only reactionary, we're set up to fail and our buildings will continue to metaphorically burn down.

ON HABIT

The justice argument presented above—that behavioral expectations and clear consequences protect an individual right to learn—is something of a rhetorical safety net when all other arguments fail. There are, in fact, positive reasons for clear routines, expectations, and consequences beyond a mere negative protective measure.

First, consider that most states require around 180 days in a school year with about seven classes a day. If we can work with an efficiency that saves five minutes during each of those classes—slipping in one more discussion question or a few extra pages of reading—that amounts to 6,300 minutes in a school year or 15 hours per class. Such efficiency will not alone save the American education system, but leveraging every minute of class time towards learning—ensuring that entrances and exits, distribution of materials, discussions, and the like flow well— could make a dent in the achievement gap by adding the equivalent of 15 extra days of learning in a year. Efficiency doesn't preclude breaks or necessitate draconian measures. It merely means that we should save time and mental space where possible.

Second, when a million things call for the attention of our students, clear routines cut down on the cognitive clutter. They know where to sit, what to do, what direction to follow, and are saved from the stress, inefficiency, and potential misdemeanor that comes with indecision and ambiguity. In my own experience, students act out the most and infringe upon each other's rights to learn when directions are most ambiguous. This could result from my own unclear directions during an academic activity or from a time of few boundaries, like indoor recess. It inevitably leads to frustration and an unhealthy learning environment.

More importantly, however, clear behavioral expectations are a question of habit. We can form our students' characters through routine. Invoking Aristotle, Jonathan Porter, the former deputy head of Michaela Community School in London, said, "Actions become our habits and habits become our character."[38] Progressivist theorists shudder at the word "habit." Rousseau wrote:

> *The only habit the child should be allowed to acquire is to contract none. Prepare in good time for the reign of freedom and the exercise of his powers, by allowing his body its natural habits and accustoming him always to be his own master and follow the dictates of his will as soon as he has a will of his own.*[39]

Rousseau's vision for education was negative: we must prevent children from learning the habits and prejudices of society. Rather, we are born with inclinations that "extend and strengthen with the growth of sensibility and intelligence but under the pressure of habit they are changed."[40] Education, then, ought to either protect us from the outside or return us to these natural inclinations, to uncover the diamond in the rough.

In place of habit, Rousseau prized will and consciousness. He believed that his approach to education would result in an adult who would be entirely cognizant of every decision, weighing the pros and cons always, and fully intentional in every action. All choices would be made with volition. Perhaps this sounds like an ideal: some sort of philosopher-king who has achieved perfect self-mastery. Perhaps. Or it could be exhausting and result in little to no critical thought.

It's a person's ability to make coffee from habit that allows them to think of things of more importance in the morning. It's a child's ability to kick the grass thoughtlessly while walking that is a sign of wellbeing. Instead, the man who must deeply ponder the implications of kicking the grass or brewing coffee would find himself paralyzed, immobilized by the endless task of consideration and introspection.

Professor Daniel Willingham has spent a career summarizing how our brains actually work. He argues that our brains are designed *not* to think, and this isn't a condemnation.[41] If our working memory only has a few slots then it's crucial that we save those for essential tasks, consigning to routine and habit anything we can accomplish thoughtlessly. Researchers have studied the brain activity of lab rats as the little rodents learn a simple maze.[42] In the first few run-throughs, as the rats sniff about and turn all around, their brain activity flares. After a few practices, their brain activity spikes only in the beginning and when they receive their treat upon completion. They have learned the routine of the maze and needn't think much while scampering through to cheese or chocolate.

A human equivalent is driving. I'm young enough to remember first learning to drive. I had to consciously consider every movement of my hands, every acceleration, every step on the brake. I had to consciously set the car into reverse and to then slowly ease up on the brake. It was slow. It was tedious. It consumed all my mental energy. Today, while not entirely a thoughtless task, driving is something I can do while also talking or thinking about the workday ahead. We can get a taste of this original cognitive overload while driving through a busy, unfamiliar city. Suddenly, our working memory is inundated with new street signs, swarms of pedestrians, cars behind us honking, all while we're trying to figure out if we need to turn right or continue straight. A cab driver in that city knows the streets and flows of traffic so well that they can attend to the aberrations that require attention. The rest of us are thrust back to our early driving days, unable to think about everything that demands our attention in those moments.

One summary paper on the role of habits in our daily lives summarizes their benefits well: "Without habits, people would be doomed to plan, consciously guide, and monitor every action."[43] When reviewing daily logs, these authors estimate that as much as 45% of our daily actions are entirely habitual—and that's exactly as it should be.

Now, this might seem like a tangent into self-help and esoteric discussions of individual volition. Not so. The bestselling book by Charles Duhigg, *The Power of Habit*, identifies the ways in which countless industries have revolutionized themselves through institutionalized habits, routines, and procedures. So, too, can people change their lives for the better by concentrating on small, incremental changes. When schools focus on habits—when we perfect our behavior management systems and encourage beneficial habits in our students—the effects compound each other.

At the institutional level, Duhigg gives the example of the aluminum company Alcoa. By spotlighting something as mundane as worker safety, the company reworked its communication process, allowing workers quick access to executives and a faster turnaround action plan after injuries.[44] This slowly exposed other areas of inefficiency and ineffective routines. By focusing on small changes, every aspect of the company began to change. So it is with individual decisions. When people start to work out daily, they also tend to eat better, lead more productive lives, and adopt other beneficial habits. Even something like making the bed in the morning correlates to productivity, health, and wellbeing later in the day.

Duhigg refers to these as "keystone" habits. When we concentrate on one area, this can instigate self-control and changes in other areas. He posits that the mechanism through which this works is small wins. Changes in one area beget changes in another, and soon larger wins seem possible. Duhigg provides as an example a woman who managed to quit smoking, which made exercising easier and thus getting in shape an achievable goal. These keystone habits occur in school as well.

In one particularly rowdy and even violent school I worked at, we had a stand-in assistant principal for one month while another was on leave. While there, he pushed for an aggressive focus on clear hallways and timely class attendance. When fights in the lunchroom, tanking reading scores, and chaotic classrooms called for attention, he focused entirely on attendance. It may have seemed like there were bigger fish to fry, but when we concentrated on attendance, a keystone habit, the very culture of the school began to change. When the bell for class rang, the administrators and hall monitors patrolled every hall and sent every tardy student to our building's theater. There, the students checked in with another assistant principal. If they had less than three tardies, they went to class with a hall monitor. If they had more, they spent an hour in silence in the theater.

Quickly, other areas of school began to change. When teachers could begin in a timely fashion, their own classrooms developed smoother routines. When the hallways were clear, it changed the atmosphere inside and outside classrooms; this was no longer a place for play but one for learning. Students who usually spent hours ambling the hallways attended class, developed new goals, rubbed shoulders with their more academically minded peers, and developed relationships with teachers. Unfortunately, this administrator was only with us for a short time, and when he left the routine left with him. Our school returned to chaos.

It's important to note that an aspect of this attendance routine was a punitive consequence. It wasn't large: merely spending an hour silently in a room. Nonetheless, it was one pillar on which this cultural change stood. We had to take away what drew students into absenteeism. They wanted to walk the halls, joking with friends. If that was no longer an option—and what's more, if any attempt at this brought with it boredom—then class quickly became the preferred alternative. A common argument against exclusions of any kind is that students are missing out on learning; by excluding them, they receive a consequence in place of the instruction they need. But in this case, few of these students attended class anyway— we merely removed the positive benefit of skipping out. Turns out, a handful of students also brought other students into absenteeism with them; like stones around a swimmer's neck, they drew their friends away from learning.

Rousseau considered habits akin to thoughtlessness, a precursor to automatons. One review of the literature on neuroscience and habits acknowledges that previous conceptions of habit consider them opposed to "teleological action."[45] That is, they are unconscious, automated behavior opposed to intentional action. Aristotle and further investigations into cognitive science consider habits the foundation of virtuous behavior and action, able to be crafted with intention and volition.

Even if habits are unconsciously followed once established, we can consciously form them. If someone wants to be a courageous individual, it requires more than intellectual assent to the importance of courage.

Aristotle writes:

> *For the things we have to learn before we can do them, we learn by doing them, e.g., men become builders by building and lyre players by playing the lyre; so too we become just by doing just acts, temperate by doing temperate acts, brave by doing brave acts.*[46]

Any habit, virtue included, requires training and practice. A person does not become a skilled chef because someone convinces them of the utility of cooking. Rather, they become skilled through training and practice. Similarly, someone might develop the virtue of courage through facing situations that require courage, considering how to be courageous in their daily life, and reading stories of courage. We learn virtue through habit. We could reason our way into a proper definition of courage or humility, but it requires practice and repetition to bring this virtue into our life and daily actions.

Aristotle says we are what we do repeatedly. If someone is reflexively cruel with their words, spends no time considering others, and ignores the needs of others, they will not live a virtuous life. However, if someone makes time for reflection and journaling wherein they consider other people's needs, habitually hold doors open for others, and reflexively say please and thank you, they will live a conscientious, polite, and respectful life. I think of Fred Rogers, famed host of the children's TV show *Mister Rogers' Neighborhood* and a man known for his selflessness. He spent hours writing letters to others and praying for them; this habitual consideration of others then manifested itself in a selfless life. Our habits form our character, for good or for ill.

Rousseau's aversion to habits is futile. When almost half our actions are performed habitually, we will learn them regardless. Suggesting we don't learn habits is akin to asking us not to eat. It's a question of *what* habits we form, not whether we choose to or not. Habits can be "innate or learned."[47] It's better that we intentionally learn virtuous, beneficial, useful habits. We can control our emotions and characters; habits solidify that control into routine.

Our routines and expectations in school can help to develop these intentionally built, virtuous habits. Encouraging in students daily exercise, healthy eating, reading before bed, and putting phones away at a certain hour can keep them well, physically and mentally. Requiring that they remember a pencil for every class will develop the habit of always bringing what they need to meetings. Helping them to keep track of a planner will make them the kind of people who thoughtfully plan their day and leave nothing undone. Asking that they work silently will instill a habit that will serve them throughout their schooling, allowing them to naturally focus on tasks and respect others' work environment when appropriate. There are also intellectual habits of a sort—what might be colloquially called muscle memory. Musicians spend hours practicing their scales, not so they can play their scales well, but because perfect finger placement and fine motor movements allow them to play with the finesse of Oscar Peterson or Chopin. Requiring students to clearly state a thesis or run through their math facts makes these intellectual habits routine.

Finally, we can help students to develop emotional habits. Not blurting out, pausing to process emotions before reacting in anger, seeking wise counsel when confused—these sorts of routines and behaviors will serve them for the rest of their lives. Behavior expectations and routines are loving guides for students. Contrary to Rousseau's distaste for habits, it is incumbent upon adults to help children develop the habits that will make for a productive, virtuous life. And this includes the negative consequences built into behavior systems. If blurting out elicits no disincentive, it will become a habit, whereas, if students know it will bring a detention, they will learn to pause and allow others to finish speaking.

Rousseau would have us learn virtue and control through experience. He gives the example of a tutor who hopes that their student will learn the necessity of self-control; rather than preach some ethical lecture, expose the child to one man beset with rage—screaming, shouting, pushing, shoving—and the child will learn their lesson. What grand advice. Even if a student took away the proper lesson from that experience, there's still the question of how to encourage whatever emotional regulation into the future. They might intellectually assent to the need to curtail anger, but how does that play out in action? Mortimer Adler, an Aristotelian philosopher and educational theorist, writes:

> *It is not by preaching moral homilies or by giving little lessons in ethics that moral character is formed. The moral sense develops under the discipline and examples that define desirable behavior.*[48]

Like Aristotle, Adler knew that discipline was necessary. Aristotle rightly identified the nature of laws to shape man. They are not themselves the arbiters of morality, but they do signal to citizens what a society considers just or unjust and so can modify behavior. Consider mask mandates. It may or may not have been beneficial to wear them at the height of the coronavirus pandemic, but after the imposition of mandates it become, for a time, socially unacceptable not to. The law modified behavior. So, too, our expectations and sanctions on students establish a culture of acceptable and unacceptable behavior in schools. They encourage, foster, and facilitate habits. However, there is a second half to Adler's counsel: we need examples of desirable behavior.

READING AND CHARACTER EDUCATION

In the previous section, I argue that virtuous behavior requires more than persuasion. That being said, persuasion is still a necessary element of character formation. No one will act justly if they are not convinced of its worth. Understood so, right living almost necessitates thoughtful reading, wrestling with grand ideas, ethical dilemmas, heroes and villains, successes and failures, and competing theories of life. In the previous chapter, I outlined the importance of reading books for what they offer in themselves. The final step in literacy instruction that I often felt was lacking, even as a student myself, is helping students to intentionally incorporate the lessons of literature into their own lives.

With Robert Frost's *The Road Not Taken*, after analyzing the poet's portrayal of decision-making—showing how he portrays the two roads as really quite similar, in the way they bend off into the distance so he cannot see the future—I ask my students two questions: do they agree with Frost's conclusion and how can we then make wise decisions? They brainstorm the major decisions people have to make: who to marry, what job to take, where to go to college, where to live. They identify the road most taken and its natural appeal and even benefits. Then, most importantly, we discuss how to make wise decisions. Who can we turn to for advice? What literature or scripture can we go to for insight and wisdom? What habits should we develop to make wise decisions regularly? What role should emotions play versus the conscious weighing of pros and cons?

When I treat literature this way, students are enthralled. While education currently debates social-emotional learning (SEL), I find engaging with robust literature to be an eminently effective form of character education. The most comprehensive review I have found on SEL comes from the RAND Corporation. It identified only eight SEL interventions with any positive outcomes, and each of these didn't even meet the requirements for the most rigorous evidence.[49] True character education is a deep, almost spiritual thing. It requires more than a few little lessons in ethics and signs around the building that encourage a growth mindset.

Character education is as old as education itself. The Ratio Studiorum was an early attempt at a mass system of education set forth by the Jesuits in 1599. When reading it, their approach to literary instruction always strikes me. Much of the time is occupied by the teacher explaining to students what a given oration from Cicero or a passage of scripture means. The Jesuits believed that within these texts were essential pieces of wisdom and forms of rhetoric worth imitating. More important than learning the "skills" of analysis was gleaning the knowledge and wisdom that these authors had to offer. Where students had independent activities, they imitated the style of their intellectual forebears, memorized key passages, or pulled their own quotations. These works and the ideas within them then became worked into each student's own intellectual framework— the first principles upon which they built their lives. As they went about establishing their own habits, like proverbs, students would reflexively be slow to speak and quick to listen; they would choose to be gracious to all men.

Daily behavior routines and reminders play a part in this, as I acknowledged above, but a deeper reflection is necessary. In the past, this reflection came from churches, families, and other institutions. More and more, schools are being asked to provide this too. If we teach great literature, we'll get literacy development and character education almost follows naturally. If we gut our schools of robust academic content to focus on a few mini-lessons about emotional regulation, I fear we will get neither. The English professor Karen Swallow Prior emphasizes the transformative power of great literature, writing: "A book that requires nothing from you might offer the same diversion as that of a television sitcom, but it is unlikely to provide intellectual, aesthetic, or spiritual rewards long after the cover is closed."[50] Books entertain; great books transform.

The question is not if schools should address character education, but rather how and to what end. Leveraging our literary classrooms to this purpose seems the best way to do so. After a lesson in which we used the story of Juliet to consider how students should handle disagreements with their parents, one student told me it was the first time a book ever gave her insight into how to handle a situation in her life. The benefit of using literature is that it presents students with profound worldviews and scenarios through which they can explore potential paths and outcomes, without having to do so in real life. Prior argues that "great books offer perspectives more than lessons."[51] Almost like a video game, in reading them, students can see how a worldview or personal change might play out in their own lives, but can return to a saved spot.

Using literature also keeps things comparatively free of ideological inculcation. SEL, too, often bases itself on utilitarian theory. Tolerance and open-mindedness replace courage and prudence. Students are told to practice emotional self-control, not because it will necessarily lead to right living, but because it will aid them in the workplace. There is a worldview that underlies it. When we ask students to apply books to their own lives, however, we can avoid this pitfall. A multitude of books guarantees a multitude of perspectives. A student who uncovers the meaning of a book is free to adopt its premises or reject them, but they are always aware that it is one set of beliefs among many. No implicit worldview is foisted upon them.

CONCLUDING ANECDOTE

A sober-minded approach to these competing theories would eschew an overreliance upon any. A student should not be suspended for burping in class once, but neither should a student return to class within the same hour of cussing out a teacher; it undermines the teacher's authority to ask their students to comply with even the simplest of directions. The most successful schools maintain aspects of both, but more on that in the next chapter.

Allow me one final anecdote. A student of mine had a bad reputation in our school and a list of office referrals that would take an afternoon to read through, including numerous suspensions and expulsion. I taught him for three years in a row. He acted out in my class and I doled out regular consequences. However, he also spent time in my room, chatting through his problems during study halls. Eventually, he dropped out and I thought he would always remember me, if he did at all, with derision. A year after he dropped out, he sent me an email asking me to be his mentor and, in one meeting, thanked me for being tough on him. He said he knew I cared because I wouldn't let him off the hook. No one enjoys being the disciplinarian—but our kids need us to be.

REFERENCES

1. Cook, H. & Houston, C. (2018) "Student accused of sexually assaulting teacher has expulsion overturned," *The Age,* www.theage.com.au/national/victoria/student-accused-of-sexually-assaulting-teacher-has-expulsion-overturned-20180303-p4z2p3.html

2. Smythe, A. (2017) "My daughter had to share a classroom with her rapist," BBC News, www.bbc.com/news/education-41486776

3. Bigham, B. (2018) "I'm a teacher not a boxer, and I'm tired of being beat up by students," *Ed Post,* www.edpost.com/stories/im-a-teacher-not-a-boxer-and-im-tired-of-being-beat-up-by-my-students

4. Hudson, M. (2019) "Public education's dirty secret," *Quillette,* https://quillette.com/2019/02/10/public-educations-dirty-secret

5. Hattie, J. (2008) *Visible Learning,* Routledge

6. Kamenetz, A. (2017) "School suspensions have plunged: we don't yet know if that's good news," NPR, www.npr.org/sections/ed/2017/03/23/521070924/school-suspensions-have-plunged-we-don-t-yet-know-if-that-s-good-news?t=1660899825794

7. Lewis, C.S. (1970) "The humanitarian theory of punishment," *God in the Dock: essays on theology and ethics,* Eerdmans

8. Foucault, M. (1977) *Discipline and Punish: the birth of the prison,* Pantheon Books

9. Lewis, C.S. (1970) "The humanitarian theory of punishment," *God in the Dock: essays on theology and ethics,* Eerdmans

10. Ibid.

11. Arendt, H. (1978) *Between Past and Future: eight exercises in political thought*

12. Ibid.

13. Ibid.

14. Lewis, C.S. (2017) *Surprised By Joy: the shape of my early life*, HarperCollins

15. Rousseau, J-J. (2005) *The Social Contract,* Barnes & Noble

16. Jensen, E. (2009) *Teaching with Poverty in Mind*, ASCD

17. Zill, N. & Wilcox, W.B. (2019) "The black-white divide in suspensions: what is the role of family?" *Institute for Family Studies*, https://ifstudies.org/blog/the-black-white-divide-in-suspensions-what-is-the-role-of-family

18. Letter from Arne Duncan dated January 8, 2014, www2.ed.gov/policy/elsec/guid/secletter/140108.html

19. Anderson, K.P., Ritter, G.W., & Zamarro, G. (2017) *Understanding a Vicious Cycle: do out-of-school suspensions impact student test scores?*, University of Arkansas, www.uaedreform.org/downloads/2017/03/understanding-a-vicious-cycle-do-out-of-school-suspensions-impact-student-test-scores.pdf

20. Ibid.

21. Ibid.

22. Lacoe, J. & Steinberg, M.P. (2019) "Do suspensions affect student outcomes?", *Educational Evaluation and Policy Analysis*, 41(1), pp. 34-62

23. Lacoe, J. & Steinberg, M.P. (2018) "Rolling back zero tolerance: the effect of discipline policy reform on suspension usage and student outcomes," *Peabody Journal of Education,* 93(2), pp. 207-227

24. Eden, M. (2019) *Safe and Orderly Schools: updated guidance on school discipline*, Manhattan Institute, https://files.eric.ed.gov/fulltext/ED594263.pdf

25. Kamenetz, A. (2017) "School suspensions have plunged: we don't yet know if that's good news," NPR, www.npr.org/sections/ed/2017/03/23/521070924/school-suspensions-have-plunged-we-don-t-yet-know-if-that-s-good-news?t=1660899825794

26. Eden, M. (2016) "In defense of suspensions," *Education Week*, www.edweek.org/education/opinion-in-defense-of-suspensions/2016/08

27. Eden, M. (2017) "Backsliding on school discipline: how de Blasio's suspension reforms are producing classroom disorder," *New York Daily News*

28. Hattie, J. (2008) *Visible Learning*, Routledge

29. Hwang, N. & Domina, T. (2021) "Peer disruption and learning: links between suspensions and the educational achievement of non-suspended students," *Education Finance and Policy*, 16(3), pp. 443-463

30. Eden, M. (2017) "Backsliding on school discipline: How de Blasio's suspension reforms are producing classroom disorder," *New York Daily News*

31. Ibid.

32. Camera, L. (2019) "Study contradicts Betsy DeVos' reason for eliminating school discipline guidance," *U.S. News and World Report*, www.usnews.com/news/education-news/articles/2019-01-04/study-contradicts-betsy-devos-reason-for-eliminating-school-discipline-guidance

33. Augustine, C.H., Engberg, J., Grimm, G.E., Lee, E., Wang, E.L., Christianson, K., & Joseph, A.A. (2018) *Can Restorative Practices Improve School Climate and Curb Suspensions? An evaluation of the impact of restorative practices in a mid-sized urban school district*, RAND Corporation, www.rand.org/pubs/research_reports/RR2840.html

34. Way, K. (2020) "Can't imagine a world without police? Start here," *Vice*, www.vice.com/en/article/9353ky/what-is-transformative-justice-police-abolition

35. Riley, J.L. (2020) "Good policing saves Black lives," *Wall Street Journal*, www.wsj.com/articles/good-policing-saves-black-lives-11591052916

36. Eustachewich, L. (2020) "Seattle sees 525 percent spike in crime thanks to CHOP," *New York Post*, https://nypost.com/2020/07/02/seattle-sees-525-percent-spike-in-crime-thanks-to-chop-mayor-durkan

37. Bennett, T. (2020) "Teachers need to be taught to teach students to behave," *Education Next*, www.educationnext.org/teachers-need-to-be-taught-to-teach-students-to-behave-excerpt-running-the-room

38. Michaela Community School. (2017) "Jonathan Porter: no excuses discipline" (video), YouTube, https://youtu.be/N0H91smFiBg

39. Rousseau, J-J. (1979) *Emile: Or on Education*, Basic Books

40. Ibid.

41. Willingham, D.T. (2010) *Why Don't Students Like School?*, Jossey-Bass

42. Duhigg, C. (2014) *The Power of Habit*, Random House

43. Neal, D.T., Wood, W., & Quinn, J.M. (2006) "Habits—a repeat performance," *Current Directions in Psychological Science*, 15(4), pp. 198-202

44. Duhigg, C. (2014) *The Power of Habit*, Random House

45. Bernacer, J. & Murillo, J.I. (2014) "The Aristotelian conception of habit and its contribution to human neuroscience," *Frontiers in Human Neuroscience*, 8(883)

46. Aristotle. (2009) *The Nicomachean Ethics*, Oxford University Press

47. Bernacer, J. & Murillo, J.I. (2014) "The Aristotelian conception of habit and its contribution to human neuroscience," *Frontiers in Human Neuroscience*, 8(883)

48. Adler, M.J. (1982) *The Paideia Proposal: an educational manifesto*

49. Grant, S., Hamilton, L.S., Wrabel, S.L., et al. (2017) *Social and Emotional Learning Interventions Under the Every Student Succeeds Act: evidence review*, RAND Corporation, www.rand.org/pubs/research_reports/RR2133.html

50. Prior, K.S. (2018) *On Reading Well: finding the good life through great books*, Brazos Press

51. Ibid.

Part III.
Ideas Applied

6. TRADITIONALISM IN ACTION

I can make all the arguments I want about the ideal philosophy of education. I can lay out syllogisms and build theories up from first principles. I can cite all the research that isolates individual instructional practices. Even so, none of this would necessarily justify any one system, theory, approach, or anything else. What's more, I doubt it would leave many convinced. Schools are such complex systems with such a variety of moving parts that it's near impossible to justify any one approach entirely in the abstract.

Falsifiability remains a cornerstone of intellectual interrogation. Any theory must be proven right or wrong, and be able to be proven right or wrong. The most persuasive justifications for a traditionalist approach to education come by way of the schools that are doing it and doing it well. They are proof of concept; they are the grand experiment that proves the theory's viability. I can write books. Authors can write op-eds. Educators can debate in the teachers' lounge. Social scientists can run experiments. But it is the institutions that have built themselves upon these principles and succeeded wildly that are the most persuasive. Moreover, since the educational scale is tipped heavily towards progressivism, one lone voice, op-ed, or book standing on the opposite side can do little; institutions, schools, and curricula act as a counterweight.

In this chapter, I will explore a few of these institutions. There are charter school systems that far surpass their traditional public school counterparts precisely because of the traditional practices they employ; there are top-shelf sequenced curricula that outperform any haphazardly thrown together lesson plans. I will also discuss how these ideas play out in my own classroom—a section I include simply because I can show how I have applied the theory of traditionalism to the nuts and bolts practice of classroom teaching; I can only speculate on how other teachers have brought these ideas into their classrooms.

SEQUENCED CURRICULUM

I'm no great cook. Even so, over the summer my table is full of culinary delights. When my wife and I replace our standard store-bought fare with locally grown vegetables and meats from the farmers' market, our breakfasts, lunches, and dinners resemble something like a feast. Despite our mediocre skills in the kitchen, we can rely on the knowledge and expertise of the producers along with recipes from the internet to enhance our meals. The quality of the produce, spices, and meats are not alone sufficient for a great meal, but they are crucial elements.

So, too, with curricula. The skill of producing a meal from ingredients is an entirely different job from the production of the ingredients themselves. Our job as teachers is to take the materials and craft them into coherent lessons that respond to student needs. At times, these jobs can overlap: many private school teachers in small districts are expected to produce materials as well as teach, but the opportunity cost of that arrangement makes it an unideal option. Conversely, the benefits of a sequenced curriculum—separating the job of the teacher from the job of the curriculum developer—are many.

First, it ensures coherence. Without a sequenced curriculum—where classes are left to run on a teacher's whim or preference—districts run the risk of kids learning about dinosaurs or nebulas in multiple grades without ever experiencing covalent bonds. A RAND Corporation report found that 90% of teachers said they sourced materials from the internet;[1] reviews of online content find most of these materials to be "mediocre" or "probably not worth using."[2] In place of a team of experts, Google or Teachers Pay Teachers become our curriculum developers. Like Newton's law, we cannot destroy curriculum development; we can only change its point of creation.

Second, a sequenced curriculum saves time. I've been on curriculum hunts before. In my first year of teaching, I stayed up well into the night and woke up so early I could get to Starbucks when the doors first opened. I put in 80- to 90-hour weeks just trying to develop lesson plans, worksheets, assessments, and other curricular documents. Teachers spend up to seven hours a week selecting and developing materials online.[3] Frequently, this is an exceptionally fulfilling task; at other times, it is simply tedious. Someone might enjoy gardening enough to grow 100% of their own produce, but that would consume all their waking hours. Instead, if they sacrificed some autonomy to local growers, they would find an abundance of time opened up for other things. Without the need to craft every question or activity anew, teachers could give more meticulous feedback, reflect on their practice, and communicate with parents.

Third, the research is rather conclusive: a core curriculum benefits students. In his book *The Schools We Need and Why We Don't Have Them,* E.D. Hirsch meticulously documents the ubiquity of what he calls core curriculum among the world's most successful school systems.[4] While the US is too large for one curriculum mandated top-down from Washington, there are lessons to be learned. Curriculum matters, and our students need access to high-quality curricular materials.

I've taught multiple curricula now. I've taught a district-planned curriculum that has left much to be desired: few of the teachers read entire novels from start to finish and much of the curriculum was Deweyian, skill-centric pedagogy. In another curriculum, when I knew a few of the planners on the committee, I could see where conflicting visions came into play. Because I knew their pedagogical philosophies, I could tell which teacher had planned which section; there was no coherence.

Since then, I have had the privilege of using Doug Lemov's *Reading Reconsidered* curriculum, created with his *Teach Like a Champion* team, to teach *Narrative of the Life of Frederick Douglass.* It was the difference between homegrown and frozen veggies; between chopping vegetables with a perfectly sharpened chef's knife and a dull butter knife. The curriculum would not make a poor teacher great but even a table full of raw, well-grown produce provides nourishment. I first noticed the strength of the curriculum in regards to controversial topics. Douglass' book is incredibly violent and jarring: he pulls no descriptive punches and portrays American chattel slavery in all its reality. If taught poorly, we risk a lot with this book: scarred children, upset parents, the adoption of overly pessimistic worldviews. Fortunately, with Lemov's curriculum in hand, I knew the questions had been workshopped, edited, and re-edited before I asked them. I knew that even the most violent passages could be couched within their historical context; I was not left grasping for supplementary texts that helped to make sense of the atrocities depicted. I knew that a team of educational experts had reviewed, edited, criticized, and reworked every aspect of the documents before being sent out for instruction in the world. I may have been the only teacher in the classroom but I was not alone in teaching the material–others wiser than me had produced the materials I would teach. That was a comforting thought.

At no point did I feel I had sacrificed my autonomy on the altar of sequenced curriculum. Instead, I felt I had a buffet of curricular materials at my disposal. This worry about loss of autonomy is frequently invoked in discussions of sequenced curricula. For many teachers, searching for and crafting curricula is the most fulfilling aspect of their jobs—aside from interacting with students, of course. With a pre-planned curriculum, won't they be little more than classroom automatons delivering lesson plans like pre-programmed drones?

The responses to this valid concern are many. As I've already mentioned, we cannot remove the need for curriculum creation. The question is and always will be a matter of who creates it—teachers, students, administrators, companies, or online search engines. Student-led and online-led curricular construction is unideal for every reason that I've listed previously in this book. The question then is a matter of whether the curriculum comes from teachers, companies, or administrators.

I've crafted my curricula alone before. It's busy. It's lonely. True, it can be fulfilling, and after a career working, reworking, crafting, modifying, editing, revising, delivering, and then repeating every step, it could turn into a pristine curriculum. Nonetheless, this approach is simply not scalable, as most teachers are not seasoned educators with a lifetime curriculum at the ready. It's far preferable for a number of educators or content experts to put their collective experience and wisdom into a curriculum, revise it over and again, and then offer it as a resource for teachers to use. Let the growers grow, the cooks cook, the curriculum writers write curriculum, and the teachers teach.

I concede that a teacher would have to sacrifice some autonomy with a sequenced curriculum, but that's a trade-off I'm willing to make because it saves me time and effort. I feel supported, not constrained, by the plethora of questions, activities, assessments, and guides that a well-made curriculum provides to me. Even within its confines, I still have wiggle room. One example stands out. About halfway through a unit on *Narrative of the Life of Frederick Douglass*, I could tell my students were struggling. They weren't enjoying the book: it had elicited all sorts of uncomfortable emotions, confusions, questions, and frustrations. The unit said to move forward, but I didn't. I sat down at the class's level and asked how they were doing. We spent 45 minutes of class discussing all that was on their minds. They asked each other questions and gave each other insight. This was a Catholic school, so the students wrestled with fundamental questions about how a good God could allow such atrocities to persist unpunished. As they filed out, one student came up to me and said, "I'm feeling better now. That book is still hard to read but I'm glad we are." Ever since then, students have asked me, "Mr. Buck, can we just talk for an entire class again?" I deviated from the curriculum and the class blossomed, but we could only have this conversation because of the seeds of ideas that the curriculum itself had first sown.

There are ways for teachers to scratch their curricula-writing itch. First, many schools employ a team-led method for developing district curricula. This allows teachers to still produce activities with the benefits of sequenced units. Second, even within a sequenced curriculum, there are places for teachers to supplement lessons. In the Douglass unit I used, I noticed my students struggling with the concepts of ethos, pathos, and logos, so I crafted an additional lesson on the topic. Finally, if curricular construction is truly a teacher's favorite aspect of the job, there are entire careers dedicated to this much-needed work, both within and outside districts.

There were other aspects of Lemov's curriculum that demonstrate the benefits of pre-planned curricula. For example, I found the use and reuse of vocabulary astounding. In place of a vocabulary lesson isolated from the rest of the activities, this unit taught vocabulary and then embedded these words again and again into questions and summative assignments. A student might see "apostrophe," "literary archetype," or "wallow" early in the unit, only to encounter those words again in readings, questions, and the requirements for long-answer responses. When I gave a vocabulary quiz at the end of the unit, I found no review was necessary because the unit had weaved review throughout. Because this unit had been written, workshopped, and revised time and again, incredible use was made of every single question. No opportunity for review or analysis had been missed.

I also found the supplementary non-fiction texts superb. Such readings build the historical knowledge that students need to understand any text we put into their hands, and this knowledge forms the basis of their critical thinking into the future. Finding relevant non-fiction texts was always the most difficult task for me while crafting any unit on my own. I'm an English teacher, not a historian, so not only did I lack quick recall of any relevant historical texts, but it was also difficult for me to sift through the important and the irrelevant, the high-quality and the mediocre. Using Lemov's unit, however, gave me access to other content experts in eras of which I was admittedly ignorant. The unit had excerpts from biographies, primary texts, maps, pictures, engravings, articles from the time period, and much more. My students learned far more about Nat Turner's rebellion, the effects of the cotton gin, various antebellum slave laws, contemporaneous works of art, layouts of slave plantations, nautical terminology, and other historical facts than I could have provided. In many cases, I knew of these things ahead of time but it didn't necessarily cross my mind to teach them all.

The Core Knowledge curriculum from E.D. Hirsch's foundation boasts similar strengths. Ultimately, each of these resources benefits from a team of experts intentionally crafting and revising units for use. Greg Ashman is right to say that teaching needn't be some cottage industry wherein teachers are left to cobble together resources from scratch.[5] Prefabricated materials are no more constraining to a teacher than an actor's script. There is such a thing as over-direction, but all education needn't be improvisation either. Isaiah Berlin writes about a musician who uses music such that "the player is not bound to the score ... [but] has absorbed the score into his own system ... [and] has changed it from an impediment to free activity into an element in that activity itself."[6] So, too, such resources expand a teacher's creative power.

CHARTERS

Some General Charter Statistics

Before I outline some of the more successful charter school systems, it seems pertinent to address the effects of charters as a whole on the education system. Perhaps the best meta-analyses of charters' effect sizes come from Stanford's Center for Research on Education Outcomes (CREDO).

CREDO's first major review—and one of the first comprehensive reviews of charter schools—came in 2009, early in the charter school movement in the US.[7] At the time, results were mixed. Many students in charter schools actually lagged behind their traditional public school (TPS) counterparts.

Such initial findings shouldn't be surprising. The mechanism for improvement within deregulatory policies like school choice and charter schools is not via intentionally crafted mandates that would improve schools the following year. Rather, competition and localism are the pressures and mechanisms through which charter schools improve over time. If a company starts losing money, they will improve products or cut costs. If a school begins to lose students via choice, such pressure incentivizes them to improve their services with an urgency that good intentions, goodwill, or persuasion simply cannot.

So, too, localism plays a substantial role. There are countless decisions to be made every single day; countless community preferences and local cultures. A bureaucrat or statute could not possibly account for them all. Charters have the capability to respond to these local problems and produce individual, targeted solutions. Through competitive pressure and the freedom to respond to local demands, charter schools improve organically over time, almost like an evolving organism.

The data bears this out. By CREDO's 2013 updated review, the situation had reversed.[8] Students in charter schools gained the equivalent of seven additional days of learning, with the benefits particularly strong among charters that had been open for a longer time. These institutions had built trial-and-error-type wisdom into their practices, policies, curriculum, instruction, and procedures.

However, this 2013 review still masks the most striking conclusion to come from CREDO. In reality, white and affluent students often fared *worse* in charter schools. The reality is simply that white and affluent students are more likely to have access to adequately funded schools in safe communities. We can attribute it to whatever systemic, privileged, or historical cause we want, but that's the reality. As such, the negative result among white and affluent students obscures the almost inconceivable benefit that charter schools provide to most other students. The 2013 report provides a list of the students that disproportionately *benefit* from charter schooling:

- *Students in poverty.*
- *English language learner students.*
- *Black students.*
- *Black students in poverty.*
- *Hispanic students in poverty.*
- *Hispanic English language learner students.*
- *Special education students.*[9]

One last report from CREDO in 2015 sought to hone in on this disproportionate impact. According to CREDO's analysis, "students enrolled in urban charter schools receive the equivalent of 40 additional days of learning growth … in math and 28 days of additional growth … in reading compared to their matched peers in TPS."[10] For Hispanic English language learners, the growth equated to 72 days in math and 79 days in reading.[11]

At a time when critical pedagogy is ascendant in American schools, any critical pedagogues need to reckon with this data. If the goal is equity or the closing of the achievement gap, the charter sector seems almost single-handedly capable of accomplishing just that. Nonetheless, these charter schools more often receive the opprobrium of critical theorists than their wholehearted endorsement.

It's worth briefly covering a few of the common rebuttals to charter schooling, which CREDO seeks to answer. Perhaps the most frequently cited explanation for the success of charter schools is that they "skim the cream"—they accept only the successful students and so can boast positive results. It's a matter of selectivity, not actual growth or achievement. CREDO points out, however, that charter schools tend to serve disproportionately poor students and that students tended to have falling grades before attending charters. Both those facts, while not a perfect rejoinder to the accusation, at least run counter to it. "Cream-skimming" may play a part but it is not sufficient to explain all the success of charter schools.

The other common narrative I see in response to charter schools points to the growth of charter management organizations. US president Joe Biden has claimed that he is against "for-profit" charter schools.[12] This conjures images of corporatists cashing in on children and wealthy donors using money to sway politicians—who wouldn't be against such a system? However, in reality, this is neither a moderate nor a useful stance.

The dichotomy between non-profit and for-profit originates in the difference between charter management organizations (CMOs) and educational management organizations (EMOs). Both function as umbrella networks that handle daily business and curricular management for charter schools. The only difference is a legal designation: CMOs are non-profit and EMOs are for-profit. It's a difference in paperwork. This difference is only meaningful if it impacts student learning. The few studies that have looked into the CMO-EMO dichotomy are inconclusive. One study found non-profit charter schools perform better than for-profit ones; another found no evidence for such a conclusion.[13,14] CREDO's own research found that charter schools managed by an umbrella organization outperformed local district charters.

The means by which charter schools improve is hard to pin down. Local control and deregulation allow for countless changes to be made in response to needs within the community. The decision-making power is spread out from a centralized office to parents, teachers, and administrators. As such, it is hard to account for every success. Networks of successful schools like Uncommon or KIPP point to at least one explanation that we can identify. These schools have adopted a clear vision and philosophy of education and can implement it to fidelity. Whereas many traditional public schools and districts have countless competing factions within—my own co-worker across the hall, although a friend, had the polar-opposite view on pedagogy from me—these networks of schools can advance a coherent ethos. They can build a school from first principles up.

While the most common charter school systems have a "no-excuses" ethos based on the traditionalism I've outlined in this book, others succeed based on progressive education principles. High Tech High, a school in San Diego that runs on theories of project-based learning, stands as one clear example. Even so, this is not evidence of wholesale success and it is not clear whether or not High Tech High is actually scaleable. Traditionalist schools have a proven ability to replicate their success across the country. It's worth zooming in on a few to see how they achieve their results.

Institutional Habits

A child leaves litter in the hallway; it's not picked up. A student throws something down the hall but the teacher doesn't bother to address it. Students begin to wander hallways during class. Their noise grows louder. They mock a teacher. Soon students are berating teachers. In one of my schools, a teacher had to check herself into an in-patient mental health facility because of the verbal abuse she suffered from students. The small infraction that opens this paragraph would not inevitably lead to fights and verbal abuse. However, once the mindset beneath it takes root—a lack of care or concern over the small things—it can spread and choke out any other positive growth.

Success Academy, perhaps America's most successful and thereby most hotly debated network of charter schools, takes the exact opposite approach. It "sweats the small stuff." When I taught in urban schools, I regularly heard some variation of "Well, we can't worry about some mundane complication when we have fights to deal with." Conversely, Success Academy knows that a focus on these small details is the best defense against disorder. Every blinking light bulb is replaced, every scuff wiped from the floor, every classwork display straightened.

If anything, the small things matter most. George L. Kelling and James Q. Wilson introduced the "broken windows" theory of policing in a 1982 issue of *The Atlantic Monthly*.[15] They described a social experiment wherein a car was left out in the open on a street in an affluent urban neighborhood. For days, no one touched it. But once the experimenters shattered the window of the car, passersby further vandalized and robbed it. The appearance of neglect invited further vandalism. They summarize the theory so:

> Social psychologists and police officers tend to agree that if a window in a building is broken and is left unrepaired, all the rest of the windows will soon be broken … Window-breaking does not necessarily occur on a large scale because some areas are inhabited by determined window-breakers whereas others are populated by window-lovers; rather, **one unrepaired broken window is a signal that no one cares,** and so breaking more windows costs nothing [emphasis mine].[16]

A broken window says this is the kind of place where windows are broken without consequence. There is no sanction and thus no personal cost. By contrast, Success Academy communicates to families and students that this *is* the kind of place that maintains excellence even into the small details. It's not the kind of place where misbehavior occurs, so why even try? Sweating the small stuff establishes a culture of excellence from the appearance of hallways to the content of the classroom.

Order requires construction and maintenance. San Francisco is suffering the results of abandoning a "sweat the small stuff" approach to public order after effectively decriminalizing petty theft under $950. "They've got bigger fish to fry!" One journalist tells of shoplifters swiping a few drinks to enjoy right on the sidewalk in front of the store and others stuffing backpacks full of goods with impunity.[17] And it's not just petty thieves. One multi-agency law-enforcement effort, Operation Proof of Purchase, uncovered a warehouse containing stolen goods worth millions of dollars intended to be hawked on the street or sold back to stores. The petty thievery quickly became one thread in an intentionally crafted, interwoven network of crime. In response, Walgreens has closed 22 stores in the city since 2016 and other retailers are following suit.[18] When police officers ignored the small fish, bigger fish came along, and the community suffered for it.

In December 2021, San Francisco's Democratic mayor announced that the "bullshit" plaguing the city would no longer be tolerated.[19] She increased funding to police departments and pledged new policies cracking down on the open use and sale of drugs on the streets. Other localities like Oakland also backtracked on de-policing policies to instead hire more officers and open police academies.[20] Public order is a progressive ideal. Without it, those most vulnerable suffer, and it's the same in either chaotic or orderly schools.

The impulse to sweat the small stuff extends beyond preventing heinous offenses. One line from Kelling and Wilson's article stands out: "Outside observers should not assume that they know how much of the anxiety now endemic in many big-city neighborhoods stems from a fear of 'real' crime and how much from a sense that the street is disorderly, a source of distasteful, worrisome encounters."[21] One reporter in San Francisco writes that the open drug dealing and shootings have left "children and seniors afraid to go outside."[22] Most of my own students didn't fear violence; they dreaded the constant low-level disruption. Most of my students weren't going to get punched in the face, but they lost their temper at times after yet another mean comment, another paper airplane, another student insulting the teacher. They wanted to learn and being prevented from doing so frustrated them. The constant disruptions, the litter, the vandalized bathrooms communicate to students that this school is uncontrolled and uncontrollable.

Children are naturally rebellious as they develop their own sense of self. When schools sweat the small stuff then the expression of that rebellion becomes small as well. At Michaela Community School in London, they would prefer that students express their natural sense of rebellion by attempting to bend uniform rules, rather than pursuing "big ticket" behaviors like "swearing at a teacher or bringing a knife to school."[23]

At Success Academy, everything is pre-taught and systematized. Everyone has routines—from the youngest student to the administrators. Kids walk down the hallways in silence. Administrators observe and provide regular instructional feedback, and norm their language even before the school year begins, thus ensuring that they employ the same justifications for various policies and correct students with similar redirections. It's amazing the practice that goes into it all. Teachers rehearse walking down the hallway in silence so they can provide the clearest directions and anticipate confusion. Admins practice observations in empty rooms. There is even a staff member whose job includes a detailed list of "small stuff" to sweat every day, from covered sockets in kindergarten classrooms to cleaning graffiti in the bathroom—excellence and order from top to bottom.[24]

There is also a clear behavior management system—designations of green, yellow, and red—that follows the student from classroom to classroom, all of which have normed expectations. A critic might point to the importance of teacher autonomy and personal differences in teaching styles, and thus the need for varied expectations. However, such differences cause problems. In one school, my administration left phone policies up to teacher discretion. When phones were allowed in one room but not another, the permissiveness of one teacher affected others. Teachers squabbled with children, students carried phones with them regardless, administrators struggled to dole out punishments for an infraction that was permissible elsewhere, and some teachers developed a reputation for being overly strict, thus undermining their ability to work with students.

Rather, everything in Success Academy is normed: students read in 2-2-2 (two feet on the floor, two hands on the book, two eyes on the page), levels of noise range from "zero noise" to "restaurant level," and even the colors in the buildings are constant across the system. There's a clear benefit to students in this. In her challenging essay "The silenced dialogue," Lisa Delpit, a MacArthur "Genius" Fellow, observes that there are rules in any school environment.[25] We cannot remove rules; we can only express them clearly and overtly, or leave them unwritten.

When rules are unwritten, students suffer. Delpit makes profound observations about the unspoken rules in classrooms: "The codes or rules I'm speaking of relate to linguistic forms, communicative strategies, and presentation of self; that is, ways of talking, ways of writing, ways of dressing, and ways of interacting."[26] She provides an example of a middle-class mother who might ask her child, "Isn't it time for your bath?" Although posed as a question, it is really a command and the mother expects it to be followed promptly. Similar veiled commands and unspoken rules permeate our schools. When such rules or social norms are left implicit, students can run afoul and receive what is truly an unfair consequence. The remedy is to keep expectations clear across the building, explicitly stated, and maintained.

It's the students who most need our help that suffer most in disorderly environments. The psychiatrist Bessel van der Kolk explains that when our minds experience trauma, the amygdala, which warns us of "impending danger" and activates "our body's stress response," can become overactive.[27] Stress responses are normal in the face of threatening situations. However, "when traumatized people are presented with images, sounds, or thoughts related to their particular experience," van der Kolk writes, "the amygdala reacts with alarm."[28] What one individual perceives as normal background noise or the chaos of day-to-day schooling can trigger a stress response in others with trauma in their past. Too often, these neurological realities become a justification for misbehavior. However, if we allow one student to act out because of their history, we risk another silently suffering and countless more losing out on learning.

Michaela Community School does a brilliant job of responding to this "deficit thinking." In the school's book *Battle Hymn of the Tiger Teachers*, former deputy headteacher Jonathan Porter writes:

> *A "some excuses" school argues that Tom's background explains why he behaves like he does. Of course, they are right. It is no coincidence that Tom throws chairs around the classroom: he's had precious few positive role models, his dad's nowhere to be seen, and he's grown up with few of the boundaries that have nurtured his middle-class peers.*
>
> *What is at stake here is whether you think Tom is capable of changing. WE do. But also whether you are prepared for Tom's behaviour to affect the learning of the other 30 pupils in his class. We aren't.[29]*

"Trauma-informed" pedagogy cannot mean that we lower the standards for all students. The idea that poverty leads to poor character truly is an offensive, bigoted idea. It's an argument that the philosopher G.K. Chesterton criticized as early as 1908, writing against the idea that "the physical conditions of the poor must of necessity make them mentally and morally degraded."[30] "No-excuses" models contest these conceptions of students. Critical pedagogy rightly draws attention to the varied experiences of students that underlie their ability or inability to function equally within a standard school setting. However, in place of altering the system—which invariably means lowering standards, providing excuses, and thereby facilitating for students to make poor choices—Michaela believes that all students are capable and treats them so.

Another Michaela teacher, Becky Staw, tells the story of a student who had been scared to attend his former school because of the bullying he would face. At Michaela, however, he felt "a lot safer."[31] If students have experienced trauma, they should be able to expect a school that is orderly; a school where they needn't fear unexpected chaos in the hallways; a school where they are safe. They should be able to expect that if that right to safety is infringed upon, the culprit will be properly sanctioned.

These systems needn't only be about order and cleanliness. Michaela fosters routines for building relationships between teachers and students into the school day. Teachers eat meals with their students, play games at recess, and hold restorative conversations during any suspension. Michaela doesn't leave it up to chance or individual teacher charisma to establish these relationships. They are built actively through institutional habits. And neither are these systems only about instruction in the present. Invoking Aristotle, the habits and routines we build with students now will serve them later in life. Staw writes:

> We believe that it is the duty of the teacher to help children form good habits, a duty we share with the child's parents. We want to teach children pro-social behaviour because it is this kind of behaviour—kindness, empathy and resilience—which will allow them to be successful now and later in life.[32]

When students face sanctions and so must learn to regulate their anger, when they learn to automatically say thank you, when they can make eye contact and provide a firm handshake, they develop the habits they need to be successful later in life. Many of these behaviors may be culturally dependent and arbitrary—as Delpit and other critical theorists assert— but to deprive students of knowledge of the workings of the dominant culture is to deprive them of what they need to function in this society. Perhaps we can change our cultural norms over time, but we do our students a disservice if we pretend it has already changed and neglect to instill its customs.

Discipline

Although Ken Robinson popularized the term "factory-model schooling," this criticism of modern schooling traces back at least to Foucault, and it's still the most salient critique against these modern iterations of traditionalist schooling.[33] Paul Hirschfield of Rutgers University writes: "Critical scholars have argued that strict disciplinary regimens in working class schools help to promote smooth and voluntary transitions into an industrial workplace that tightly regulates and subordinates laborers."[34] Foucault suggests that a similar undergirding structure across schools, prisons, factories, and military service serves to subordinate its constituents into a thoughtless, capitalistic workforce.

The "no-excuses" models of schooling grew in parallel to the crackdown on crime in the 1990s and directly cited broken-windows policing as inspiration. "Zero-tolerance" policies on guns and drugs increased the use of suspensions, a practice that quickly aimed its disciplinary discretion at more minor infractions—everything from imperfect uniforms to ambiguous terms like "disrespect."

Questions that underlie critical theory ask whether misbehavior occurs in response to cultural clash, to students never having learned proper behavior, or as an expression of some deeper hurt. In each of these cases, it seems cruel and unjust to impose a consequence for something that isn't really the student's fault. Instead, we need supports and academics so that students can succeed. This is a nice-sounding argument, a paean to the romantic belief in the inherent goodness of all children. But here's the harsh reality: people are going to commit crimes no matter what and children misbehave. Is it natural that one child bites another? Or is it unnatural for students to interact peacefully? The economist Thomas Sowell suggests, looking back on history, that chaos and disorder are the natural states of human civilization.[35] Rather than seeking the special causes of criminality or misbehavior—these things need no explanation—we should instead seek to understand the causes of peace and prosperity.

One analysis of broken-windows policing sought to compare the effects on crime of economic factors like minimum wage and unemployment with the effects of deterrent factors like policing and arrest rates.[36] Is criminality a result of economic hardship or licentious laws? Do students act out because they are children or because they have some unmet need? The researchers found that "while both economic and deterrence variables are important in explaining the decline in crime, the contribution of deterrence measures is larger than those of economic variables."[37] Both factors played a part. Unmet needs and economic hardship certainly encouraged criminality, but providing further economic support caused a smaller reduction in crime than simply adequate policing. Our society will never reach Eden, and until then people will commit crimes and students will call each other names. We can choose to either respond to misbehavior or tolerate it.

The pendulum of school discipline ever swings back and forth. We don't need a return to the stereotypical schoolhouse, with pupils asked to stand before the silent class to recite whatever is demanded of them while the threat of a ruler taps in some authoritarian's hand. Jonathan Porter acknowledges that "no-excuses discipline badly done can be very bad indeed."[38] Critical scholars are correct to lambast no-excuses discipline if the rules are laid out simply for the sake of rules, obedience for the sake of obedience, consequence for the sake of consequence.

Present in every "no-excuses" school that I've encountered is behavior "narration." The teacher justifies and explains every consequence, reinforcing the *why* behind every rule. To do otherwise is akin to a police officer ticketing someone without explaining the reason. We drive to the speed limit to protect other road users; we work silently to allow others to focus on their own thoughts and writing. The consequences exist for the good of the group; for the purpose of learning, not for mere control and safety. Examples of adult authoritarianism throughout children's literature clarify this point. For example, in the 1996 film of Roald Dahl's *Matilda*, the protagonist's father justifies his actions by saying, "I'm right and you're wrong, I'm big and you're small, and there's nothing you can do about it." The problem here is the imposition of authority for the sake of authority itself. To assign a detention or suspension to protect other children, to ensure safety for a bullied child, or to stymie bad habits— these are different things.

It's worth recalling here that authority and order cannot dissipate. Like energy, they only change form. If adults do not lovingly take on an authoritative role in the school or classroom, someone or something else will. In San Francisco, crime cartels have grown up around petty theft. When police drew away from the area around Seattle's Capitol Hill, roving bands declared themselves the new law. When countries lack a stable government, endless factions push them to war. When teachers do not create structure and order, all too often the social pressures of the strongest children will impose order. It's not a choice of whether schools have structure, only a matter of who wields the authority and how.

It might be fair to argue that these no-excuses models have gone too far. *The Atlantic* published a challenging article about just that, asking: "How strict is too strict?"[39] Students have complained and even protested against the extremity of certain rules, complaining of rule books 51 pages long or receiving consequences for an insufficiently straight arm while raising their hand to answer a question. In response, the charter leaders loosened their policies but still maintained the general ethos. They decreased their use of suspensions, expanded their dress code, and took the insight of student boards, but in the end they still used suspensions, still had dress codes, and still placed the final decision-making responsibility with adults.

We need to remember the underlying *difference* between prisons and schools. Both enforce routine and order but for drastically different reasons. Prisons exist for punishment and safety. Schools exist for learning. Too much routine certainly can stifle learning: student testimonies from many no-excuses schools cite their difficulty in transitioning to the independence of college (who doesn't struggle with this?). But too little routine prevents learning as well: a far greater number of testimonies cite these schools as places of love, joy, and learning. The pendulum will swing back and forth, but the focus on learning as the reason for discipline will hopefully keep that swing to a minimum.

Michaela Community School does a brilliant job of holding the pendulum steady in a space that accepts the critiques of progressive and critical theories but within the confines of a traditionalist system. Importantly, the school recasts the typical victim narratives. Whereas the media might portray a student who receives a detention or suspension as a victim of hard times suffering the oppression of their school system, Michaela shows how adult authority is lovingly expressed through expectations and consequences.

Imagine a student who cusses out a teacher and receives only a warning. This implicit acceptance of the behavior communicates a number of messages: it tells the offender and other students that what they did is acceptable, or that it's unacceptable but is what's expected of that student and no one anticipates that they'll change. By contrast, providing a consequence communicates that you care enough about the student to hold them to a high standard and correct their behavior when it deviates. It also communicates to other students that the school will protect their learning.

And that gets to the heart of it. Perhaps the most pernicious effect of progressive approaches to discipline is simply the academic costs they enact. Paulo Freire suggested that we need to free ourselves from the oppressive teacher-student dichotomy.[40] In reality, deconstructing this relationship leaves us beholden to chaos and illiteracy, and it's the students who suffer trauma or poverty who can least afford wasted class time. Michaela's Becky Staw writes: "To bemoan the attainment gap between the rich and the poor, while disempowering the teacher in the classroom, is to condemn our disadvantaged pupils to poorer life chances."[41]

Students also benefit incidentally from the freedom of mind that the teacher then has. When an administration and a behavior code place the teacher in a role of authority and back them up, the teacher can worry less about what vulgar interjection or pencil will fly across the room and instead focus on teaching. To put it in cognitive terms, their working memory will be unencumbered by behavior concerns, freeing them to concentrate on responding to student comments, crafting impromptu questions, or clarifying explanations. I've experienced this myself. In my early years of teaching, before I could run a classroom effectively, I was distracted by whispers or the anticipation of misbehavior and so my questions didn't quite land and my explanations of grammar concepts left students confused. When I have classes running well, it feels like an improvised artistic act, with my thoughts drifting nowhere except for the next question, example, or analogy.

Academics

Ironically, Eva Moskowitz, founder of Success Academy, considers the schools' pedagogy to be progressive, citing John Dewey as a major inspiration. One journalist at *The New Yorker* summarized Success Academy's goal as "to combine aspects of a very traditional approach—rigid discipline, tracking, countdowns, rigorous accountability—with elements of a highly progressive curriculum."[42] The schools' math curriculum emphasizes students discovering their own strategies for tackling problems. Their reading curriculum relies on leveled texts and centers comprehension skills like identifying the main idea. Kindergarten includes regular "block time," a hallmark of early childhood progressivism.

This block play seems fitting. A child might ask to build bridges and the teacher responds, bringing up different pictures of bridges and teaching the basic names in response to the child's interest. This is project-based, student-led learning, progressive to its core. No one argues, though, that play-based, experiential learning is *all* bad. Rather, the concepts are taken too far. Children do first learn through trial, error, and experimentation. Misconceptions arise when we attempt to extend that type of learning into higher grades and more complex concepts. Humans are naturally preconditioned to learn certain basic skills, and so learning those will appear natural. As cultures developed and our knowledge grew more complex, these natural processes no longer sufficed, and so learning everything else—the stuff of school—will require at times contrived and unnatural learning environments and practices. Tom Bennett, the founder of researchED, agrees:

> *Classrooms are unnatural to some extent, of course, given that they are unique to our species. They are also highly evolved, efficient methods of imparting a lot of knowledge to a lot of people at once.*[43]

That being said, Success Academy, despite its claims to progressive pedagogy, has many hallmarks of a traditionalist approach. The schools have a set, sequenced curriculum. Anna Switzer, who helped to design units at Success, told *The New Yorker* that "'shared texts' play a more prominent role than they would at a very progressive public school."[44] Success Academy's own English curriculum opens with a paean to great texts:

> *Our English curriculum exposes scholars to the great texts, ideas, and events that have shaped our modern world, and it prioritizes Platonic-style discourse; incisive analysis; and powerful, cogent writing. By studying works of lasting and urgent value, our students learn to grapple with complex ideas, appreciate diverse cultural perspectives, and experience the joy of the written word.*[45]

Courses include "Survey of great books," "Canonical works of American literature," and "Canonical works of global literature," none of which would fit neatly into a workshop-style approach nor a critical classroom that wants to deconstruct the canon itself.

In his book *How the Other Half Learns*, Robert Pondiscio confirms that, in many ways, Success Academy is not the bastion of progressivism it claims to be. Moskowitz has "adopted the language of progressive education more than its practices," he argues.[46] In her memoir, Moskowitz wrote that "you are more likely to succeed if you accept the fact that schooling often requires getting children to act contrary to their natural inclinations."[47] Rousseau bristles and Dewey turns in his grave. Pondiscio also draws attention to the fact that the children at Success schools have learned their times tables by heart and their supposed project-based learning is really more like "cross-curricular units."[48]

Two other elements of Success Academy are worth drawing out. First, much of education has formed itself into the image of standardized tests, allocating more and more time to reading and math. In one school where I worked, students had up to three English classes a day. Yet Success Academy has not bent itself to fit the tests and has allocated more time than typical public schools to music, science, history, the arts, and even chess.[49] Second, Moskowitz is a champion of field trips. Taken together, these two aspects of the system ensure students build a diverse schema of background knowledge that likely pays dividends as they continue their schooling.

Michaela Community School, the British counterpart to Success Academy, is traditionalist from the first to the last bell. Curricula are sequenced. Teachers employ direct instruction. The emphasis is on knowledge over skills. Drill and practice permeate the building. To go into the detail would be an unneeded review of everything I've already covered in this book, but it's worth outlining a few aspects of the school's ethos.

Michael Taylor, a history teacher at Michaela, expounds on the school's knowledge-rich approach. He worries that "the 'doing' of history has become the essence of history teaching so much, we no longer teach the substantive knowledge."[50] Progressivist fads emphasize the use of primary source documents over the "rich knowledge base that is required to understand a source and analyse it."[51] Academic historians use the tools of knowledge to analyze the source document, whereas children are left trying to do pull-ups without the critical muscle mass they need to do so. The role of the history teacher is not to create academic historians there and then, but to give students the training to become one in the future.

Michaela makes use of "knowledge organizers," a traditionalist practice that I haven't yet addressed. A knowledge organizer is a single sheet of paper that lists the essential vocabulary, concepts, quotes, and historical events that a teacher expects their students to have learned by the end of a unit. It's essentially a study guide that teachers hand out at the *beginning* of the unit for reference throughout the following classes. I have used knowledge organizers with reservation. They have acted as a sort of scaffold, encouraging me to refer back to previously covered historical events, to use and reuse unit vocabulary, and to work in review practice. The organizers were but one more tool or resource, not the sole activity and guide.

Teachers at Michaela incorporate regular knowledge checks and self-quizzes throughout their classes. Research into the benefits of periodic quizzing is substantial. In one study of middle school students, researchers implemented low-stakes quizzes before units, after lectures, and prior to tests. They found that even "a single low-stakes review quiz produces potent testing effects" and, notably, this learning "persisted to the end of semester exam and to the end of the school year."[52] Direct instruction best helps students to learn a concept, and regular opportunities to retrieve that knowledge from long-term memory help it to stick. This persistence of memory is crucial. We've all had the experience of cramming for a test only to forget the knowledge within days; regular, low-stakes recall and review works against that natural phenomenon. Doug Lemov's *Reading Reconsidered* unit, which I referred to earlier in the chapter, made frequent use of knowledge checks and self-quizzes, incorporating regular reviews into bellworks, short activities, and quick homework assignments to help the history, quotes, and themes stick in students' minds.

MY CLASSROOM

To conclude this chapter, I think it's worth expounding on how I incorporated these ideas into my own instruction. My professional journey has been a process of growing skeptical of the progressivist, project-based, student-led practices that I learned in teacher training to first discovering traditionalist theories and then struggling to implement them in my day-to-day teaching. That imperfect process is precisely what sets us, teachers, apart from academics and advocates: I don't just discuss and consider these ideas in the abstract; they affect what I will do come Monday. How will I incorporate knowledge-rich theories or worked examples into a unit on *Romeo and Juliet*? What does long-term memory have to do with a literature classroom? How can direct instruction pair with a novel study? I'll try to answer some of these questions. To do so, it might be best simply to explain how I run a typical unit in my classroom.

We always begin by building a bit of essential background knowledge. If we're studying *A Christmas Carol*, students read articles from the BBC about Victorian England and we consider what life was like, who Charles Dickens was, what poorhouses were, and other such questions. Before studying *Romeo and Juliet*, students learn about the Globe Theatre and Victorian England. Any unit begins with basic historical information, so students have images to furnish in their minds as they read and a knowledge base with which to begin analyzing the text. Making connections or envisioning a story are not skills. Students cannot imagine a Victorian street out of the wisps of thought. They need to see images in real life before they can see them in their mind's eye.

As we're reading, I incorporate more short readings on various topics related to various chapters: Elizabethan wedding customs, fugitive slave laws, Victorian social customs, famous images from related eras, and so forth. These take the form of entire class activities (paraphrasing the preamble to the US Declaration of Independence), short bellwork-type activities (an image with a single question), or homework (a reading with comprehension and analysis questions). Sometimes we discuss the reading at length; at other times, they are short and provide just enough information to help students understand a scene.

In every unit, the texts are always central, classic, and linguistically rigorous. I taught Shakespeare to English language learners for a number of years and many opted to memorize passages just for fun. If they can handle that level of rigor, any student can. As we read, I make use of group reading, independent reading, and even partner reading. Generally, the most important passages we read together, narrative chapters or sections students read independently, and partner reading is kept to supplementary texts.

For group reading, I've learned much from Doug Lemov. I spend an above-average amount of time reading out loud and believe it's the most important part of instruction. To keep the words flowing efficiently, instead of round-robin reading wherein students call on each other, I bounce back and forth between reading myself and calling on students. It's a classroom habit that we build and they know how it goes. I will say, "Pause, thank you," and then call on the next student. For more difficult texts, I allow students to opt out of reading aloud, but with less rigorous texts all students are expected to read. If a student struggles with reading or has a learning disability, I take them aside at the beginning of the year for a quick chat. They know that I will pre-mark easier passages for them or, if they request it, I'll tell them ahead of time when they'll be called on so they can practice a passage beforehand. By the end, where in former English classes these students would not participate – isolating them in a sense from the community of the class – they prefer this pre-planned reading, finally able to join in with everyone else. No one is left out; no one is left asking why their classmate never gets called on; no one is forced into an embarrassing situation.

As we read, students usually have a "reading guide"—pre-planned questions that foster both establishing meaning and analyzing meaning. Students cannot analyze something that they don't first comprehend. Once meaning has been established and sufficient knowledge built, I find the simplest questions often elicit the best responses. What is the author doing in this chapter? What are you thinking as we finish this section?

I also incorporate professional analyses of texts into my classroom. We want students to think for themselves and come to their own conclusions, but it's hard to do so if they've never encountered a professional analysis or have nothing to compare their own thinking to. At middle school level, we'll read passages from online analysis sites or watch video essays to compare. Like the teachers in the Jesuit schools of the Ratio Studiorum, I'll also analyze passages for them and explain what I'm doing as I speak or write. These are the equivalent of worked examples; they model the process of analysis for students.

I'm sure many will bristle at this, but I make use of multiple-choice tests in my classes. I don't use them in every unit but I do use them. If I'm serious about the centrality of knowledge, it's imperative that my students learn a book—its characters, themes, images, figurative language, famous passages—and not just the ambiguous skill of "how to analyze." Reviewing characters, quotes, plot developments, historical or current events, analyses, famous similes or metaphors, and the like will help those to stick in long-term memory. A multiple-choice test helps to ensure that students have learned the book and can use this knowledge to analyze other texts in the future.

However, not every unit ends with a test. Most of my "projects" take the form of extended responses (on-demand or essays), presentations, or something that can house extended written responses, like "dust jackets"—these resemble projects but also require students to write extended summaries, quote analyses, reviews, and justifications for the pictures they draw, so are really just an excuse to practice structured writing. In each case, the project is not the means by which students learn, but a final demonstration of the learning.

Currently, I teach three separate grades in succession, which allows me to build students' writing proficiency from strictly outlined paragraphs to more creative essays. In the sixth grade, I teach a basic format for literary analysis responses:

- Theme.
- Context.
- Quote.
- Explain.

The first few times, I always provide an example of my own. I color-code it along with the above structure as a "worked example." After students have written a few, I take exemplars to demonstrate what was done well, but I also take mediocre examples and improve upon them. I pre-prepare these "improvements" on a slideshow presentation and track my improvements on consecutive slides. I include bullet-pointed details of what I'm changing. Did they need to introduce a quote? Did their paragraph stray off into too many unrelated tangents? Could they have chosen better words? In the end, students have an exemplar with bullet-point reviews for their own reference. It's constraining at first but so are any introductory exercises.

As they start to grow proficient in structured writing, I begin to require knowledge components to the writing. Before the final essay on *Romeo and Juliet*, we read four separate articles that outline various perspectives on love: the various Greek words for it, famous passages from Christian scripture, and scientific analysis of the neurochemicals involved. I add requirements like "reference at least one non-fiction article from our unit," "include an anecdote," or "use 'pathos' and 'ethos' somewhere in the response." Students need to practice writing and making choices, but they require knowledge and models from which to choose. If we do not provide knowledge and strategies, they are choosing in scarcity. By eighth grade, I begin to work in professional essays as the "worked examples," asking: how do they balance factual analysis and entertaining anecdotes? How do they incorporate the personal pronoun? What's the undergirding structure of the essay?

It's a continual process of reflection, modification, improvement, and further reflection. Even this year, as I write this book, I'm modifying. Take, for example, my grammar instruction. I noticed my students not only failing to grasp the concepts initially, but also losing mastery by the time of the test. With cognitive psychology in mind, I started to consider what could be causing this problem. I had grown lax in my behavior expectations during the direct instruction, allowing a low-level whisper and perhaps joking with students too much. These small allowances seem like no big deal in the moment, but when students aren't paying attention they aren't learning the material. My responsibility is to teach them, not entertain them.

But it didn't end there. When structured practice came around, I always let students shift to working in pairs immediately. While this makes the practice more enjoyable, it also works to overload their working memory. With a din in the classroom and conversations drifting to and fro, students are busy thinking about everything but the content—and if they're not thinking about it, they're not learning it! Finally, I didn't work in enough review. Students learned the content for the day and didn't see it again until the test came around. Far preferable would be a quick two- or three-problem review once or twice a week, mixing up old and new concepts.

None of these concepts are revolutionary. Read books together and discuss them. Set up classroom routines with behavioral expectations and hold students accountable. Teach students directly through explanations, models, and examples. Ask questions to ensure they are following the concepts. Expose students to the best literature that humanity has produced, the most important scientific concepts, and the most significant events in history, so they can go into the world armed with an outline of knowledge.

All this returns me to an anecdote from chapter 1: my student who complimented my "new way" of teaching. Education doesn't need a redefinition of what it means to be educated, nor a drastic overhaul of the system. It needs to rediscover tradition—a tradition of teaching methods that value the role of the teacher, of order and discipline, of knowledge worth knowing, and of wisdom worth learning.

REFERENCES

1. Tosh, K. & Kaufman, J.H. (2020) "New teacher survey shows that digital materials were not optimal before the pandemic. Now that they are front and center, how should they be used?" RAND Corporation, www.rand.org/blog/2020/05/new-teacher-survey-shows-that-digital-materials-were.html

2. Polikoff, M. & Dean, J. (2019) *The Supplemental Curriculum Bazaar: is what's online any good?*, Thomas B. Fordham Institute, p. 11, https://fordhaminstitute.org/national/research/supplemental-curriculum-bazaar

3. Goldberg, M. (2016) *Classroom Trends: teachers as buyers of instructional materials and users of technology*, MDR, https://mdreducation.com/reports/classroom-trends-teachers-buyers-instructional-materials-users-technology

4. Hirsch, E.D. (1996) *The Schools We Need and Why We Don't Have Them*, Doubleday

5. Ashman, G. (2021) "Practical people," *Filling the Pail* (blog), https://fillingthepail.substack.com/p/practical-people

6. Berlin, I. (1958) *Two Concepts of Liberty: an inaugural lecture delivered before the University of Oxford on 31 October 1958*, Clarendon Press

7. Center for Research on Education Outcomes. (2009) *Multiple Choice: charter school performance in 16 states*, Stanford University

8. Center for Research on Education Outcomes. (2013) *National Charter School Study 2013*, Stanford University, https://credo.stanford.edu/wp-content/uploads/2021/08/ncss_2013_final_draft.pdf

9. Ibid.

10. Center for Research on Education Outcomes. (2015) *Urban Charter School Study*, Stanford University, http://urbancharters.stanford.edu/download/Urban%20Study%2041%20Region%20Workbook.pdf

11. Ibid.

12. Strauss, V. (2022) "What Biden's proposed reforms to U.S. charter school program really say," *The Washington Post*, www.washingtonpost.com/education/2022/04/06/biden-reforms-charter-school-funding

13. Center for Research on Education Outcomes. (2017) *Charter Management Organizations*, Stanford University, https://credo.stanford.edu/wp-content/uploads/2021/08/cmo_final.pdf

14. Wolf, P.J. (ed.) (2018) *School Choice: separating fact from fiction*, Routledge

15. Kelling, G.L. & Wilson, J.Q. (1982) "Broken windows," *The Atlantic Monthly*, www.theatlantic.com/magazine/archive/1982/03/broken-windows/304465

16. Ibid.

17. Williamson, K.D. (2021) "The ORC invasion," *National Review*, www. nationalreview.com/magazine/2021/11/15/the-orc-invasion

18. Riley, J.L. (2021) "San Francisco has become a shoplifter's paradise," *The Wall Street Journal*, www.wsj.com/articles/san-francisco-shoplifters-theft-walgreens-decriminalized-11634678239

19. Schwartz, I. (2021) "SF mayor London Breed announces crackdown, policies 'less tolerant of the bullshit that has destroyed our city,'" *RealClearPolitics*, www.realclearpolitics.com/video/2021/12/15/sf_mayor_london_breed_announces_crackdown_policies_less_tolerant_of_the_bullshit_that_has_destroyed_our_city.html

20. Brinkley, L. & Johns, T. (2021) "Oakland City Council approves 2 more police academies for OPD amid surge in violence," ABC 7 News, https://abc7news.com/oakland-city-council-police-hiring-meeting-mayor-libby-schaaf-plan-department-opd/11308286

21. Kelling, G.L. & Wilson, J.Q. (1982) "Broken windows," *The Atlantic Monthly*, www.theatlantic.com/magazine/archive/1982/03/broken-windows/304465

22. Har, J. (2021) "San Francisco DA, others denounce mayor's plan for police," AP News, https://apnews.com/article/business-health-elections-crime-san-francisco-ffa1a0660f791a3a9242f7f11afcadd0

23. Michaela Community School. (2017) "Jonathan Porter: no excuses discipline" (video), YouTube, https://youtu.be/N0H91smFiBg

24. Pondiscio, R. (2019) *How the Other Half Learns*, Penguin Random House

25. Delpit, L.D. (1993) "The silenced dialogue: power and pedagogy in educating other people's children" in L. Weis & M. Fine (eds.) *Beyond Silenced Voices: class, race, and gender in United States schools*, State University of New York Press, pp. 119-139

26. Ibid.

27. van der Kolk, B. (2014) *The Body Keeps the Score: brain, mind, and body in the healing of trauma*, Viking

28. Ibid.

29. Porter, J. (2016) "No-excuses discipline changes lives" in K. Birbalsingh (ed.) *Battle Hymn of the Tiger Teachers*, John Catt Educational

30. Chesterton, G.K. (2007) *Orthodoxy*, Barnes & Noble

31. Staw, B. (2020) "We believe in authority" in K. Birbalsingh (ed.) *The Power of Culture*, John Catt Educational

32. Ibid.

33. RSA. (2010) "RSA ANIMATE: Changing education paradigms" (video), YouTube, https://youtu.be/zDZFcDGpL4U

34. Hirschfield, P.J. (2008) "Preparing for prison? The criminalization of school discipline in the USA," *Theoretical Criminology*, 12(1), pp. 79-101

35. Sowell, T. (2007) *A Conflict of Visions*, Basic Books

36. Corman, H. & Mocan, N. (2005) "Carrots, sticks, and broken windows," *The Journal of Law & Economics*, 48(1), pp. 235-66

37. Ibid.

38. Michaela Community School. (2017) "Jonathan Porter: no excuses discipline" (video), YouTube, https://youtu.be/N0H91smFiBg

39. Carr, S. (2014) "How strict is too strict?" *The Atlantic*, www.theatlantic.com/magazine/archive/2014/12/how-strict-is-too-strict/382228

40. Freire, P. (1970) *Pedagogy of the Oppressed*

41. Staw, B. (2020) "We believe in authority" in K. Birbalsingh (ed.) *The Power of Culture*, John Catt Educational

42. Mead, R. (2017) "Success Academy's radical educational experiment," *The New Yorker*, www.newyorker.com/magazine/2017/12/11/success-academys-radical-educational-experiment

43. Bennett, T. (2020) "Teachers need to be taught to teach students to behave," *Education Next*, www.educationnext.org/teachers-need-to-be-taught-to-teach-students-to-behave-excerpt-running-the-room

44. Mead, R. (2017) "Success Academy's radical educational experiment," *The New Yorker*, www.newyorker.com/magazine/2017/12/11/success-academys-radical-educational-experiment

45. Success Academy Charter Schools. (2021) *The High School Curriculum*, www.successacademies.org/wp-content/uploads/2021/11/COM21_008_CurricGuide_HS_2v11-1.pdf

46. Pondiscio, R. (2019) *How the Other Half Learns*, Avery

47. Moskowitz, E. (2017) *The Education of Eva Moskowitz: a memoir*, Harper

48. Pondiscio, R. (2019) *How the Other Half Learns*, Avery

49. Success Academy Charter Schools. (2021) *The High School Curriculum*, www.successacademies.org/wp-content/uploads/2021/11/COM21_008_CurricGuide_HS_2v11-1.pdf

50. Taylor, M. (2020) "History at Michaela" in K. Birbalsingh (ed.) *The Power of Culture*, John Catt Educational

51. Ibid.

52. McDaniel, M.A., Agarwal, P.K., Huelser, B.J., McDermott, K.B., & Roediger, H.L. (2011) "Test-enhanced learning in a middle school science classroom: the effects of quiz frequency and placement," *Journal of Educational Psychology*, 103(2), pp. 399-414

7. REHABILITATING EDUCATIONAL MISCONCEPTIONS

Bad ideas prevail in education. Couched in euphemistic language, notions like "creative thinking" or "21st-century skills" can be hard to contest. Although they quickly crumble under interrogation and analysis, those who question them immediately position themselves against a concept that at the very least sounds beneficial to students—and so the ideas spread. Who could possibly be against creativity or training students for the future?

For much of my career, I contested these ideas directly. However, I am starting to believe that a more effective strategy is to reclaim them for proper use. Creative thinking may be a vacuous notion but we still ought to value creativity. Rather than merely contesting the former, I wonder how we can foster the latter? Rather than critiquing "21st-century skills," I wonder how we can effectively prepare our students for the future? That is a valuable end goal of education, after all.

At the very least, I hope this chapter acts as something of an inoculation. If glittering generalities do spread like the common cold, time spent interrogating them can act as an effective defense. What's more, through analyzing and critiquing contemporary thought, this chapter can accomplish some sort of interleaving—an idea in education where teachers and students mix up and return to old concepts, thereby solidifying learning. If I introduced many arguments and concepts in the initial pages of this book and fully extrapolated them in part II, this chapter puts them into practice in a final review.

CREATIVE THINKING

Regardless of whether it's read for its religious or literary merit, Genesis, the first book of the Bible, provides a beautiful image of creativity. Adam and Eve work the garden, bring order from chaos, and make something from raw materials. Where God creates something from nothing, humans create from material. Adam and Eve work with seeds, dirt, and water to bring forth food, and so it is with all professions. An artist works with paints and canvas to create a landscape. A banker produces wealth. A teacher works with information and children to grow knowledge within the human mind. Understood such, creativity is the creation of goods, services, knowledge, or anything of the sort, not mere artistic creation. In this sense, we could consider creativity the end goal of education—to develop students who are able to create in our society and bring order to chaos.

There are two questions to answer here: what exactly is creativity and how do we foster it?

A progressivist understanding of creativity returns to the understanding of childhood as a state untarnished by society's strictures and rules. It underlies phrases like "Children are always asking why" and "Children are naturally curious." The child's mind is inherently creative and schooling snuffs out that spark; if we would only stand out of the way and provide it space, creativity would flourish. "Creativity is not learned but rather unlearned," writes one university lecturer.[1]

Defending this approach to creativity is the oft-cited paperclip study.[2] In 1968, George Land and Beth Jarman asked participants to develop as many possible uses for a paperclip as they could think of. Children far outperformed adults and performance on this task dwindled with age; the older the individual, the fewer unique purposes they could think up for the paperclip.

This type of thinking is often called creative or divergent thinking—the ability to think outside the box, to consider new uses for old things, to dream up unique ways of accomplishing tasks. Children are naturally better at this. When they encounter a fork, perhaps they haven't yet learned table manners and so that fork has no meaning to them. It could be a makeshift play-weapon, a utensil for eating, a noisemaker, or a great implement for poking their sibling.

Convergent thinking—thinking along predefined paths typically associated with truth—naturally comes with adulthood. We learn that a fork is used for eating certain foods, even if it may have other uses like fishing something out of the drain. We learn that there's an explanation for why the sky is blue, and that a water molecule is made up of two hydrogen atoms and one oxygen atom. We learn objective truths and cultural norms that confine our paths of thought.

It's rather silly to blame this loss of divergent thinking on schooling and to consider it a negative. Regarding the cause, it's a natural process of life. Adults have responsibilities and so cannot spend time experimenting with the uses of a fork. They learn cultural norms to smooth over social interactions. They learn more and more about the world, and their experience does not necessitate a constant posture of "why?" We divide the thoughts that are worth our time from those that are distractions. To some extent, we *ought* to develop convergent thinking: I don't want my financial planner playing make-believe, nor do I want an engineer to sketch out a project with the complexity of a noodle bridge. When I worked at a coffee shop in high school, my perpetually stoned coworker had plenty of divergent ideas but no capacity to bring them into being. He could think outside the box but had no creative capacity to manifest his energies.

A teacher's capacity to foster divergent thinking is often analogized to flexing a muscle. Progressivists argue that we can retrain our brains into divergent thinking through mind-mapping, loose-association exercises, question-asking, art projects, journaling, and free-writing. Popular conceptions of creativity portray it as a skill that can be trained, like critical thinking. Perhaps these activities would stimulate creativity, but I think cognitive science and knowledge-rich ideas provide a far more robust understanding of creativity.

There's a captivating video in which Paul Simon explains his process of writing the song *Bridge Over Troubled Water* (I owe thanks to Carl Hendrick's Twitter account for pointing this out to me). It's a beautiful introduction to such an understanding of creativity and a rare peek into artistic genesis. Simon begins by explaining that the original melody came from a Bach canon; he merely wrote a variation. Then he was stuck, but upon hearing some blues chords found inspiration for the next section. Finally, the lyrics came about from a concert he attended; he admits he stole the lines from someone else. He's a living example of T.S. Eliot's dictum: "Immature poets imitate; mature poets steal; bad poets deface what they take, and good poets make it into something better, or at least something different."[3]

It's not just Simon who works in this way. In Elizabethan times, it was understood that knowledge and literary references were necessary to craft a work of art. In that era, individuals would collect compelling and interesting quotes as they read; reading focused as much on the discovery of great one-liners as it did on plot and character development. From this type of reading, Shakespeare crafted many of his great works. Far from relying on divergent thinking, Shakespeare pulled stories from *Holinshed's Chronicles* and *Plutarch's Lives*. He even lifted entire passages from other works to include in his own.

The list of individuals who created from a base of knowledge is endless. The speeches and sermons of Martin Luther King Jr. read like a veritable who's who of references. In one paragraph in his "Letter from Birmingham Jail," one of the most eloquent and well-reasoned works of non-fiction in the American canon, he references three passages in scripture, as well as Martin Luther, Thomas Jefferson, and Abraham Lincoln. Such knowledge-rich creativity goes beyond the written word. It's a common motif in jazz improvisation to "reference" another song or solo: a musician will work in the melody from another song and alter it as they improvise, modifying the melody itself or working it through several different keys. In fact, many jazz classics derived from Broadway show tunes like *Summertime* or *Brotherhood of Man*. In poetry, Eliot's *The Waste Land* is functionally a collage of literary references and inspirations from mythology, other poems, philosophy, Christianity, and works of art.

In each case, these creatives drew on their vast knowledge of their own craft and domain to create something new. Few works of art come *ex nihilo* from a mind that has mastered divergent thinking. One should not think of artistic creativity as a work of literature popping into existence, but rather as someone gathering lines, images, motifs, and archetypes like buckets of paint to use in crafting their own work.

The axiom from Ecclesiastes that "there's nothing new under the sun" seems pertinent.[4] We cannot create anything entirely new, but must apply ancient wisdom and tradition to our modern norms. We express the same truths and hold the same arguments over and again, in our modern context.

This knowledge-dependent approach to creativity has been demonstrated in research. In the introduction to one such study, the authors look back over art history and affirm that great artists develop their capacities through "encounters with others' artworks," allowing "artists [to] create their own original artworks and expression styles."[5] In the study itself, the researchers asked participants to draw a control picture. On the following day, they were asked to either draw another picture from scratch, copy an artist's example and then draw their own, or model their own drawing on another artist's work. Professional artists scored these drawings using metrics like technique and creativity. In each case, technique did not improve but the participants who copied another artist's work showed signs of creative growth in their second drawing, while still producing unique works of art. Like looking to a Greek muse, these participants had increased their ability to think creatively not by practicing creative thinking or running a loose-association exercise, but by considering deeply the work of another artist.

It's not merely domain knowledge that allows creativity. Structured practice is essential. There's a common phrase in jazz, "shedding," which means spending hours running scales, long tones, and rehearsing memorized passages. It comes from Charlie Parker, who spent up to 12 hours a day in his woodshed practicing the minutiae on his saxophone. Shedding has since become something of a rite of passage for musicians. Have they put in the drill-and-kill-type practice to master their instrument?

Any creative art requires technical mastery. Even abstract artists like Pablo Picasso and Salvador Dalí first had to master the techniques of the masters before them. The need for this mastery returns us to the cognitive idea of automaticity. For Charlie Parker and Dizzy Gillespie to invent the fast-playing subgenre of jazz called bebop, they had to master the motor movements on their saxophone and trumpet. Once they can run their major, minor, dominant, chromatic, blues, and other scales, that opens up working memory to consider what melody they could sample, what should be the shape of the next run of their notes, and other such creative questions. They don't waste space in their working memory thinking about finger placement.

Cognitive science and knowledge-rich thinking provide a more mature understanding of adult creativity. We can employ this creativity even as the divergent thinking of childhood recedes and the convergent thinking of adulthood takes precedence. True creativity requires domain-specific mastery. Even a classical pianist would likely struggle with jazz music. The technical skills may overlap but without that domain-specific knowledge of jazz music, they lack an element necessary for creativity.

Consider a poetry unit. There's a place and time for the rote practice of scansion, marking out the rhythm pattern of a poem. There's also a time to run linguistic drills of sorts, asking students to write isolated lines in iambic pentameter or with certain assonance. To expect students to use each of these skills in concert while crafting original poetry risks cognitive overload. They would be balancing too much in their working memory all at once.

When I learned to juggle, it first took all my focus. I couldn't talk or walk. Once mastered, juggling itself became almost mindless and I could walk or converse while doing so, although my conversation remains a bit stilted. If I want to learn a new trick, I have to practice it in isolation before I can incorporate it and perform it mindlessly. So it is with poetry. Our students need to practice isolated techniques before they can incorporate them into their poetry. Once they have mastered the technique, they can begin to work it into their own poems almost without thought; it has been automated.

We still accept that athletic prowess and musical brilliance require drill-and-kill-type practice. It's the same for any creative work. To play Beethoven requires familiarity with the major scale. To keep our students from rote practice or domain knowledge in favor of more "authentic" writing or performance experiences is to deprive them of the very material they need for mature artistry.

THINK LIKE AN EXPERT

There's a common turn of phrase that goes something like this: "I want to teach my students to think like…" and insert a field of expertise—think like a scientist or mathematician or historian or author. The sentiment has some validity. Scientists apply the scientific method and historians read primary source documents to develop their own narratives and conclusions; there is a process to each profession. However, to mimic this process-oriented, abstract-skill understanding of a profession in the classroom itself is to do our students a disservice, instilling neither love of content nor expertise.

This injunction to have our students think like experts parallels the idea that the best way to teach students history or science is to ask them to do the work of a historian or scientist. Provide them with primary source documents or a question to research and set them to work. However, the simple reality is that children are not adults and novices are not experts. We wouldn't teach a child to ski by sending them straight off the jumps any more than we should teach students science by having them "do" the work of an expert scientist. Unfortunately, many experts have such a passion for their field that they want to share its delights, forgetting the simple beginnings that it takes to get there. We want our students to experience the exhilarating freedom of going airborne off a jump, forgetting the hours spent on bunny-hill ski runs that it took to get there. We cannot achieve the former without the latter.

So, what exactly makes an expert an expert? When a historian does their job and analyzes a primary source document, they bring to bear upon it a wealth of knowledge—a vast neurocognitive network of ideas, theories, competing theories, images, facts, quotes, related documents, and pertinent events. That's the short answer. A few seminal studies in cognitive psychology elucidate all the more what exactly makes an expert.

One such study presented undergraduates and PhD candidates in physics with various problems regarding the laws of nature.[6] The researchers asked these participants to categorize and talk through their thought processes as they answered the questions. The novices organized the problems into superficial categories, while the professional physicists grouped them according to the physical laws at work and the equations behind them. The PhD candidates also identified how the problems were similar to others they had seen before and then followed a predetermined process. Speaking more broadly, the experts categorized based upon a knowledge of the field that the novices lacked and solved problems by identifying processes that they already knew. Novices are not just budding experts: the thought processes of the experts and novices differed substantially. To reach expertise, a novice must learn the factual knowledge upon which expertise hinges, as well as the standard practices and procedures common to a field of study. Skills-based theories of learning focus only on the second half and arrive there through trial and error. Unfortunately, to do one without the other is to ride a bike with one wheel.

John Dewey wanted to teach students the scientific method but scoffed at the transmission of factual scientific knowledge. He thought that knowledge of any process—historical analysis or scientific analysis—was better than the knowledge of the end result of the process; he would rather students know how to run experiments than know the scientific facts arising from these studies. "An ounce of experience is better than any theory," he wrote, a pithy turn of phrase lacking in substance.[7] No amount of looking at, picking apart, or experiencing a leaf will help students to understand how a leaf converts carbon dioxide and sunlight into sugar via photosynthesis. They could spend days and days analyzing documents from the French Revolution to discover the amount of information that a teacher could impart in a single lecture. Even if we focus on the process, however, the study that presented participants with problems regarding the laws of nature shows that experts have mastered particular processes, lines of thought, and categorization. The ability to problem-solve comes from a familiarity with similar problems that have already been faced within the discipline; these are not skills to be taught in the abstract but rather domain-specific capacities. In other words, even so-called "problem-solving skills" are forms of knowledge specific to a field that can and should be explicitly taught.

A common retort might be that engineers frequently look up less-common equations or doctors check back over manuals for how to handle a particular case. The argument runs that we should teach students how to ask questions and discover information like an engineer or doctor does. However, in the course of my years of teaching, even the ability to search the internet or ask good questions relies upon familiarity with a topic. During research units, many students struggle to search for pertinent information because they don't even know the terminology of a debate. It would be easier for someone who knows phrases like "carbon emissions," "greenhouse gasses," and "fossil fuels" to begin looking into research than someone without access to these words. Doctors and engineers may still need to double-check manuals or google a specific phrase, but they have the vocabulary to help them search manuals and databases and a schema with which they can understand the information they discover.

Teachers as experts can explicitly help students to make the connections that their novice minds may not see. We take for granted the insight that we have into our own discipline. It's a common practice to ask students to make text-to-text or text-to-world connections in the English language arts classroom, thinking that practicing this connection-making skill may help. However, I think about my unit on C.S. Lewis' Chronicles of Narnia books. A Christian author, Lewis frequently builds an allegory to biblical passages. In *The Magician's Nephew* the creation of Narnia reflects the creation story in Genesis, and Aslan's self-sacrifice in *The Lion, the Witch and the Wardrobe* near-perfectly mirrors the death and resurrection of Christ. I could ask my students to practice making connections or I could read passages from Genesis and the Gospels. The former leaves them guessing for a correct answer; the latter equips them with the content knowledge that any literary scholar takes for granted. Armed with this teacher-provided material, students can identify other allusions to the Hebraic creation story and Christ's Passion—two of the most common allusions in Western literature—in their future reading. They will be closer to thinking like a literary scholar than they would if I had merely taught them skills.

The same goes for text-to-world connections. We could ask students to make connections based by chance on modern experiences they may have had or news stories they might have heard. Or, while reading Harper Lee's *To Kill a Mockingbird* or Ernest J. Gaines' *A Lesson Before Dying*, a teacher could provide articles and documentaries related to specific cases of injustice within the court system. Abstract practice leaves students with neither skill nor knowledge. Providing the connection for them and fostering a discussion or written reflection accomplishes both.

In all this discussion of expertise rests a fundamental question: is the goal of universal public education to foster expertise? Surely, in the long run, we want all our students to develop expertise in something, be it in abstract domains like history or mathematics or vocational skills like carpentry or baking. However, I wonder about the utility of this deep knowledge—the process and factual knowledge specific to any one domain—to the average citizen or student. What's the utility of superficial versus deep knowledge?

Take, for example, a student who develops a keen interest in post-Reformation monarchy in England and the murders that come with it. Seeing this interest, a project-based-learning teacher would have their student begin drafting a list of sources to read and perhaps designing some final project. The student may learn a lot about English monarchy and perhaps gain some familiarity with crafting a PowerPoint presentation, but all class time has an opportunity cost. If critical thinking depends upon knowledge, what is lost when schools, especially in earlier grades, value deep knowledge or broad knowledge? We should want our students to be able to think critically about a variety of topics, and this requires broad knowledge.

Perhaps the opposite of a student delving deep into the drama of English monarchy might be the typical AP US or European history class. A common critique of these classes is that they spend so little time on any one event or figure. Towering figures of US history like Abraham Lincoln or Franklin D. Roosevelt might only get a few days of instruction and perhaps a section of a single chapter dedicated to them. These classes can only ever cover superficial knowledge. While that characterization is true, I wonder if it's really a criticism. Deep knowledge is all well and good for experts who have chosen to specialize in a field at the postgraduate level, but we cannot possibly lift every student into expertise in every field. Returning again to my newspaper test from chapter 3, considering the vast quantity of things someone needs to know in order to read and grasp an op-ed, a cursory overview of history and science seems like a decent way to educate the average citizen. They don't need expert-level knowledge in everything, rather familiarity with various ancient civilizations, major US presidents, the wars that shaped our country, and so on. In the language arts classroom, I could spend a year diving deep into my favorite sub-genre of literature, Russian novels, reading the entire corpus of Dostoyevsky. Or I could take students through a sampling of literary eras: Romantic poetry, the Harlem Renaissance, Elizabethan plays, American slave narratives, Victorian novels, contemporary fiction, and the like. To me, the latter seems like a better approach for the average citizen. And even a graduate student in literature would benefit from this outline of literary history, becoming able to contextualize their own focus of study.

In sum, the thinking of experts and the thinking of novices are fundamentally different; their modes of learning will be, too. An expert will gather vast amounts of literature related to any one topic to read on their own, and run experiments on the fringes of human knowledge to discover something new. Novices need to learn the basics of a field—the factual and procedural knowledge common to experts—before they can effectively act or learn like one. To skip over that process is to leave our students unable to reach the expertise we desire for them.

21ST-CENTURY SKILLS

Surely, with the dawn of the internet and the rise of artificial technology, schools must change and radically so. The popular education documentary *Most Likely to Succeed* uses the story of Watson, the *Jeopardy!*-winning supercomputer, to make this case.[8] After four years of designing algorithms and programming, by 2011 computer scientists had developed a machine that could beat Ken Jennings, who had won the TV quiz show 74 times. This supercomputer was not connected to the internet during the game, but the programmers had downloaded Wikipedia, World Book Encyclopedia, internet movie databases, the archives of *The New York Times*, the Bible, and other such texts onto its memory.[9]

This task was a far more complex achievement than former supercomputer challenges like beating a human at chess or Go. To win these games, the computer simply had to run every possible outcome of a chess game, and this is a calculation of chance run over and again very quickly—a task at which computers are adept. To play *Jeopardy!*, Watson needed to understand spoken language full of partial sentences, puns, metaphors, jokes, and questions.

If these machines, the documentary asks, are able to accomplish these most mundane of tasks, what use are the skills and factual information we can get from traditional education? We need to instead capitalize on our unique human capacities—creativity, critical thinking, collaboration, problem-solving, communication, reasoning, and question-asking—or so the argument runs.

Serendipitously, this supposed need for inculcating such abstractions always ends in the justification of project-based learning. Never do I see the connection. Proponents of 21st-century skills acknowledge the real impending difficulty that AI and machine learning will pose, then merely assert that progressive education is the way. How progressive education fosters such skills is left to the imagination.

Throughout this book, I've expressed my skepticism about non-academic abstractions like "creativity" or "question-asking." However euphonious they may be, they're nebulous and impossible to measure. I'm not sure how one could test the effects of an intervention on a student's "collaboration;" I know how to measure if a student understands single-variable algebraic equations. Along similar lines, as far as studies and meta-analyses have attempted to measure such non-academic abstractions, it seems as though traditionalist approaches and a focus on the basics are precisely the foundation kids need to build "21st-century skills." In Project Follow Through, discussed in chapter 4, direct instruction, derided as a "basic skills" approach, beat the competition in "problem-solving skills" and "self-esteem" as well as basic skills.

The other common quip in defense of "21st-century skills" asks: why must we learn the dates of World War II in high school when we can just look it up? I think about my faltering attempts to read Spanish in college. Eventually I developed near-fluency, but those early years were rough. I would sit in the library, googling every third word or grammatical construction, working my way through a short story like chugging cold molasses. By the time I'd managed to parse out some clause or look up one word, I'd forgotten the former words and the sentence became opaque again.

"Just look it up" runs right into the difficulty of limited working memory. If my students are presented with a text on World War II but don't possess even a cursory knowledge of the dates of the conflict, the world leaders and military weaponry of the time, or other basic factual knowledge, it's not entirely unlike reading a second language. They don't know many of the words or even what familiar words mean in this context. The ability to "just look it up" does not replace a breadth of knowledge stored in long-term memory, for both basic literacy and critical thinking. It limits the ability of a student to read critically and think in the moment. If they're watching the news, historical knowledge within easy grasp in the memory would allow them to more critically analyze what is being discussed. Are there other historical analogies to this event? How have we as a civilization approached similar struggles before? These cannot just be "looked up."

Another approach to "21st-century skills" focuses on exactly the computing and engineering that will supposedly run our society in the future. In elementary school, students are still more than a decade out from the workforce. I remember the clunky computers and software I used in elementary school; no familiarity with that outdated technology helps me nowadays. Academic basics, however, do help me. Even advanced coding relies on algorithms and logic, thus further emphasizing the need for math and literacy.

Returning to the real difficulty that the furthered automation of our economy will present, it seems to me that if machines do threaten to upend our society, a return to traditionalist approaches to education will best face down this challenge. We cannot match the computing power of software, the efficiency of machines, or the knowledge store of computers. We can, however, develop the prudence, wisdom, discernment, patience, and other virtues that come with a liberal arts education. Of all the people I interact with within the education space, the classical education types are the kindest. They have read every book that they both agree with and disagree with. It's hard to be angry, hopeless, or petty when the words "Be still and know that I am God" are seared into your memory.[10]

Certain ideas, bits of knowledge, works of literature, and the like have persisted through the ages, deemed important over and again despite former tectonic shifts. Software comes and goes. Shakespeare remains. Perhaps, in the last syllable of recorded time, when eyes no longer see, great authors too will pass. But until then math facts, literature, history, science, phonics—these things will be timeless necessities, the essential building blocks of any culture for schools to pass along.

SOCIAL-EMOTIONAL LEARNING

Character education goes back to antiquity. Plato said that "education is teaching our children to desire the right things;" it forms children such that they "hate what ought to be hated ... and love what ought to be loved."[11] The McGuffey Readers, elementary school reading books used in the 19th and early 20th centuries, pointed on every page to some moral to be learned. Education without character development is like water without hydrogen. It simply cannot be. The question is only: what kind of people shall we form? What shall they love and hate, and how do we form them?

Alas, moralizing is controversial. What virtues are we to pick? Professor Allan Bloom traced the development of value ethics within the university. It's a relativized ethics. Whereas justice and prudence were absolutist virtues and our only job was to manifest them in the actions of our lives, one can value family or friends while strangers value their own vocation. Neither is right nor wrong, so ethics becomes a matter of personal preference. It is far beyond the scope of this section to discuss character education in its entirety—doing so would require several volumes—so I offer here a few hesitations to at the very least slow the widespread and wholesale adoption of social-emotional learning (SEL) into our schools.

In practice, SEL transforms the classroom from a space of academic learning into a glorified therapy session. Robert Pondiscio of the American Enterprise Institute succinctly summarizes the approach as shifting the role of teaching from "pedagogue" to "therapist."[12] Before I hopped onto the traditionalist train, I used to run restorative circles in my classroom to discuss everything from behavior to class content; I believed this would bring the class together. And then one student on the fringes of the school's social circles brought up his suicidality and I quickly realized what it was to so manipulate the teacher's role. We are trained in academic instruction. I worry deeply about the effects if we choose to deputize teachers, experts in their fields and instruction, into a therapeutic role far beyond their training. What does it mean for education when we establish a system that incentivizes and rewards not academic excellence but the disclosure of personal feelings and trauma? That looks very little like what I would consider an institution of "education." It may be a worthwhile endeavor, but not within a classroom's walls.

The research into SEL resembles much of the rest of progressive pedagogy. In short, there is very little. A meta-analysis from the RAND Corporation, the most comprehensive review of the literature that I've found, broke the evidence down into tiers, from the most reliable and rigorous to the least.[13] Although there is some evidence for the efficacy of SEL in the elementary grades, it's almost entirely lacking at the secondary level. The researchers found eight total interventions with some positive results, but not a single one of them fell into their category of rigorous research: randomized controlled trials. In other words, there is little evidence about SEL's effects on academic, social, or emotional learning, and what little evidence has come up is lackluster in its quality.

In my estimation, SEL will be the next "growth mindset." A few years ago, growth mindset—the idea that if students *believe* they can learn then they are more likely to—was the new fad. My school adopted language to encourage growth mindset and my assistant principal had a shelf full of the seminal book on the topic to offer to anyone who strolled by his office. Who could be against growth mindset?

Then a few meta-analyses came along and dampened the fad like wet blue jeans.[14] The interventions that sought to alter the presence or absence of a growth mindset in students were largely ineffective. Our intelligence may be malleable but our views *about* intelligence are relatively fixed. And this result shouldn't come as a surprise. These non-academic goals in education are Gordian knots of sociology and psychology. Friends, family values, schools, culture, literary texts encountered, popular media, passing comments, tweets, Facebook posts, movies, genetics, and so much more influence our emotional states and beliefs. A few black-bordered posters reading "You can do it" or "Kindness is cool" probably won't do much in the way of social, emotional, or growth mindset development.

As I alluded to in chapter 5, SEL falters because it's too flimsy a thing. The Renaissance philosopher Michel de Montaigne wrote that our students must study "what are valor, temperance, and justice; what the difference is between ambition and avarice, servitude and submission, license and liberty; by what signs we may recognize true and solid contentment; how much we should fear death, pain, and shame."[15] These are the questions of a lifetime and cannot be extracted from the very content of our other classes. In discussing great literature and historical anecdotes, students will have before them the very examples they need in order to grapple with these ideas. We must direct their minds first away from themselves before they return for introspection. If, instead, we set them loose on their own interests, reading their own interpretations into everything, they will have only rumination and brooding as options, no way beyond themselves. Character education must be a central tenet of our very curriculum, not a prepackaged add-on.

Even if we adopt the utilitarian approach of SEL, I remain unconvinced of the common elements of it. If our goal is to develop students for a functioning society, why does something like the "success sequence" get such short shrift? Enough studies have confirmed as to make it almost fact that if young people graduate high school, get a job, get married, and have kids in that order, their likelihood of living in poverty drops to almost zero.[16] But SEL programs never make mention of this societal reality and so I'll make little mention of SEL in my own classroom.

LIFELONG LEARNING

I have sat through professional development sessions that place "lifelong learning" as the primary goal of education. Perhaps it is. Perhaps it isn't. What I find more concerning in these meetings isn't any philosophical discussion of the ultimate goal of education, but a causal link that is skipped over. Lifelong learning is used as the justification for whatever instructional technique that follows, not an actual end goal. There's rarely a discussion of how to encourage or allow for lifelong learning beyond mere posturing.

Where specific attempts are made, they follow two broad approaches: motivation and academic thinking skills. The former really turns the inculcation of lifelong learning into a matter of persuasion. Through engaging lessons, we want to instill in students the perspective that personal reading and research are worthy ways to spend their time. That seems an endlessly complex task to achieve, and one that focuses more on how we can make our instruction as engaging as possible so students leave our school doors with positive sentiments toward academic pursuits. I find this a worthwhile goal but unquantifiable and near impossible to break down into any achievable component parts. If that is what lifelong learning is then really it's an emphasis that we just teach well.

The second explanation of lifelong learning tends to come by way of instilling our students with the capacity for various academic skills. Can they ask good questions? Can they evaluate a source for credibility? Can they analyze a historical document or literary text? Provide them with practice in these skills and then they can go about their lives learning on their own. However, as I've shown throughout this book, these academic skills are mirages—appealing rhetorically but lacking substance. The skill is not the tool, the knowledge is the tool, and if we focus too much on skills at the cost of content then our students will find themselves unable to analyze, evaluate, or think critically in any robust sense of the words.

One study, which sought to determine how prior knowledge affects the acquisition of new knowledge, suggests a different manner of creating lifelong learners.[17] The experiment had two parts. In the first, researchers assessed participants' prior knowledge of baseball and movies, presented them with new facts in each of these topics, and then assessed them on these facts. Unsurprisingly, individuals who showed high prior knowledge of movies or baseball recalled more of the new information about movies or baseball.

In the second part, the researchers attempted to create experts. To do this, they selected more obscure topics (professional beach volleyball and off-Broadway musicals) and had the participants learn various facts about these topics. Some learned lots of information about volleyball but little about the musicals, and other participants the opposite. The participants returned two days later to learn yet *more* about each topic and then be tested on their knowledge. Those who had learned more about volleyball recalled more new facts about volleyball, and those who had learned more about the musicals learned more about the musicals. A schema of knowledge had been created in the minds of participants, which then allowed them to better learn new material.

The conclusion? Knowledge facilitates learning. To learn new things, we need to fit them into our pre-existing schema. E.D. Hirsch uses the image of Velcro to explain this phenomenon.[18] If I learn a new fact about World War II, I might relate it to the countries involved, the images in my mind of trench warfare, or any world leader. Each of these connections helps me to hang onto and remember the new fact. Thus, like Velcro, our prior knowledge acts as a collection of little hooks that grab onto new knowledge. Each new fact we learn expands the number of hooks on our Velcro and helps us to grab yet more.

This importance of prior knowledge played out recently in my own life. I was reading a book of history, *Modern Times* by Paul Johnson, and followed his chapters on the Russian Revolution, the rise of Hitler, and World War II with interest. Upon reaching a chapter about India, however, my reading slowed, my comprehension faltered, and my interest waned. Having learned less about Indian political history in high school, I knew fewer of the names, dates, and historical events and so naturally struggled to read. What's more, I remember many of Johnson's conclusions about Lenin and Hitler because I already knew much about them. I didn't even recognize the names in the chapter on India and so remember little. My prior knowledge in one area facilitated my "lifelong" learning, while my lack of knowledge in another area hampered it.

If we want to develop lifelong learners, teaching them explicit knowledge would be an excellent way to accomplish this. I think of it as building the frame of a house. We don't know what they will need to learn in the future, but knowing even a little bit about something can aid future learning. Thus, our history curriculum needs to build a basic framework like the structure of a house. If the supports and boards are all in place—if they know generally about the French Revolution, slavery, the American Civil War, the World Wars, the Renaissance, and so on—then later in life they can return to that section of the house and furnish it with new information. They can build a wall, add hooks, and hang pictures as they learn more about each of those eras. If they know a little bit about them then learning more will be easier later in life.

As a final note, consider the curiosity that comes naturally with learning a little bit about something. I think about students walking around a library. A student who knows a little bit about the Himalayas— they picture snowy, billowy peaks and Mount Everest—might see a nonfiction title about this mountain range and think to themselves, "Well, I know a little bit about them. Let's see what else I can learn." A student who has never heard of the Himalayas will walk right by, their interest unpiqued, the book never reaching recognition.

CRITICAL THINKING SKILLS

I've already spent a chapter debunking "critical thinking," arguing that it isn't a skill but rather a knowledge-dependent, natural process. It's a human faculty that we can only improve through the acquisition of new, domain-specific knowledge. However, I do believe there are certain *habits* that can facilitate so-called critical thinking. These aren't skills but routines to follow. They cannot be perfected and honed like a skill, but if carried out time and again will likely result in knowledge-rich critical thinking. If we run with a sports analogy, these habits are not like running drills to perfect a "skill," but rather habits like training every day and studying the techniques of the great players. There are certain intellectual habits and routines that we can adopt when approaching any idea, content area, or controversial topic.

To begin, we must always seek out and consider various perspectives. It's not enough to read the work of someone with whom we agree that engages with counter-opinions. To paraphrase John Stuart Mill, we must consider alternative opinions from someone who *believes* them. In no other way can we receive a contrasting opinion put forth with force, conviction, or coherence. A dissenter, however honest, always has an incentive to weaken the case. Mill also said, "He who knows only his own side of the case, knows little at that."[19] They know neither the counterargument itself nor the honing and perfecting of one's own opinion that comes when faced with ideological contention. Like a rock turned to diamond, when pressurized with dissenting opinions forcefully expressed, our own beliefs grow stronger. As such, it's a powerful habit to not only subscribe to news sources that regularly disagree with each other but also to actively seek out dissenting views on any topic. I myself subscribe to typically left and right magazines and also have a list of sites that I check before I write any article. In doing so, not only do I better develop my own ideas but, importantly, I also develop empathy for my ideological opposite. In the classroom, this means presenting both sides of an issue to students and remaining neutral as a teacher. I have "controversial questions" for every unit—ethical dilemmas that relate to the themes of the book we're reading—and when discussing them, I always take the least popular side in the class, regardless of my own opinion on the issue. We must model these habits for our students.

Second, we must teach the official structures and terminology of academic, critical thought. Knowledge of a topic certainly trumps all. I'd trust a virologist on the topics of infectious diseases over a philosophy undergrad who has memorized every logical fallacy. However, I'd trust an expert virologist who knows formal logic the most. Content expertise supersedes training in the structure of academic thought. Even so, these are powerful tools. The ability to discern an ad hominem attack, genetic fallacy, or red herring from a cogent argument may not constitute critical thinking but it can certainly act as a safeguard against poor thinking. A vaccine is not equivalent to health but it is certainly a safeguard against disease.

Reading widely is the final habit of critical thought that I'll outline here. Students learn to read and then spend their lives reading to learn. Like gasoline to an engine, knowledge is the fuel to critical thought; there simply is no other means as powerful as wide reading. Reading about history, reading about current events, reading the thought of the great philosophers, reading literary fiction—all provide us with the arguments, stories, facts, logical syllogisms, and ideas we need for critical thought.

I want to emphasize here the importance of books. Almost anyone can produce an 800-word article; however, a book put forth by a publisher is at the very least a sign that someone has given extended thought to an idea before they put it down on paper. It is no guarantee of quality but it's certainly a predictor. And if we read 50 books in a year over an 80-year life span, we only have time to read about 4,000 books in our lifetime. We should choose wisely.

These three simple habits—engaging with opposing opinions, learning the academic language and structure of formal thought, and reading extensively—do not automatically lead to critical thought. Someone could practice soccer for hours and hours a day and never amount to much. Even so, they are the habits most likely to result in critical thinking. Even if they never go professional, someone who spends hours a day practicing a sport is likely to be well above average. They may not best Lionel Messi but they'll trounce just about anybody else on the field.

These habits also make use of what we know about the importance of knowledge. Reading widely and considering alternative points of view are not really means to facilitate and hone a skill. Rather, they are regular practices of garnering, seeking out, and acquiring knowledge of both sides of a debate and general knowledge about topics. The importance of the former knowledge—that of opposing sides—is obvious. The importance of general knowledge is not always so clear. The student question "When will I need to know this in the future?" gestures at the uncertainty. Sometimes we have an answer; other times, if we're being honest, we cannot predict when they'll need to know something. Nonetheless, I know that when rioters stormed the Capitol on January 6, 2021, I was glad to have read the final pages of *Macbeth*, as the fallen king sat holed up in his castle, facing defeat but unwilling to admit so. Similarly, learning about the knowledge problem in libertarian economics as an undergraduate has informed my opinions about education policy and pedagogy. Knowing a few things about camping, cooking, and sports allows me to create analogies to explain complex concepts to students. Broad knowledge has utility even if we cannot pin it down into concrete examples.

DIFFERENTIATION

A simple cartoon, one that was common fare in education circles, sparked online outrage in 2021. It depicts various animals—a monkey, a fish, an elephant, and a few others—and behind them is an oak tree. In front of them, a teacher sits behind a desk, saying, "For a fair selection everybody has to take the same exam: please climb that tree." Making use of common parlance in professional development sessions and teacher prep programs, this little cartoon drove a short media cycle and warranted several national op-eds written as explainers, defenses, and critiques; one Facebook post garnered more than 2,500 comments and 104,000 shares.[20]

Superficially, the cartoon throws shots at standardized testing: how could we consider it a fair system to judge all students according to the same standard when human beings are so varied and multifaceted? Surely a test cannot capture all that constitutes an individual human. What about their creativity? Their compassion? Their communication skills? There's truth to this criticism but assumptions are built into that cartoon that are at best misguided and at worst quite troubling.

The most troubling is also the most obvious. Human beings are varied, yes, but what does it suggest to compare our differences to those that divide a dog, cat, fish, elephant, and monkey? There is some genetic variability in human beings but of the approximately three billion base pairs that constitute our genome, we share 99.9% of those in common. All variability in humanity springs from that remaining 0.1%.[21] Perhaps that should be the emphasis of our discussion even as we acknowledge varied differences, abilities, and inclinations.

This brings us to the simply misguided assumption in that cartoon. Not just in regards to genetics but also in learning, human beings share far more in common than not. With standardized tests, we're not asking different species to complete an arbitrary task like climbing a tree. Rather, we're asking human beings to complete tasks that we all consider fundamental to society: reading, writing, and arithmetic. It would be far more helpful to focus on those aspects of learning that would benefit us in common than to wave our hands and suggest that differences of interest or superficial abilities are tantamount to the challenge presented in the cartoon.

There's a common sentiment that teachers ought to personalize the learning for each and every student. Perhaps best encompassed in the idea of the "zone of proximal development"—the ideal challenge or next concept for each student—the suggestion is that we must meet students where they are and push them to the next level. On its surface it's appealing, couched in humanistic rhetoric, but a concept's validity lies not in how euphonious its name is. "What kind of monster would treat every student the same?" asks Greg Ashman wryly.[22]

However, when the superficial cover is pulled back and the concepts interrogated, we find many snags and confusions. In a history class, how could one possibly determine a zone of proximal development (ZPD)? Must students learn about Napoleon before George Washington? Do we always have to go chronologically? Or perhaps in reverse? In science, certainly, some concepts are foundational to others, but a student could learn the nature of the solar system before the laws of gravity and vice versa. ZPD makes more sense within a "skills-centric" philosophy of learning, involving various analytical skills or reading levels. But even there the skills are so interwoven—constructing a thesis, analyzing a quote, drawing inferences—that ZPD becomes meaningless when applied to concrete situations.

Let's assume, for the sake of argument, that there is some credence to these ideas. A common practice is differentiation. This can happen at either the level of the task or the goal: students receive varied end assessments or some sort of modified material or learning environment along the way to the same goal. I worked for a number of years as an ESL (English as a second language) support teacher; my job was differentiation. I would review various activities and assignments for teachers in order to isolate and identify difficulties that students might encounter. I would suggest various groupings, provide alternative or simplified readings, and modify activities with sentence frames, color-coded outlines, or multiple-choice responses.

Before we get into the research, the difficulties buried within this approach are legion. The school system, administrators, and society at large already ask a lot of schoolteachers. The task of differentiating pushes their job to impossibility. How can one teacher adequately account for a room full of students with reading abilities ranging from a few years behind to a few years ahead, multiple individualized education programs (IEPs), and behavior problems? In one classroom, I had a range of ESL students, a few with behavioral IEPS, a student with significant learning disabilities, and another with severely limited vision. Just differentiate! I might as well just cut the Gordian knot, too. Perhaps some teachers could successfully run such a classroom, but they would have to be an Alexander the Great. Any policy or approach needs to be feasible for the average teacher, who already works 54 hours a week.[23] Can we reasonably expect them to work more?

One common policy to alleviate this concentrated workload is the expansion of ESL and special education departments to include auxiliary and support teachers. Again, great in theory, but not necessarily so in practice. With ever more regulations, I found many of my colleagues in these departments became glorified paper-pushers for administration or errand-runners for teachers. What's more, I wonder if their time wouldn't be better spent teaching their own mixed-ability classes, thereby shrinking class sizes and accomplishing the same task of lessened workloads.

Another obvious difficulty of differentiation in practice is that of drawing attention to those students who need extra support. Even in my best attempts to modify materials such that they resembled the standard worksheet or test, students quickly picked up on who got what. Another process for differentiation is through grouping, either intentionally mixed-ability or single-ability groups. In both cases, even when I was in school, we knew who the teacher considered the academically gifted kids and those who needed help. And let me tell you, children do not use the same polished, politically correct language that adults do to describe such groupings.

In reality, in my time as a lead classroom teacher and as an ESL support teacher, I've come to one conclusion: it is both ethical and effective to treat all students pretty much the same. If I want sentence frames, I provide and require them of all students. I may even provide just two separate options: something simple like *"I think _____ because..."* and something more complex and open-ended like *"Although _____, ..."* If I'm going to provide a structured paragraph outline, I'll project it along with an example for all students. Of course, I only do this after modeling my thought process and instructing students in what exactly the "worked example" does and why. All the modifications I used to provide as an ESL teacher, I now give to all students and offer them the option to use them as they may or may not see fit. Also, it's worth noting that while I may still provide instruction or examples, the supports largely come away by the final assessment.

We're not without research in this arena either, although it is limited. Universal Design for Learning (UDL) is an entire system of instruction that works in differentiation throughout the process. It stresses the need for student selection, multiple alternatives for auditory and visual information, varied methods for responses, and other such personalization. Almost beyond parody, one meta-analysis comes to this profound conclusion: "Results from this analysis suggest that UDL is an effective teaching methodology for improving the learning process for all students. The impact on educational outcomes has not been demonstrated."[24] In the same breath, the reviewers say that UDL is "effective" and yet the impact on academics "has not been demonstrated."[25] And so proceeds so much education research. Where evidence is lacking, efficacy is asserted regardless because it fits the prevailing vision of how things *ought* to work.

Quite to the contrary, there is at least circumstantial evidence that a "mostly the same" approach to instruction benefits students, and this would fit into the cognitive architecture we all share that I've outlined throughout this book. In his analysis, Ashman found that the countries that score highest on international exams are also the least likely to have teachers personalize learning for students.[26] While not explanatory, this association—less personalization with higher international scores—should at least cause one to pause and reconsider. A 2016 review of scores from the Programme for International Student Assessment (PISA) found a positive association with teacher-led instruction and "inconsistent" outcomes for student-directed strategies.[27] Of course, all this evidence is correlational and not causal. Where researchers have tried randomized controlled trials, the results are mixed, confounding variables abound, and they almost always compared differentiation strategies with "nothing," not necessarily a different intervention.

Why exactly differentiation doesn't work is a question near impossible to answer, because differentiation is such a multi-factorial phenomenon. It could be that those teachers who differentiate could have better spent their time considering a more clear example, reflecting on their practice, communicating with parents, providing feedback, or some other high-leverage practice. Also, any intervention when compared with nothing will usually lead to some positive results. Something is better than nothing. But, alas, education works within a scarcity of time and so we must always compare any intervention with how time could be spent otherwise. In this case, there is weak evidence that differentiation works but it should not be treated as the panacea for education.

DIRECT INSTRUCTION POTPOURRI

The cliches above serve to positively frame ideas that lack substance. Words are powerful things. If we rename something bad, it loses the negative connotations it formerly carried. The effect is common in the language of war: enhanced interrogation techniques, targeted strikes, or boots on the ground. In his famous essay "Politics and the English language," George Orwell mocked how the use of machine guns, bombs, and incendiary ammo might be called "pacification." However, the action can proceed in the reverse as well. If we call something by a derogatory or ugly name, it can turn us off otherwise good ideas.

Much ideological contention is a war over words. How we define and name ideas sets the starting point for any intellectual exchange. An interlocutor is primed, swayed before the conversation even begins if the words to be used carry positive or negative connotations.

In college, my roommate and I, whenever we wanted to discuss a controversial issue, would lay out a list of words that we weren't allowed to use. If we wanted to use the phrase "social justice" or "objective truth," we had to pick something more concrete or explain what we actually meant. No conversation can truly proceed in this way—we rely on shorthand and assumed definitions to speak and write in understandable sentences—but it's an interesting exercise to show just how slippery many terms are. It forced us to clarify what exactly we meant and, more often than not, worked to expose either the sturdiness or flimsiness of many of these words.

In the following sections, I work in the opposite direction than I did above, exposing the positive ideas behind derogatory cliches. They are a series of words associated with direct instruction and laden with negative connotations. Explicit instruction has no fighting chance when the theory must first contend with the associations heaped upon it. Instead, like the discussions I had with my roommate, I try to expound on what exactly each buzzword means and suggest a replacement term that is both accurate and value-neutral. Perhaps "drill and kill" is a bad practice, but let's come to that conclusion after considering its true meaning and efficacy, not because negative connotations encumber the phrase.

Drill and Kill

Critics portray structured practices either as dull and thereby prone to "killing" a love of learning, or as thoughtless "drills" that don't facilitate higher-order thinking skills. But practice needn't kill any love of learning, and students who *don't* practice extensively cannot hope to accomplish "higher-order thinking," however one chooses to define that infinitely nebulous phrase. One review reads: "All evidence, from the laboratory and from extensive case studies of professionals, indicates that real competence only comes with extensive practice."[28] Daniel Willingham writes: "As far as anyone knows, the only way to develop mental facility is to repeat the target process again and again and again."[29] Barak Rosenshine confirms that "students need extensive, successful, independent practice."[30]

It's not only the basic skills that are mastered in repeated practice. Through these drills, students develop automaticity with the basics, which in turn allows them to focus on more advanced concepts. I have listened to students in middle school without a solid base in phonics struggle through reading. With pronunciation and fluency dominating their working memory, they're left unable to comprehend the text in hand, let alone deeply analyze its meaning or implications. Instead of "drill and kill," it's better that we call it *structured practice*.

I see independent practice as some of the true moments in learning. Just as I might squeeze a pillow to let out the fluff and thereby find a rip, in doing practice problems for, say, prepositional phrases, students and I discover the gaps and confusions in learning. Often, students assume that they have mastered a concept and so disengage, but through practice they discover their inability to finish a problem or, upon correction, copious errors. In these moments, answering questions, providing new examples, and clarifying confusions accomplish much of the learning in my class.

Unfortunately, many skills require what cognitive scientists call "overlearning" and that can only come through repeated practice. This practice into automaticity will not always be "fun" or "engaging." There are two ways to address that hesitancy. First, I question why learning must always be necessarily fun or engaging. Surely nothing in life will always be so, especially the important things. That learning should ever be "fun" falls into the naturalistic fallacy. Children may learn spoken language and group dynamics through wordplay and yard games, but I see no reason why students should be able to learn mechanical physics in the same way. Second, we can retrofit some aspects of primary learning into the process of more unnatural secondary learning. For example, various games or competitions can harness the power of primary learning and thereby make extended practice a more enjoyable endeavor. It's worth questioning still if a student will gain as much from, say, a Blooket or Kahoot game as they will from silent, independent practice when the software and competition draw their working memory away from the actual content before them. Allowing students to complete practice in pairs or small groups can capitalize on our naturally communitarian tendencies, making the learning environment more welcoming, but, again, this approach isn't without flaws. In their efforts to help each other, students lacking expertise can misdirect their peers and, as with games, a noisy classroom can stymie a student's working memory, capacity to focus, and thus their ability to actually learn.

Finally, it's worth noting that for independent practice to work well, students must practice accurately. If they have a low success rate in their practice, it can instill bad habits that then necessitate unlearning and relearning—a substantial task in a short school day. If a teacher is answering too many questions or dealing with too many misconceptions, it's better to simply pause the class and re-explain.

Chalk and Talk

A stranger said to me recently, "The moment I stop teaching, I feel like my students stop learning." Although an imperfect statement—students need to practice and read on their own—it struck me nonetheless. It runs so counter to the cliches and platitudes thrown around at many staff meetings. Common discourse denigrates any instruction wherein the teacher spends more than five or 10 minutes giving an explanation; instead, teachers need to get out of the way and just let their students learn. If only it were so easy. But here was someone who thought of the teacher's role as absolutely vital to learning—and it is. Rather than a dull, necessary evil that comes before the learning by "doing," chalk and talk is where the learning first happens in a classroom.

Knowledge is not formed in the mind of a student *ex nihilo*. Even if we accept an epistemological framing such as constructivism, students cannot construct a schema from nothing. Nothing comes of nothing. Rather, they need building blocks of information and all new knowledge must come from without. Most often, a teacher, a video, or a text of some kind presents to the student new knowledge that they then acquire and retain in their long-term memory. Even in the case of student-directed learning, in reality, the students are merely choosing their external source of information and what is contained therein. There is still some external source from which they glean new information.

Phrased differently, students need a teacher. If they are to learn, they cannot avoid the necessity of direct instruction of some kind; we can only change who or what fills that instructional role. Often denigrated as a method that reduces teachers to mere automatons following a script, direct instruction and explicit teaching place a primacy on the role of the teacher. Compared with the idea of a teacher as an arranger of classroom experiences, it's an entirely different conception of the profession. The teacher's role is not one of a facilitator but one who provides clear explanations and structured practice, checks for understanding, encourages review and recall, and assesses mastery.

The direct instruction part of that process is foundational. Without explanation, children cannot learn. In fact, without sufficient instruction, students often learn incorrectly and then practice incorrectly as well, ingraining misconceptions and errors into their thinking and problem-solving. As Rosenshine says, "Practice can be a disaster if students are practicing errors," and so we must ensure they're not practicing errors because of insufficient direction.[31]

In my own classroom, *any time* my students must complete an extended piece of writing (by extended writing I mean anything that warrants a structured response, typically a paragraph or longer) I provide an example of my own. I outline, often color-coded, elements in my own paragraph or in professional examples, think aloud to explain my process as I'm writing, and even provide some prompting for their own responses. If we're in the middle of the unit and students have written longer responses already, I choose exemplars to highlight what has been done well. I also select intermediate responses to demonstrate and explain what could have been done better. In grammar, I provide examples, non-examples, and complete practice problems.

Rosenshine provides a succinct summary of the importance of chalk-and-talk instruction:

> *In a study of mathematics instruction, for instance, the most effective mathematics teachers spent about 23 minutes of a 40-minute period in lecture, demonstration, questioning, and working examples. In contrast, the least effective teachers spent only 11 minutes presenting new material. The more effective teachers used this extra time to provide additional explanations, give many examples, check for student understanding, and provide sufficient instruction so that the students could learn to work independently without difficulty.*[32]

Rosenshine goes on to explain that the less successful teachers then spent more time visiting students during work time, re-explaining the concepts that they had not mastered the first time.

Two common criticisms of chalk-and-talk instruction point to the supposed short attention span of students and the supposed retention rates garnered by differing types of learning. The former criticism is quick and easy to refute. Common statistics are thrown around without much grounding, like the idea that we can expect a student to pay attention for about however long they've been alive: five-year-olds can manage five minutes, six-year-olds six minutes, and so on. The idea of an attention span is really something of a misnomer, however.[33] It's entirely context-dependent. I've seen students check out before their teacher even began teaching and heard talk of kids playing *Fortnite* for hours on end without interruption. In my own personal experience, the best teacher I ever had spent almost every class entirely in lecture. He was a history teacher who taught us history as though he were spinning a story around a fire. He worked in jokes, took on voices, ran about the room, and partook in other such antics. He also gave lots of notes, assigned readings, drilled us with questions, and required incredibly analytical writing in response to complex questions. Conversely, I had a college lecturer in whose class I worked a regular nap into my schedule. Whether students can pay attention to a lecturer has little to do with the lecture format itself and more to do with the content and person providing it.

The second contention against chalk and talk points to the supposedly poor retention of knowledge that outright lectures achieve. A common graphic employed to defend this assertion is the so-called "learning pyramid." There are countless iterations of the learning pyramid and the actual statistics applied to it are as varied as the snowflakes in my backyard, which should itself be a tell about the dubiousness of this oft-cited "research." Invariably, "listening" or "lecture" are placed at the top of the pyramid with a 5% retention of information rate, and "doing" at the bottom with something around 90%.

Even before I get into the research, it's worth noting that such a portrayal of the numbers is clearly absurd. If something like a student "teaching" another allows 80% comprehension and they use a mixture of demonstration and lecture, would that garner more than 100% retention? Furthermore, if a student teaches another, where do they get this information to be taught? Did they receive it via lecture (5%) and then demonstrate it to another student (30%) resulting in peer retention amounting to a fraction of a percent of the original? What a silly framing.

Shifting to a more academic treatment of the matter, the "pyramid of learning" comes from Edgar Dale's "cone of experience."[34] The original graphic in his book includes no numbers and he warned his reader to not take it too literally. It proceeded not from low retention to high retention, but rather from concrete sensory experience to abstract experience like word representations. Dale intended his graphic to be descriptive, not prescriptive, of different classroom activities for teachers to use and for their own reflection. Since then, various advocates have mapped sourceless data onto the pyramid and turned it into a prescriptive graphic, not describing how various classroom activities are but informing how classrooms *should* be. Framing the learning pyramid so provides it with a veneer of esteemed, psychological research that can then be used as a cudgel against any traditionalist forms of instruction. In reality, as one academic review of the "retention chart"—a similarly framed, popular graphic—put it, "there is within education psychology a voluminous literature on remembering and learning from various mediated experiences. Nowhere in this literature is there any summary of findings that remotely resembles the fictitious retention chart."[35]

Isn't it ironic that so many professional development sessions that denigrate chalk and talk so often take the form of a lecture or direct instruction? Droning on in a monotonous voice with no examples, no jokes, no humor, no stories is obviously a poor use of class time; few would dispute this.

In place of chalk and talk there should be no one replacement word. Rather, we should simply be more specific about what exactly we mean. Is the teacher asking questions? Are they lecturing? Are they providing clear examples? Are they explaining a concept with analogies or realia? These strategies all have their place in the classroom. We can debate the efficacy of one over the other as it relates to this or that concept, but the words used must be clear in their meaning and neutral in their connotations. Referring to mere chalk and talk or some other generalized phrase is not only unhelpful but could quickly encompass and thereby cause us to look over many effective teaching strategies.

In his book *The Power of Explicit Teaching and Direct Instruction*, in a review of the literature, Greg Ashman provides a cogent outline of what behaviors are associated with student learning:

> *... effective use of time; a coherent curriculum in sequence; active teaching—"Do teachers actively present concepts and supervise students' initial work, and then encourage them to build and to extend meaningfully on teachers' initial presentations?"—a balance between conceptual and procedural knowledge; proactive management; teacher clarity; enthusiasm and warmth; pace; teaching to mastery; review and feedback; and teachers' possession of adequate subject matter knowledge.*[36]

What again and again stands out to me as I read the literature about direct instruction is simply how integral the role of the teacher is. I watched a video recently of a classroom that had fully incorporated a "gamification" model of education. Students sat in small clusters around flat-screen televisions, each with their own laptop, and played some online game. The video had thousands upon thousands of views and positive comments underneath. I recoiled. How depressing to send students into school to stare at screens yet more, focused not on their peers, teacher, or content but on their laptops. I use games in my classroom but either as a final review or the day before an extended break, knowing that they're far from academic activity. What really stood out to me in that video, however, was the teacher standing in the back of the class doing effectively nothing. Even if we accept progressive education's principles, it reduces the teacher to observation. We are to babysit while students complete their projects or, in this case, play their games. Whether or not that is academically effective is another question—one that I've addressed throughout this book—but it's worth noting that it does effectively erase the role of "educator."

Rote Memorization

Every year I ask my students to memorize a poem, but I intentionally avoid using the word "memorize." Rather, they must learn Robert Frost's *Stopping by Woods on a Snowy Evening* or Langston Hughes' *A Dream Deferred* by heart. Poems when memorized become something we hold dear in our hearts and minds, growing almost into a mental keepsake. But there are also demonstrable, educational reasons to do so.

Throughout history, literary and artistic greats have employed memorization as part of their creative development. A common practice in jazz circles is the act of memorizing and transcribing famous solos; there are articles online dedicated to listing the classic improvisations that any aspiring musician ought to have memorized. Charlie Parker famously memorized Lester Young solos, transposed them into every key, and practiced them at double or triple their original tempo. Shakespeare would likely have spent time memorizing *Holinshed's Chronicles*, where he drew inspiration for his history plays. Augustine would have learned entire passages of Virgil by heart. Each of these literary, musical, and philosophical masters, through memorizing the best of their predecessors, thereby developed a palette for sound, rhythm, imagery, and melody.

In his book *How to Think Like Shakespeare*, Scott Newstok outlines many of the presuppositions of enlightenment and medieval education and emphasizes our altered understanding of creativity nowadays. "If anything," he writes, "creative imitation … has been the hallmark of art and industry" for most of human history.[37] Upon discovering a piece of writing they admired, Robert Louis Stevenson, Benjamin Franklin, and countless other authors would perform imitative practices to perfect their own craft—reproducing it directly, memorizing it, or attempting to mimic its style. "By trying to sound like someone else," Newstok writes, "you begin to sound 'like yourself.'"[38] In memorizing literature, our students implicitly adopt the best that is in authors and can begin to employ these skills, patterns of thought, lines of argumentation, and knowledge in their own thinking and academic work.

There's a strong knowledge-rich justification for the memorization of literature, too. Perhaps students may learn the words of the Preamble to the US Constitution or a poem of Wordsworth without profound understanding at first. Nonetheless, young children can delight in nursery rhymes—the rhythm, the symmetry, the sing-song nature—even before they fully understand the words. These words, locked into their memory for recall, then allow them to compare and analyze later when they do have the capacity to fully understand them. If "critical thought" is a process of making connections, as Rousseau contends, then students need nodes to connect, and memorized verse forms powerful nodes that can supercharge thinking later when connected. They serve as models as we focus on every word, detail, image, grammatical construction, passing emotion, punctuation or lack thereof, and poetic or rhetorical detail.

In reality, pure rote knowledge—memorization without learning—is probably relatively rare or nonexistent. Even before a child fully grasps the meaning of a nursery rhyme, they develop a sense of rhythm, order, and balance. They get fleeting images that store in their memory even if some of the finer points elude them. They also store complex syntax and familiarize themselves with unique grammar constructions to employ in their own writing. Complex language becomes second nature.

Memorization doesn't inhibit the growth of the self or critical thought. Rather, it strengthens the mind, focus, and attention to detail as drills and strength training do the body. It enhances the self, providing students with knowledge and language that they can use against lazy thinking and propaganda. Memorization does not stifle freedom but, through difficulty now, allows students to make better use of that freedom later on. It enlarges, strengthens, and frees the self.

My own students demonstrate the fulfillment and creativity that come with memorization. They have to memorize literature every year in my class, sometimes a poem for speaking to the class and at other times lines from Shakespeare for performance. The poetry this year was just delightful to watch. Students paced the room, speaking to the sky, to the crowd, to different students depending on the line. Some spoke in accents and performed pre-planned motions. One student practiced with her friends so they could act out Edgar Allan Poe's *Annabel Lee* as she spoke it. In my Shakespeare unit, the performance of a scene is the final assignment and students must memorize their lines. The laughter that echoes from the halls as they plan their costumes, setting, and performance paints the exact opposite of the false caricature of students sitting dully at their desks reciting lines of Homer in choral response to a teacher in front.

REFERENCES

1. Vint, L. (2005) "Fresh thinking drives creativity innovation," *Quick*, 94, pp. 20-22

2. Land, G. & Jarman, B. (1998) *Breakpoint and Beyond: mastering the future today*, Leadership 2000 Inc

3. Eliot, T.S. (1998) "Philip Massinger," *The Sacred Wood (1920)*, Dover Publications

4. Biblica. (2011) *The Bible*, New International Version

5. Okada, T. & Ishibashi, K. (2017) "Imitation, inspiration, and creation: cognitive process of creative drawing by copying others' artworks," *Cognitive Science*, 41(7), pp. 1804-1837

6. Chi, M.T.H., Feltovich, P.J., & Glaser, R. (1981) "Categorization and representation of physics problems by experts and novices," *Cognitive Science*, 5(2), pp. 121-152

7. Dewey, J. (2015) *Democracy and Education*, The Free Press

8. Whiteley, G. (2015) *Most Likely to Succeed* (film)

9. PBS NewsHour. (2011) "A: This computer could defeat you at 'Jeopardy!' Q: What is Watson?" (video), YouTube, https://youtu.be/dr7IxQeXr7g

10. Biblica. (2011) *The Bible*, New International Version

11. Plato. (1980) *The Laws of Plato* (translated by Thomas L. Pangle), Basic Books

12. Pondiscio, R. (2021) *The Unexamined Rise of Therapeutic Education: how social-emotional learning extends K-12 education's reach into students' lives and expands teachers' roles*, American Enterprise Institute, www.aei.org/wp-content/uploads/2021/10/The-Unexamined-Rise-of-Therapeutic-Education.pdf?x91208

13. Grant, S., Hamilton, L.S., Wrabel, S.L., et al. (2017) *Social and Emotional Learning Interventions Under the Every Student Succeeds Act: evidence review*, RAND Corporation, www.rand.org/pubs/research_reports/RR2133.html

14. Sisk, V.F., Burgoyne, A.P., Sun, J., Butler, J.L., & Macnamara, B.N. (2018) "To what extent and under which circumstances are growth mind-sets important to academic achievement? Two meta-analyses," *Psychological Science*, 29(4), pp. 549-571

15. De Montaigne, M. (*c.*1575) *Of the Education of Children*

16. Haskins, R. & Sawhill, I. (2009) *Creating an Opportunity Society*, Brookings Institution

17. Van Overschelde, J.P. & Healy, A.F. (2001) "Learning of nondomain facts in high- and low-knowledge domains," *Journal of Experimental Psychology: Learning, Memory, and Cognition*, 27(5), pp. 1160-1171

18. Hirsch, E.D. (1996) *The Schools We Need And Why We Don't Have Them*, Doubleday

19. Mill, J.S. (2022) *On Liberty*, Dover Publications

20. www.facebook.com/235761613111516/photos/a.297318953622448/4048268065194166

21. National Human Genome Research Institute. (2018) "Genetics vs. genomics fact sheet," www.genome.gov/about-genomics/fact-sheets/Genetics-vs-Genomics

22. Ashman, G. (2021) *The Power of Explicit Teaching and Direct Instruction*, Corwin

23. Najarro, I. (2022) "Here's how many hours a week teachers work," *Education Week*, www.edweek.org/teaching-learning/heres-how-many-hours-a-week-teachers-work/2022/04

24. Capp, M.J. (2017) "The effectiveness of universal design for learning: a meta-analysis of literature between 2013 and 2016," *International Journal of Inclusive Education*, 21(8), pp. 791-807

25. Ibid.

26. Ashman, G. (2021) *The Power of Explicit Teaching and Direct Instruction*, Corwin

27. Caro, D.H., Lenkeit, J., & Kyriakides, L. (2016) "Teaching strategies and differential effectiveness across learning contexts: evidence from PISA 2012," *Studies in Educational Evaluation*, 49, pp. 30-41

28. Anderson, J., Reder, L., & Simon, H. (2000) "Applications and misapplications of cognitive psychology to mathematics education," *Texas Education Review*, 1(2), pp. 29-49

29. Willingham, D.T. (2010) *Why Don't Students Like School?*, Jossey-Bass

30. Rosenshine, B. (2012) "Principles of instruction: research-based strategies that all teachers should know," *American Educator*, 36(1), pp. 12-39

31. Ibid.

32. Ibid.

33. Maybin, S. (2017) "Busting the attention span myth," BBC News, www.bbc.com/news/health-38896790

34. Dale, E. (1969) *Audio-Visual Methods in Teaching*, Holt, Rinehart & Winston, p. 108

35. Subramony, D.P., Molenda, M., Betrus, A.K., & Thalheimer, W. (2014) "The mythical retention chart and the corruption of Dale's cone of experience," *Educational Technology*, 54(6), pp. 6-16

36. Ashman, G. (2021) *The Power of Explicit Teaching and Direct Instruction*, Corwin

37. Newstok, S. (2020) *How to Think Like Shakespeare*, Princeton University Press

38. Ibid.

8. A CANON OF TRADITIONALIST EDUCATION

Everyone has their canons and catechisms. There's a jazz canon featuring Miles Davis, Herbie Hancock, John Coltrane, Dizzy Gillespie, Count Basie, and more. There's a canon of existentialist philosophy ranging from Kierkegaard and Dostoyevsky to Sartre and Camus. Canons can be as broad as "the Western canon" to as niche as Japanese role-playing video games from the nineties. Even those who criticize the hegemony of "canons" will in the same breath recommend a list of books to read that prove their point. We cannot avoid having intellectual forebears; we can only choose different ones.

In this chapter, I will lay out what a traditionalist canon for education might include. The list is far from exhaustive but I employed some crowdsourced help, reaching out to Twitter for recommendations. So, some of these recommendations come from me, and others from friends established in institutions or working happily as classroom teachers.

This canon is broken down into, first, the big 10: essential reads that don't fit into any one category. Next, three sections follow—essays, classical and liberal education, and neo-traditionalism—the last of which consists of cognitive psychology, direct instruction, and modern teaching manuals. Included with each entry is a short synopsis, so any reader can sift and winnow through what interests them and what doesn't.

The real inspiration for this list came from Twitter, of all places, where people continue to ask me, "What else should I read?" Similar to my experience early in my career, these teachers have grown disillusioned with the ideas they learned in the university. This short canon begins a larger project of providing not only a counternarrative to progressivist ideas, but also canonizing and systematizing traditionalist ideas. Classical education, a liberal education, and neo-traditionalism have their differences. I myself find the strict adherence to the trivium and quadrivium of the classical folks a bit constraining. Conversely, those in the liberal tradition do wonders for the defense of knowledge and books but come up short on the question of instruction—great books are all well and good, but how are we to teach them? Lastly, the knowledge-rich and direct instruction folks, while great on instruction, are simply too utilitarian; certainly there must be more to an education than just reading scores and a job at the end. Regardless, they all have something to learn from each other—and we have yet more to learn from them.

THE BIG 10

1. Any E.D. Hirsch

While the tenets of classical education reach back as far as Aristotle, Hirsch is often credited with effectively starting a movement. His bestselling book *Cultural Literacy* (1987) was an initiating shot in the battle against the progressive education that had dominated schools since John Dewey and William Kirkpatrick. Often associated with Allan Bloom, Hirsch takes a different approach—a pragmatic one. Shakespeare may not be better in himself than any other author, but cognitive science and sociological data suggest that his work is better for literacy—and that's not to mention the unifying influence that a shared, common culture has on any society. Since Hirsch's first book, he has published a handful of others, each as insightful as the first. *The Schools We Need and Why We Don't Have Them* (1996) traces our contemporary woes in education to the Romantic movement and its reverence for the "natural," before outlining in meticulous detail the success of sequenced curricula and teacher-led instruction. His other books include *The Knowledge Deficit* (2006), *The Making of Americans* (2009), *Why Knowledge Matters* (2016), and *How to Educate a Citizen* (2020)—each equally worth reading.

2. The Abolition of Man (1943) – C.S. Lewis

The Abolition of Man is first and foremost a philosophical work that defends our belief in objective reality. It begins, however, with a discussion of education. In short, all our instruction inculcates some sort of worldview, whether or not we are consciously aware of it. When we imply that no works are inherently beautiful, no knowledge is worth knowing, and no truths supersede our cultural moment, then we will create men "without chests." If we disparage virtues like courage then we shouldn't be surprised to find cowards in our midst. The brevity of the work, fewer than 100 pages, makes it a distinctly digestible read.

3. The Crisis in Education (1978) – Hannah Arendt

This essay is something of a two-punch combo, addressing the place of both tradition and authority in schools. First, Arendt argues, schools no longer adhere to traditional content, thereby keeping students from the robust knowledge that they need to function in and think critically about society. By relativizing away all content, we deprive students of the very answers we need. We cannot go on questioning everything, but at some point have to start seeking out answers. Second, when we decenter adult authority, we leave students beholden to the unchecked whims of the boldest, and often cruelest, of their peers. Taken together, by deconstructing these ideas, we leave our schools places of chaos and little learning. There are few other works that so effectively discredit progressive education and do so with such cogency and brevity.

4. Principles of Instruction (2012) – Barak Rosenshine

It's all well and good to discuss and write about direct instruction in theory, but teachers need to know how this ought to inform their instruction on Monday when 25 pupils are staring at them in earnest. How do the principles of cognitive science manifest themselves in day-to-day instruction? Rosenshine's essay—another work that can be read in one short sitting— lays out 10 basic principles *and* draws out the practical implications. It perfectly walks the line between theory and practice, providing teachers with the theoretical undergirding so they can understand why they should adopt these practices, as well as clear directions for how to alter teaching according to the principles. It's also worth mentioning Tom Sherrington's *Rosenshine's Principles in Action* (2019), which augments the original work. Just as E.B. White took his professor's haphazard textbook, *The Elements of Style,* and then modified, organized, added to, and republished it as the canonical manual on writing, Sherrington took an already brilliant work and updated it into something yet better.

5. Why Minimal Guidance During Instruction Does Not Work (2006) – Paul A. Kirschner, John Sweller, and Richard E. Clark

This academic essay is worth reading and rereading. Where project-based and discovery learning often receive gold-standard-like status in contrast to "fact-cramming," "chalk and talk" methods of instruction, this essay pillories PBL with ruthless efficiency. The central thesis reads: "The past half-century of empirical research on this issue has provided overwhelming and unambiguous evidence that minimal guidance during instruction is significantly less effective and efficient than guidance specifically designed to support the cognitive processing necessary for learning." From there, the authors outline the evidence of PBL's mediocrity and explicate its failures using the principles of cognitive theory. It is both a forceful denunciation of progressivist-type instruction and a useful primer on concepts like cognitive load, working memory, automaticity, and long-term memory.

6. Why Don't Students Like School? (2009) – Daniel T. Willingham

To answer that titular question, Willingham proposes a simple answer: the methods of curriculum and instruction that we typically use do not align with how our brains actually learn. Although he ostensibly intends to answer a handful of common questions, the outline functions more as a conceit for him to introduce essential ideas in cognitive science.

7. Teach Like a Champion (third edition 2021) – Doug Lemov

I'm not sure a better endorsement of Lemov's work exists than a blog post from Greg Ashman. He writes that anyone who picks up this book will notice a contrast between its "specific and detailed observations and advice" and "the kind of nonspecific ideological navel-gazing that constitutes much of the content of education courses."[1] Ashman adds that this book is a "practical guide" that is "interested in helping teachers to become more effective." Through a process akin to ethnography, Lemov has spent years observing teachers. Over time, he started to notice similarities in the pedagogy of the best and lays out these techniques in this book. I know countless teachers who felt woefully unprepared for the job but found direction and competence in *Teach Like a Champion*.

8. The Silenced Dialogue (1993) — Lisa Delpit

Delpit's essay is provocative and insightful. Straddling the line between critical and traditionalist pedagogy, she shows how progressive theories of education fail the students they most claim to help. Regardless of how arbitrary our society is, our students must function within it. As such, it's imperative that they receive direct instruction into this "culture of power." Students cannot intuit written grammar or choose their way into powerful cultural knowledge; only through instruction and guidance can they access the knowledge they need to succeed in our culture. It's a controversial essay that makes the case for traditionalist pedagogy on progressive, critical grounds.

9. Nicomachean Ethics — Aristotle

There are few books that speak with such a dense, electrified force, the kinds of books that can become the basis of an entire society and culture: Christian scripture, Lao Tzu's *Tao Te Ching*, Plato's *Republic*. Aristotle's *Nicomachean Ethics* is such a book. His central question is: how can we live a good, ethical life? Aristotle is the cornerstone of classical education and his thought remains relevant today.

10. Emile: Or on Education (1762), Democracy and Education (1916), Pedagogy of the Oppressed (1968) — Jean-Jacques Rousseau, John Dewey, Paulo Freire

Know thy enemy. I find these authors are frequently referenced but rarely read. John Stuart Mill famously said, "He who knows only his own side of the case, knows little at that."[2] As many teachers provide examples and *non*-examples of new concepts to their students, it's essential that we read those with whom we disagree in order to understand our own beliefs. I may disagree with these authors but I respect them still, and through reading them have come to understand traditionalist education all the better—both its strengths and shortcomings.

ESSAYS

The Lost Tools of Learning (1947) — Dorothy Sayers

In this short essay, Sayers delivers both a work of classical education evangelism and a roadmap for such an education. Her central thesis is this: we have come to focus so much on content that we have deprived our students of the very tools they need to grasp that content. What good would a pile of wooden boards be if a carpenter had no hammer, saw, screws, or nails? Although I have bristled throughout this book at the prioritization of academic skills and "learning how to learn"-type language, Sayers takes a classical approach to these concepts. Her tools are grammar, rhetoric, formal logic, and language—far more robust concepts than the modern skills-based education, which amounts to little more than watered-down intellectual milk.

Strengthening the Student Toolbox (2013) – John Dunlosky

Dunlosky distills mountains of research into effective and ineffective learning strategies down to 10 readable, quickly implementable pages. His essay outlines high-leverage practices in the classroom based on advances in cognitive science, like self-quizzing, interleaving, distributed practice, and self-explanation. Although these are framed as techniques to teach students for use in independent study, I found them equally as usable in my own instruction. For example, I need to give students opportunities for regular review and mix in a variety of types of problems. Dunlosky also explains *why* these strategies work. For example, mixing different types of problems helps students to differentiate between different concepts; distributed practice leverages retrieval and thereby long-term retention of knowledge, whereas massed practice (all the same kinds of problems in one go) fosters mastery in the moment but results in quick forgetting.

The Tyranny of Three Ideas (2016) – E.D. Hirsch

Yes, I've already told you to read Hirsch, but this essay, the prologue to his book *Why Knowledge Matters*, has been published separately and is a succinct introduction to his thought. He opens with a brief history of a monumental change in French education, a shift in the 1980s to a progressivist approach, thus making something of a natural experiment. He concludes: "An entire educational theory has been put to the test in France, with incontrovertible results that everyone in France now calls 'the crisis of the school.'" From there, Hirsch outlines the "tyranny of three ideas" that pervade the American and now French systems of education:

- *Early education should be appropriate to the child's age and nature, as part of a natural developmental process.*

- *Early education should be individualized as far as possible—to follow the learning styles and interests of each developing student.*
- *The unifying aim of education is to develop critical thinking and other general skills.*

In short, naturalism, individuals, and skills-centralism are three philosophical foundations that must be rooted out if our schools are to improve.

The Mighty River of Classics (2001) – Camille Paglia

To Paglia, the intellectual heritage is something of a river, with tributaries, side bends, countless sources, and moments where it seemingly disappears only to reappear further down the mountainside in fuller force. This is perhaps one of my favorite texts that I read for this book. Paglia excoriates the poststructuralism that undergirds much of modern educational theory and makes the case for a liberal arts tradition without succumbing to a "West is best" closed-mindedness.

The Storm Over the University (1990) – John Searle

An academic philosopher himself, Searle chronicles the canon wars of the 1980s as something of an outside observer. He astutely contrasts the philosophies of traditionalists like Allan Bloom with the radicals in the university, suggesting that neither side ever clearly states their point and so our debates over canon, curriculum, and education falter. Searle closes the essay with a list of what he thinks a substantive education ought to entail: knowledge of our own cultural tradition, a basic grasp of the sciences and political theory, a second language, the outlines of philosophy, and the skills of writing and speaking—a back-to-basics curriculum that I imagine few would dispute.

Of the Education of Children (c.1575) – Michel de Montaigne

Reading Montaigne is like viewing a baroque painting: full of color, image, swirl, and flair. This essay is a sprawling meditation that covers everything from the purpose of education to the contents of it and the manner of instruction. In many ways, Montaigne stumbles upon practices that modern cognitive psychology only confirms: a pupil must be able to re-explain the passage he read for himself if he is to learn the contents; a mind full of substance will more easily put words to paper or speak before a crowd. Montaigne's imagery is unparalleled. He knows that not all things worth learning will be immediately appealing to students and so "healthy foods must be sweetened for the child." Like a bee that collects nectar only to form it into honey, so we must expose our students to learning, but they must acquire and construct it in their own minds. And one added bonus: Montaigne strays into humor, too. One can't help but laugh at his comparison of rearing a child to gardening; it's easy to plant a seed but a far harder, far more confusing task once the thing has sprouted. Thankfully, Montaigne provides direction, insight, and levity to guide us.

At a Loss for Words (2019) – Emily Hanford

Hanford expounds on American education's "little secret about reading: elementary schools across the country are teaching children to be poor readers—and educators may not even know it." What follows is an unparalleled example of education reporting and theory that skewers many misconceptions about how children learn to read. Ironically, the reading strategies that schools are actively teaching—using context clues, memorizing words, guessing—are precisely the strategies that *struggling* readers use. What struck me most in reading Hanford's article was a short embedded video where two students—one taught phonics and the other the three-cueing approach to reading—are asked about how they read.[3] The first student says she reads by "looking at the words" and the second by "looking at the pictures." The first student has learned to read and the second has learned to guess.

CLASSICAL AND LIBERAL EDUCATION

The Paideia Proposal (1982) – Mortimer Adler

Although classical education and Adler both have something of an elitist reputation, this is a false stereotype. Adler believed that what society considers the best education for those considered the best is the best education for all. More straightforwardly, everyone deserves an education rooted in the liberal tradition. Whereas many books get lost in theory, Adler has his mind always on the instructional practices in the classroom: any good system needs didactic instruction (lectures and textbooks) wherein students acquire new knowledge; coaching and supervised practice (writing and working through problems) wherein students develop intellectual skills; and Socratic questioning (open discussions) wherein students enlarge their own understandings and ascertain their own values. He is a progressive traditionalist.

The Great Tradition (2007) – edited by Richard Gamble

Classical education has so many roots in the work of so many Greek and medieval philosophers that the idea of even beginning to hack away at such a reading list is daunting to the point of being off-putting. Gamble's book compiles excerpts from many such authors to provide an introduction to the long tradition of classical education; he reaches back to Plato through Seneca and Cicero and up to John Henry Newman and Michael Oakeshott. Anyone who has perused this volume could rightly call themselves well-read in the classical education canon.

Trivium 21c (2013) – Martin Robinson

There's nothing new under the sun; rather, our task is to continually rediscover, reinvigorate, and defend ideas worth defending. Robinson's book is an attempt at just that. He contests that the grammar, dialectic, and rhetoric of traditional classical education are the same groundings that our children need today to live a good life. He believes this approach can cut through the noise and fads of modern education and unite the progressives and traditionalists.

The Trivium (1948) – Sister Miriam Joseph

Developed as an introductory textbook for Saint Mary's College in Indiana, *The Trivium* outlines the basic concepts of classical education and then delves into nuts-and-bolts instruction in grammar, the functions of language, logic, and rhetoric. This is a textbook—and an advanced one at that—but it can provide the grounding necessary for any teacher interested in classical education or the curriculum for upper grades.

How to Think Like Shakespeare (2020) – Scott Newstok

As much a book of brilliant quotations as an original thesis, Newstok elucidates the philosophy and approach to education common in the Renaissance era. One chapter on imitation lays out a number of writing practices from days of yore that any teacher could quickly incorporate into their own lessons. More than anything, the book sets out a coherent vision of an education that was routine in the past but contrasts starkly with ideas commonplace today, thereby teaching us as much about the present as it does the past.

The Closing of the American Mind (1987) — Allan Bloom

This is a compelling, infuriating, at times inscrutable, and yet unendingly profound work of nonfiction. While the first third of the book reads like a professorial curmudgeon complaining about kids these days, the middle and final section ought to be read and reread. Bloom traces the philosophical descent of American culture into what he calls value-relativism and away from the hard truths and morality that we call virtues. The final section is a paean to great books: the insights they provide us, the way they remove us from ourselves and our insular eras, the companions they can be.

Two Concepts of Liberty (1958) — Isaiah Berlin

While not ostensibly a tract on education, Berlin's thought in this essay informs the field regardless. He establishes the difference between negative and positive liberty—the difference between freedom *from* and freedom *to*. Importantly, these two conceptions of liberty need each other. Freedom from constraints is meaningless unless we can then live a positive, meaningful, fulfilling life. Concurrently, we cannot live a positive, meaningful, fulfilling life if others are continually infringing upon our liberties. Similarly, healthy constraints facilitate positive liberty. A musician who has trained another's musical score into memory has expanded his own freedom. "The player is not bound to the score," Berlin writes, "[but] has absorbed the score into his own system ... [and] has changed it from an impediment to free activity into an element in that activity itself." The essay is endlessly informative in our discussions of both behavioral structures and the methods of training our students.

NEO-TRADITIONALISM

Reading Reconsidered (2016) — Doug Lemov, Colleen Driggs, and Erica Woolway

Teach Like a Champion is Lemov's bestselling book but, call me a hipster, I think *Reading Reconsidered* is his best. After reading Hirsch, I knew my classroom practices were ineffective but I wasn't sure how these traditionalist ideas should manifest in instruction. How does one build a knowledge-rich English classroom? Lemov answers just that question in *Reading Reconsidered*. He moves from curriculum selection to effective questioning, structuring reading times, and the incorporation of non-fiction supplementary texts. I often say that E.D. Hirsch taught me how to think about education. Well, this book taught me how to teach.

Visible Learning (2008) – John Hattie

Visible Learning is quite a tome to tackle but it's broken up such that it needn't be read front to back. Hattie attempted an ambitious feat: where a meta-study synthesizes the data from a few different studies, Hattie undertook a sort of meta-meta-study. He crunched the numbers of 800 meta-studies, thereby accounting for thousands of original studies, in an attempt to determine what were the most effective educational interventions. He found that much of what makes it into popular discourse—funding, class sizes, and the like—has a comparatively negligible impact, while that which is often disparaged—like direct instruction—is wildly effective. *Visible Learning* is particularly useful for two reasons. First, a discussion of research early in the book is an exquisite primer to the strengths, weaknesses, and norms of social science research. Second, Hattie demonstrates the need to find practices that aren't only beneficial but those that are the *most* beneficial. Any implemented routine usually has positive effects, but we cannot do everything and so must incorporate that which works best.

The Power of Explicit Teaching and Direct Instruction (2020) – Greg Ashman

Ashman perfectly straddles the line between esoteric research and engaging writing. A doctoral student himself, he is awash in research and does an effective job of covering the relevant studies without boring the reader. By the end, he presents a teacher-led classroom—one with direct instruction, structured practice, worked models, analogies, and other such practices—as one no less full of creativity, rigor, and importance. Ashman has done the thankless task of sifting and winnowing through mountains of modern research and studies to isolate and sort out the best for his readers.

Make it Stick (2014) – Peter C. Brown, Henry L. Roediger III, and Mark A. McDaniel

The central thesis of this book is simple: many of the most effective learning strategies seem counterintuitive. Students spend time rereading, highlighting, or mass-practicing the same kind of problem to mastery. Unfortunately, these are ineffective strategies; tedium and seeming rigor are not synonymous with learning. With the role of memory at the forefront of their thinking, the authors of *Make it Stick* present the theory and practical applications of recent advances in cognitive science. It's another book with takeaways that are easy to implement come Monday morning.

Seven Myths About Education (2014) – Daisy Christodoulou

Christodoulou tackles, unmasks, and subsequently skewers the fallacies rampant in schools of education and the system writ large. They are:

- *Facts prevent understanding.*
- *Teacher-led instruction is passive.*
- *The 21st century fundamentally changes everything.*
- *You can always just look it up.*
- *We should teach transferable skills.*
- *Projects and activities are the best way to learn.*
- *Teaching knowledge is indoctrination.*

Tackling orthodoxy is always controversial, but Christodoulou does so with an erudition that keeps her above the tumult.

Inside the Black Box (1998) – Paul Black and Dylan Wiliam

This essay begins with a transformative question: "Why is it that most of the reform initiatives mentioned in the first paragraph are not aimed at giving direct help and support to the work of teachers in classrooms?" Too many policies have treated the classroom as a black box; we change the inputs, measure the outputs, and hope something works. In reality, everything happens *inside* the classroom and so that's where we must focus. Black and Wiliam present the case for and the foundations of a classroom practice based upon regular formative assessment and modification.

How Learning Happens (2020) – Paul A. Kirschner and Carl Hendrick

How Learning Happens is something of a canonizing work in itself. While I am here trying to lay out a canon of traditionalist education, Kirschner and Hendrick review the seminal works of cognitive psychology as they relate to education. In doing so, they reveal where many of the concepts of cognitive psychology find their genesis. Perhaps the most important aspect of this book is simply its mere existence. Even if someone has not read every study referenced in the book, the authors are making it harder to consider oneself well-read in educational theory if one is not familiar with concepts like cognitive load and working memory. Many teachers make it through teacher-prep without a robust understanding of cognitive theory. Hopefully, this book will begin to remedy that shortcoming.

The Reading Mind (2017) – Daniel T. Willingham

In *Why Don't Students Like School?*, Willingham writes about cognitive science and learning in general. He outlines basic principles of cognitive science and applies them to instruction writ large. In *The Reading Mind*, he delves specifically into how the mind learns to read, answering clearly and succinctly the question so many people are asking: how can we get kids to read?

How the Other Half Learns (2019) – Robert Pondiscio

Success Academy is arguably America's most successful charter school system. Pondiscio spent a year observing classes, meetings, and field trips to discover just how the organization accomplished this. Although an advocate of Success Academy, Pondiscio never strays into uncritical fawning. It's an insightful, entertaining look at the nuts and bolts of how a successful school does it.

The Power of Culture (2020) – edited by Katharine Birbalsingh

When I finished this book, written by the teachers of Michaela Community School in London, I wanted to fly across the Atlantic Ocean to apply. With silent corridors, sequenced curriculum, and authoritative teachers paired with family-style lunches, constant praise of students, and a culture of inside jokes, Michaela is perhaps the best argument for traditionalist education. Here's a group of teachers putting the ideas into practice and succeeding wildly. This book is a collection of essays that explain what they do and why they do it. Thus, not only are they educating their students well, but they're also spreading their ideas beyond their walls.

A Nation at Risk (1983) – National Commission on Excellence in Education

This report falls into no pedagogical camp necessarily, but the introduction to *A Nation at Risk* remains crucial reading for anyone involved in American education reform. Framed in terms of the US position on the world stage, the report argues that "if an unfriendly foreign power had attempted to impose on America the mediocre educational performance that exists today, we might well have viewed it as an act of war." Almost humorous in its dark portrayal, *A Nation at Risk* acts as a clarion call for the purpose of education: building a well-functioning society and ensuring everyone within it has the capacity to live a successful life. That is the purpose for which I write today, and the reason why we must look back to tradition in order to progress forward as an educational system.

REFERENCES

1. Ashman, G. (2020) "No, you are not cancelling *Teach Like a Champion*," *Filling the Pail* (blog), https://gregashman.wordpress.com/2020/06/12/no-you-are-not-cancelling-teach-like-a-champion

2. Mill, J.S. (2002) *On Liberty*, Dover Publications

3. APM Reports. (2019) "Words or pictures?" (video), YouTube, https://youtu.be/27E6kkNJY_o